D1564074

The Montana Frontier

March 4, 2004

to Karen

Best Wishes

Joyce Litz

The Montana Frontier

One Woman's West

JOYCE LITZ

UNIVERSITY OF NEW MEXICO PRESS
ALBUQUERQUE

Library of Congress Cataloging-in-Publication Data

Litz, Joyce, 1928–

The Montana frontier : one woman's West / Joyce Litz.— 1st ed.

     p.   cm.

ISBN 0-8263-3120-3 (cloth : alk. paper)

   1. Weston, Lillian, 1865-1949.

   2. Women pioneers—Montana—Gilt Edge Region—Biography.

   3. Pioneers—Montana—Gilt Edge Region—Biography.

   4. Frontier and pioneer life—Montana—Gilt Edge Region.

   5. Ranch life—Montana—Gilt Edge Region

   6. Gilt Edge Region (Mont.)—Social life and customs—19th century.

   7. Gilt Edge Region (Mont.)—Social life and customs—20th century.

   8. Gilt Edge Region (Mont.)—Biography.

   9. Montana—Social life and customs—19th century.

  10. Montana—Social life and customs—20th century.

I. Title.

F739.G53 L58 2004

978.6'03'092—dc22

                        2003018561

Printed and bound in the United States of America
Typeset in Centaur MT 11.75/14. Display type set in Nuptial and Serlio
Design and composition: Robyn Mundy
Production: Maya Allen-Gallegos

CONTENTS

PROLOGUE

What an elegant Thanksgiving feast Lillian cooked for two of her husband's visiting nephews in 1935 in Lewistown, Montana! Amazed, I watched a grandmother I hadn't seen before—an attractive, vivacious seventy-year-old woman, who lit an after-dinner cigarette and described a life and cities I couldn't even imagine. Because she didn't dwell in the past and seldom talked about her life before moving to Montana, relatives and close friends knew little about her beginnings.

When, years after she died in 1949, my father sent me a battered rusty trunk filled with her manuscripts, diaries, and scrapbooks, many of my questions about her were answered. These along with personal memories, family stories, and a bit of speculation helped me piece together her life story as truthfully as one can when telling another person's life. My father, Richard, who was her son, furnished many personal insights before he died in 1984.

After my article "Lillian's Montana Scene" appeared in *The Montana Historical Magazine,* 1974 summer edition, her old ranch neighbors were surprised. In 1978, Bob Lange of Lewistown wrote to Richard:

> Her story fascinated me since it was about someone I knew so well, but knew so little about. . . . We got together quite a bit in their last years in Lewistown. . . . We drove out to Gilt Edge one Sunday afternoon and was that an interesting afternoon. There were a few tumbled down buildings then and they told about the town when they lived there, and showed us the spot where their little shack sat.

Although my brother, Dick, and I spent our early years with our grandparents, we didn't know any more about Lillian than Bob Lange did. She mentioned her father occasionally, but it was years before we realized he was a top athlete of the late nineteenth and early twentieth centuries, a pedestrian named Edward Payson Weston. Once she described his walk from New York City to California in 1909 and how he followed it with a return trip the next year when he was seventy-one years old. We couldn't quite fathom anyone taking such a long hike.

Among her papers was her 1924 article about him in *Strength Magazine.* Her admiration was obvious, although I don't think she realized what a giant ego she was describing. Certainly, he was a big influence in her life. She admired his eccentric ways and tried to imitate him. She also said he encouraged her to pursue a career in a time when Victorian women were cautioned to be ladylike, shy, and retiring. He made sure she had a decent education, something she appreciated and often wrote about later—the need for women to be educated.

Lillian's professional life, from 1885 to 1930, was a pivotal era for women as more entered higher education and pioneered careers in journalism, social work, medicine, and teaching. There was Jane Addams, who led the way in social work. In 1889, she and Ellen Gates Starr established Hull House in a poor immigrant neighborhood in Chicago. In the late 1800s, Elizabeth and Emily Blackwell established the Woman's Medical College of the New York Infirmary for Women and Children. Anita Newcomb McGee, M.D., was the first woman appointed assistant surgeon general in the U.S. Army in 1898. Nellie Bly (Elizabeth Cochrane Seaman), who was the same age as Lillian, was an investigative reporter noted for her sensational exposés of social conditions in the late 1800s.

During this time when these women were gaining national recognition, Lillian was busy developing her own writing career. As I organized the contents of her trunk, I found two scrapbooks pasted full of her column, "Lillian's Letter," as well as clippings, greeting cards, and pictures of people in the news. The blue book is dated October 13, 1888, with "High Bridge" written in her large angular handwriting. The phrase "Noblesse Oblige" is penned in above her name, "Lillian Marie Weston." Perhaps she did feel a cut above the crowd if she defined the words according to *Webster's Dictionary:* "The obligation of honorable, generous, and responsible behavior associated with high rank or birth."

The gray scrapbook was started sometime after she married. Along with the usual interesting clippings and pictures, on the inside cover she glued a draft of her request for a New York City minister to marry her and Frank Hazen in 1895. Pasted next to it is a letter from Frank's brother, John, who often visited them over the years. Lillian appeared to be very fond of him, and he never married.

She also saved her fiction manuscripts, most of which were never published. These reveal things Lillian probably never meant others to see. Many of her diaries were missing, because I knew she kept one for each year of her life. Only six were saved. Her manuscripts are undated unless they were published, and many of her nonfiction pieces were. Then each was labeled with the date of acceptance, amount received, and name of publication.

Along with her papers I found sepia-tinted photos of Lillian as a teenager, as a young woman in New York City, and as a young married woman with her husband and their children, pictures I had never seen before. Although she was sixty-three years old by the time I was born, as a child I could still see the beautiful blond woman she had been. Even in old age, she had nice legs, though her plump, five-foot-two figure had lost its graceful shape. Her face was kind, with large expressive gray eyes and a determined chin set below a sensitive mouth with a slight overbite.

She and my grandfather were a good-looking couple. He was a slender man only a few inches taller than she and had a handsome, stoic face with the high cheekbones suggesting an Indian ancestor, which, indeed, he did have. He was voted most handsome in his class of 1889 at Dartmouth. He was always kind to us, but silent. To this day, my brother and I agree we never got to know him, and we lived with them until we were teenagers.

As I read Lillian's writings, I was surprised to learn she had worked seriously toward a career as a concert pianist. She wrote of wonderful daydreams of fame and fortune, how she saw herself sitting at a grand piano playing the works of the great masters as no one had ever interpreted them before. In her fantasies, she heard the large brilliant audiences applauding her.

Nevertheless, somewhere along the way, Lillian abandoned her plans to become a pianist. Beginning in 1885, she worked in New York City as a freelance writer and roving reporter, producing a weekly column, "Lillian's Letter," for several newspapers, including the *New York Sunday Herald*, the *Richmond (Virginia) Star*, and western papers like *The Helena (Montana) Record*.

In one edition, the Montana editor wrote, "Our New York correspondent 'Lillian' is a young lady not yet twenty years of age. Her father has for a number of years been connected with the great dailies of the metropolis. Her letters are being well received and favorably commented on. An enthusiastic miner in the Coeur d'Alene [Idaho] area has decided to name his new mine the 'Lillian.' As the mine is a rich one the honor will be doubly appreciated."

I could tell from Lillian's columns that she loved New York. She made her small-town readers see the city through her eyes. Her writings exuded energy and a spirit of adventure as they covered everything from the arts to the city's problems with the huge influx of immigrants at the end of the nineteenth century. She appeared to be everywhere, from riding the new toboggan in Fleetwood Park to sitting in the front row at Buffalo Bill's Wild West Show in Madison Square Garden.

Her life, however, took a sharp turn after she married, one she didn't expect. She had been so careful in her choice of a husband, because she knew her life depended on marrying the right man. A century later, Phyllis Rose wrote the same premise in her book *Parallel Lives: Five Victorian Marriages:* "I believe that marriage, whether we see it as a psychological relationship or a political one, has determined the story of our lives more than we have generally acknowledged."

Even when Lillian began to realize her marriage was far from perfect and financial problems loomed, she chose to follow Frank wherever he might lead her, and by 1916, she found herself living on an isolated wheat-and-cattle ranch in central Montana. Nevertheless, according to her writings, she turned that disastrous move into another adventure.

Early in life, Lillian thought she wanted an upper-middle-class existence when she married, but would she have liked the humdrum, narrow life of a Victorian matron who spent her days on domestic chores and calling on friends? She was a pioneer at heart and craved excitement and change. Montana, in the raw late 1800s and early 1900s, was just that, an exciting place on the last American frontier. It sparked Lillian's creative energies, forced her to be strong, physically and mentally, and fed her adventurous soul.

The Pedestrian

*My father and my grandmother had a hand in developing
my rebellious, independent nature.*

"Weston's Early Life"
Strength Magazine. June 15, 1924

Lillian grew up adoring her father, internalized most of his advice and opinions, and even inherited, or acquired, his charm. She resented the attitude of the rest of the Weston family, who considered his a low-class profession. They never accepted him as the great athlete he was, who played a major role in developing the long-distance walking matches of the late 1800s and early 1900s. She was proud of him and the fact that she was like him in many important ways: "His respectable relatives didn't understand him; they regretted he did not embrace a dignified occupation like banking, or selling groceries, insurance or dry goods. . . . To make a man with my father's erratic disposition lead a humdrum life would be like hitching a race horse to a plow."

Even his father, but never his mother, and his maternal grandparents were ashamed of his being a pedestrian.

E. A. Southern, a leading Broadway actor of the 1800s, once said, "It was the theater's loss when Edward Payson Weston became a Pedestrian rather than an actor."

He was so right, because Payse was a real showman, a handsome charmer, dandy of the nineteenth-century sporting world. He was a little guy, five feet, eight inches tall, never weighing more than 140 pounds, and he always acted and dressed his part. He wore high gaiters (leather leggings), a smart hat, a black velvet tunic—his chest covered with his many sports medals—and carried a small swagger stick. He liked to look good and liked nice clothes but wore what he wanted even if it was out of style. Lillian took particular pride in the fact that he didn't let public opinion or fashion sway him.

It's not surprising Weston had an unusual approach to life. His mother, Marie Gaines Weston, was not the average Victorian lady. She was a delicate-looking nineteenth-century novelist, who often wrote under the name M. D. Gaines (a pseudonym Lillian later used in Montana). She was also active in the abolitionists' movement in Boston just before the Civil War along with John Greenleaf Whittier and other literary types. Most of her writings, like the novel *Kate Felton*, published in 1859 and now in the University of Virginia historical archives, were romantic stories, but they also took a strong stand against slavery.

This probably accounts for Lillian's unprejudiced attitude toward black people, an unusual one in the nineteenth century. Although she didn't judge a person by his or her skin color, she did have other biases. She despised liars and cruel people and displayed a haughty disdain for people with poor taste in clothes, furnishings, and entertainment choices. She said she disliked phonies, but interestingly enough, she herself was easily manipulated by a charming person, which is no surprise, considering her father was about as charming as a man could get.

Lillian's grandfather, Silas Weston, was an unsuccessful Boston businessman, a large man—six feet, four inches tall—who played the bass viol and wrote poetry. Ed was their only son, born on March 15, 1839, in Providence, Rhode Island. His later accomplishments are even more amazing, because he weighed only four and a half pounds at birth and wasn't expected to live. He was a semi-invalid by the time he was fifteen.

At that time, the family moved to Boston, where a family friend, who was a sports trainer, asked if he could work with the teenager to improve his health. He took Ed off coffee and put him on a strict diet of vegetables and milk. Then he urged him to take short walks each day.

Soon the walks lengthened and instead of being a chore, they became Weston's recreation.

In 1855, his newfound health gave him confidence and he got a job selling candy and papers on the Boston, Providence, and Stonington Railroad. The following year, he did the same work on the New York–Fall River Steamer. For six months in 1856, he was apprenticed to a jeweler, and then he joined a circus band as a drummer.

On this last job, he was struck by lightning and saw this as a warning to change his lifestyle, so he went home. Then Ed rambled about Boston, house to house and town to town, selling his mother's books.

Weston made his first long walk, about 478 miles by road, in 1861, when he was twenty-two years old. He wrote and self-published his version of the trek, called *The Pedestrian: Being a Correct Journal of "Incidents" on a Walk from the State House, Boston, Mass., to the U.S. Capitol, at Washington, D.C.* He bet a friend he would arrive in ten days in time to attend Abraham Lincoln's inauguration on March 4.

Several creditors delayed his start on February 22 for the matter of $10 and $25 debts owed. Then in Worcester, only a few miles down the road from Boston, another creditor, a hotel owner, had him arrested and jailed for nonpayment of $50. At this point, a stranger stepped forward and signed a note for the debt so Weston could continue on his way. This was not a good beginning, and it was many miles before Weston regained his good humor.

Friends, Charles Foster and Abner Smith, followed him in a carriage, which Ed had rented for $80. His sponsors, the Grover & Baker Sewing Machine Co. and the Rubber Clothing Co., stocked the carriage with five thousand packets containing brochures featuring his picture. Delivering these to houses along the road helped Ed pay his expenses but almost finished him off as he battled a blizzard most of the way.

A crowd met them at each town they passed through, and either a hotel, café, or private citizen served them free meals. When tired, Weston and his partners would accept the offer of a free bed, but he never slept more than two hours at a time. Then they would be on their way. In one town, a woman said she wanted Weston to deliver a kiss from her to President Lincoln. Weston said he would accept the kiss but wouldn't promise to deliver it to the president.

He didn't reach the Capitol until the afternoon of March 4, a half day over the ten days, and so missed the inauguration ceremony by a few hours.

Although Weston lost his bet, he went to the President's Ball but was too sleepy to enjoy it. Later, at a levee, a reception, he talked with President Lincoln, who offered to pay his train fare back to Boston. Weston refused, saying he wanted to make the walk back to improve his record. The Civil War, however, was beginning, and he decided the trip was too dangerous, so he took the train home.

Weston didn't plan to become a professional walker. The Washington, D.C., trek had been a bit of a lark, because by that time, walking was his hobby. After the war broke out in 1861, Weston went to work for the Federal Army, using his walking ability to deliver Boston and New York mail to the northern troops in Washington, D.C.

Because Ed was so popular with his fans, companies sought to use his name for advertising their wares, even such famous stores as Brooks Brothers of New York City, who furnished his disguise as a Susquehanna River rafter. The G. W. White Hat Company gave him a hat. At least Ed was well dressed as he dodged southern sympathizers, Confederate soldiers, and unfriendly dogs.

Later he said, "I have always been afraid of dogs, especially at night."

Once, when he found a bridge guarded, he had to walk ten miles upstream to find a boat to cross the river. Then a southern farmer stopped him and insisted Ed go to work for him, saying he was too young to be on the road alone. He offered Ed 25 cents a month and room and board. Weston soon slipped away.

On one trip, he stopped in Media, Pennsylvania, at a friend's house to sleep. The friend, not realizing Ed was on a secret mission, let everyone in town know his guest was the Pedestrian. All the citizens turned out the next morning to welcome him, and Weston left town traveling fast.

That time, he was almost to Washington, D.C., when he was arrested as a Confederate spy. He had walked seventy miles in less than twenty-four hours only to be thrown into a filthy Union guardhouse cell. After many hours of interrogation, he was fed and allowed to sleep under a table in the officers' quarters, and then the Union soldiers put him on a train for Annapolis, where the New York and Massachusetts regiments were stationed.

Because Ed was small and boyish looking, this often saved his life when the Confederate army caught him between lines. He would pretend to be a local farm boy. Some more romantic newspaper accounts of his life said he was a spy, but Weston, being the flamboyant star-of-the-show type he was, probably started the rumor himself.

After the Civil War, he went to work for *The New York Herald*, first as a messenger boy and later as a police reporter. With no telephones and only horses for transportation, Weston's speedy walking ability really gave him an edge over reporters from rival papers. He would race to a story on foot and return copy to his editor, in some cases before rival reporters were even on the story's scene.

Two years after Lillian was born, her father's official walking career began on October 29, 1867, when he was twenty-eight years old. He accepted a challenge from a walking club in Maine to walk from Portland to Chicago—a distance of 1,326 miles—within thirty consecutive days (but never on Sunday because of a promise to his mother) for a $10,000 purse. The "Yankee Clipper" beat the deadline by an hour and twenty minutes.

According to the nineteenth-century *Harper's Weekly*, "This walk makes Weston's name a household word, and really gives impetus to the pedestrian mania which has become so general."

Back in New York City after setting this record, he was deluged with invitations to take part in country fairs, weekend walks, and lectures, and he organized walking exhibitions up and down the eastern seaboard. Usually a bevy of reporters and doctors followed him on his walks. The newspapermen liked to quote him, and the doctors liked to check his pulse and marvel at his physical condition.

When asked the secret of his walking success, he said, "I never was a fast walker—never tried to be."

He was a deliberate, persistent, plugging walker who was able to keep going and going with an average speed of four and a half miles per hour. He always won with a steady, even gait and stamina that withstood great fatigue. Many surpassed his speed, but none could equal him for endurance.

Payse walked with his toes turned out in what he called his "flat-foot shuffle." He was not the heel-and-toe walker of that era.

"Heel and toe will do for a time but it ruins the heel," he told reporters.

A five-day match meant fifteen days of heavy workouts: five days of exercises, five of actual walking, and five of light road work to taper off. Sports enthusiasts followed his exploits with great interest, often wagering high stakes. His fans loved him and he never disappointed them.

Weston always rubbed his feet with whiskey after a long walk and never tarried with wet shoes and socks. He was sure wet feet caused the tonsillitis he was plagued with all his life, but even so, he never wore rubber footwear for rainy weather. He said they were bad for the feet.

His shoes and boots were made to order: "Walking boots ought always to be made of fine French calfskin."

Although Ed Weston just about owned the walking sport, he didn't make much money. Advertising was in its infancy and product endorsements not yet a part of marketing strategies, and so prize money was his only income from walking. Some years he made a lot of money, and others were lean. He walked because he liked to walk, but this meant the Weston family often struggled to make ends meet.

Lillian seldom criticized her father, but she did admit he had an expensive flaw. He saw himself as something of an entrepreneur destined to make millions with his many get-rich-quick schemes that often failed. The fact was, if he wanted to walk, he had to find other ways to support his family, and he was a natural gambler.

She always remembered her father's favorite phrase and knew his bank account was low when he said, "I feel much encouraged."

This precarious existence, "turkey one day and feathers the next," as Lillian later described it, created an anxiety-charged atmosphere for his family. She sympathized as she watched her mother pinch pennies and wait for the riches that never came while her father squandered dollars on his many failed moneymaking schemes.

Unfortunately, one could not have found two more opposite personalities than Ed and his wife, Maria Fox Weston, who never understood her maverick husband or his mercurial personality. She was a conservative, genteel New Englander, a creature of habit, who clung to her routine ways all her life while Ed never recognized her struggle for an ordered life.

Maria thought this even more important after Lillian, their first child, was born on October 13, 1865, in Medford, Massachusetts. Maude was born about two years later and Ellsworth, two years after that.

In 1924, *Strength Magazine* published Lillian's story about her father. She described him as a man of character with an honest free spirit, although an eccentric one, who "walks to his own rhythm."

Though her father believed in "old-fashioned" self-discipline, he didn't believe in restricting the small acts of one's daily existence. Routine bored him, and he was forever looking for change and excitement as he noisily condemned detail-oriented people. Weston never acknowledged the fact that Maria took care of the humdrum duties, duties someone had to perform, of running the Weston family's life, often more difficult in a foreign country.

Lillian also admitted in some of her writings that Weston was a bit of a tyrant in his home but always hastened to say he was outgoing and fun loving, never mean or physically abusive. It was, however, his opinion that his likes, his comforts, and his ideas came first before those of his wife and children. Lillian wrote he rarely did anything unless he liked to do it and would never learn a game or skill because it was popular. He had his own ideas on all subjects and paid little attention to other people's opinions.

He didn't adjust his life to suit anyone else, an attitude bound to sour a relationship. The Weston marriage was not a happy one. Lillian was well aware of how her mother struggled to maintain a stable home life for herself and her children as Ed came and went as he pleased, ate when and what he wanted, and slept when he was tired. It was not unusual for him to stay up all night and sleep all day. Although Weston considered walking the finest form of exercise, he would ride if he could when he wasn't making a walk.

In her 1924 article, Lillian also wrote that Weston insisted his family follow his health rules with him, most of which she followed all her life because she saw them as pure common sense. His appetite gauged the amount he ate. If he was hungry, he swallowed a good square meal; then, if possible, he threw himself down on the couch and took a nap, "just like an anaconda," her mother used to say. Lillian thought she had read anacondas lived a long life.

He didn't eat pork but did eat beef, mutton, fish, and fowl—boiled, broiled, or roasted but never fried. He didn't like canned foods. He liked pies and very rich cakes. He loaded his bread with butter and covered his food with pepper. Simple foods, including plenty of fruit and vegetables, were his diet. He didn't eat exotic dishes with rich sauces and almost starved when he walked in France. He ate omelets twice a day for thirty days.

He drank two or three quarts of liquid each day: tea—cold or hot—lemonade, ginger beer, root beer, sweet cider. He didn't smoke and only used whiskey for "medicinal" purposes, but he didn't believe in total abstinence from alcohol. He liked wine and Bass ale or Guinness stout, but he didn't like American beer or iced claret.

Lillian, however, did skip some of his health rules, like taking a cold bath each morning. She also thought his wearing a red flannel nightshirt to bed to prevent rheumatism was pure folklore. Even so, his lifestyle and mental approach to life and walking had a lot to do with his endurance. He often said, "The condition of the whole man is basic to good health."

He told his family, "Relax when you relax and work hard when you work and don't worry about keeping up with the Joneses." And he practiced what he preached.

— TWO —

From Connecticut to London

Before I was out of my teens, I had crossed the ocean four times, studied in a French convent, lived in the Paris Latin Quarter, attended lectures at the College of France and Sorbonne, been a pupil in French national art schools.

Lillian's resumé, 1920

Weston won the jeweled Astley Belt with its $2,500 prize money, the Heisman Trophy of long-distance walking, in 1879. The six-day contest took place in London's Agricultural Hall. It wasn't an easy win, and he almost lost it. He walked long and hard for four days and fell into bed on the fifth for what he thought was going to be a two-hour nap, but his coach let him sleep six hours. This put him thirteen miles behind his nearest competitor.

Then Weston jumped out of bed and walked 127 miles in twenty-four hours to set a new world record and became an overnight international celebrity. He walked the entire 550 miles in 141 hours and forty-four minutes. He had just celebrated his fortieth birthday.

His children missed this greatest triumph because they were living in Stamford, Connecticut, with Maria's parents. Between 1876 and 1884, Maria and Ed lived alone in England and France while Weston walked in various contests and for different causes.

Edward Payson Weston, on the left, with a friend, 1879, in London, where he won the Astley Belt, the Heisman Trophy for long-distance walking.

Lillian remembered her Connecticut stay as a tranquil interlude in her life where she received a superior education at Miss Aiken's School for girls. It was also a time of treasured memories of warmth and love. Over the years when stress threatened to overwhelm her, she thought of her gentle, kind grandparents and their large white frame house filled with massive mahogany furniture, most of which had belonged to her grandfather's mother.

Lillian, a teenager in 1882, living with her grandparents in Connecticut and attending Miss Aiken's School for Girls.

Years later, Lillian wrote in an essay about inheriting her great-grandmother's Hepplewhite chair, "I always thought of it as one of the seats of the mighty. My grandfather adored his mother."

She went on to say that everyone else also said his mother was a wonderful woman, who had five sons who obeyed her as long as she lived and, because she never interfered in their lives, her daughter-in-laws thought the world of her, too. It's hard to understand how she could command perfect obedience from her sons and still not interfere in their lives.

Lillian's favorite spot in the big old house was her grandmother's sewing room with its two birdcages hanging among the lush green plants in one of its big windows. The cage doors were left open so the canaries could fly, and they sang as if they were outside. Each morning, her grandmother spread newspapers on the floor and put down shallow pans of water so the birds could have baths, an event Lillian and her brother and sister never missed.

At one point, they watched their grandmother push bits of cloth and twigs into the cage so the bird could build her nest. Then they waited as the canary mother patiently hatched her eggs.

Ruth and Sarah, Lillian's young aunts, who were her mother's sisters, still lived at home, and she tagged after them everywhere, much interested in their beauty preparations and dates. She watched with envy when they left the house with beaux, who took them riding in buggies or to shows.

The next day Lillian would follow them as "both would pace the piazza, arm in arm, exchanging confidences, until, exhausted they would at last step through the small paned French doors and throw themselves on the couch."

Once the children visited their parents in England. Lillian remembered her return trip, when she thought the Mormon prophet Joseph Smith was on board the ship. Although the man appears to have been a high-ranking Mormon official, perhaps also named Smith, he couldn't have been Joseph Smith, because he was killed by a mob in Carthage, Illinois, in 1844.

Several years later, she wrote about the shipboard incident in one of her "Lillian's Letters." She said the man was with one of his wives as they sailed down the English Channel. He got off at Queenstown, but his wife went on to New York City.

"What a fuss she did make when he left her!"

One of the other passengers said to Lillian's mother, "I do feel so sorry for poor Mrs. Smith, now her husband has gone."

Her mother said, "I suppose you know Mr. Smith is a Mormon and has several other wives."

"Is that so?" cried the other lady in astonishment. "Why, I thought she possessed his whole heart by the way she went on."

Two

In 1882, Lillian's mother returned home to the United States to accompany Lillian back to England. There's no mention in her papers whether the other children sailed with them. Although her grandparents had furnished much-needed security in her life, Lillian looked forward to a more exciting time with her parents.

When they landed, Ed was startled to find Lillian was no longer their "little girl." She was a smart, beautiful young-lady-grown. They had always sent her to the best schools they could afford and so enrolled her in the best London had to offer. Unfortunately, in England at the time, women could attend college lectures, but they couldn't earn degrees; thus female students were not prepared for higher education. English girls' schools taught "social development" and little else, as Lillian was to discover. Her major class was one of learning to curtsy.

"The height of each student's ambition was to be presented at the Court of St. James," Lillian wrote, and she knew she would never be presented to Queen Victoria. As an American, she wouldn't be required to curtsy anyway.

Queen Victoria was in the twilight of her reign, and England was in its late Victorian phase, with all the inherent snobbery and hypocrisy of the times. Both the students and the haughty teachers snubbed Lillian, something she admitted years later to us, her grandchildren. The tuition strapped her parents, and so there was no extra money to buy proper clothes. Because she knew they were sacrificing to send her to what they considered the best school, she didn't want to complain about having three dresses when the other students had dozens. And Victorian styles were expensive, because they were all alike, consisting of yards of material and rows of elaborate bows and flounces.

Lillian also was studying piano at the London Academy of Music with the idea of teaching it—or so her father thought. Because she loved music and was talented, she won several medals for pianoforte playing and harmony. Not only was she more ambitious than most girls her age, but she also needed to prove herself to negate the daily blows to her self-esteem in the English girls' school.

How disappointed Lillian was when she found she didn't like living in London! Although she doesn't say in her writings, probably the family was crammed into a small apartment. As usual, Ed Weston didn't consider whether his family liked London, because he liked the city. In the late 1800s, it was vibrant and full of activity.

Although Lillian didn't like her English school, she did enjoy London's cultural scene. There were concerts—Bach, Beethoven, and Wagner—at both the Crystal Palace and St. James Hall. New art exhibits opened regularly, often featuring the American artists Whistler and Sargent. She later wrote that London reached the zenith of its beauty and influence in the last years of Queen Victoria's reign.

In an unpublished article, "London Fifty Years Ago," written in 1940 from Lewistown, Montana, Lillian bemoaned the fact that everything wonderful about London probably would be destroyed by German bombs during World War II. She said there was no place in the world like Westminster Abbey, where Elizabeth of England and Mary of Scotland lie side by side. She also remembered a bunch of wildflowers beside a bouquet of costly hothouse roses on the slab marked with the name of Charles Dickens. Westminster Abbey did survive World War II.

She remembered climbing a narrow winding stairway to a room filled with wax figures of famous English people dressed in their own clothes. Each was an exact likeness made to deceive people into thinking they saw the actual corpse at public funerals. Prominent among these was Lord Nelson, with a patch over the blind eye he always turned toward the signal to surrender.

In her 1940 article, she wrote, "Let us hope his dauntless spirit still animates his fellow countrymen."

With sad nostalgia, Lillian remembered South Kensington Museum, with its portraits of long-dead notables painted from life:

John Kemble as Hamlet, and his celebrated sister, Sarah Siddons, queen of the English stage for thirty-three years. Peg Woffington is painted in bed, where a stroke of paralysis forced her to lie for weary years. Her face wears a sprightly expression, but a careful observer can detect tragedy lurking in her beautiful dark eyes. The likeness of Lord Byron at twenty-one is so handsome as almost to obliterate the memory of his debauchery and broken-hearted wife, while King Charles's infatuation with Nell Gynn can be better understood after seeing her deep blue, honest eyes shine out from beneath her golden curls.

Two

It took a long time to collect these authentic portraits, but, alas! One bomb could destroy them all in a minute.

It had been fifty-eight years since Lillian lived in London, and still she appeared to remember it all in minute detail.

There was, however, one aspect of nineteenth-century London Lillian never mentioned. The Thames River, which divides the city, was turning into an open sewer. Ragged barefoot children roamed the streets, and slums were ever expanding to accommodate the underclass of the period, the Irish. These poor people on London's streets were the victims of widespread illiteracy, prostitution, disease, hunger, alcoholism, and harsh labor conditions as the industrialists prospered and the workers barely survived.

This unpleasant daily scene on London's streets may have been why Lillian didn't like London. As she wandered the art galleries and museums, did she feel as Bernard Shaw did?

He wrote, "One wonders how this sordid century could have such dreams and realize them as art."

Among the many paradoxes of the Victorian period, none was more striking than the world English artists saw around them and that which they chose to paint. Sir Edward Burne-Jones, one of the most famous nineteenth-century English artists, lived close to some of the worst slums in Britain but chose to ignore both the harsh realities of life and technological progress as he said, "The more materialistic science becomes the more angels shall I paint."

This was the London Lillian saw when she joined her parents in 1882. As she struggled with her school, more and more she looked back with real longing to her grandparents' four-poster beds—"soft feather mattresses under spacious ceilings—and the bright kitchen with its yeasty baking smells."

There's no record of how long she attended the English girls' school, but several of her "Lillian's Letters" later described her disenchantment with studying how to curtsy day after day and facing the subtle, sometimes cruel abuse of her classmates and teachers. She also worried about falling behind in her studies. She wanted to develop her mind, not her social graces. She was being practical, because the Westons were not rich like the other students' parents. Lillian knew she needed a successful career to earn her own living.

Because both Ed and Maria were unhappy about Lillian's school, she didn't have to push too hard to convince them to send her to school in France. She was sure, and they knew, the tuition and board wouldn't cost them any more than the London school. It's not clear when Lillian had been to France before, but she said, "I like the French and Paris."

"Besides," she told her father, "I can improve my French."

THREE

Paris Interlude

I lived in France in the days of my youth, consequently, to me,
Paris is a city of dreams, bathed in the golden mists of romance
that soften harsh outlines and lend beauty to commonplace things.

"The Paris of Long Ago"
Ware, Montana. 1920

Stealing a few minutes from each day's endless ranch chores, how sad Lillian must have felt as she sat at her typewriter, looking out at the barren treeless landscape and writing of the beauty of Paris in her carefree teenage days. She remembered in excruciating detail "a brightly lit city starting at the Arc de Triomphe at the head of the Champs Elysées, parks, public buildings, fountains and statuary, a veritable wonderland. How she enjoyed the happy laughter, singing, rollicking students, and dainty food!"

As she read her worn copy of *Les Misérables* on a Sunday afternoon, she could still see the Seine River, spanned at intervals by beautiful bridges, flowing through the city, and into it emptying the sewers so vividly described in the French novel.

In the 1920s, as she read about Paris in current magazines, she didn't believe the French had lost their exquisite taste and sense of harmony, which, for her, was their greatest charm. She remembered the city's ladies elegantly dressed in the latest styles.

Perhaps present day French ladies parade along the boulevards in gowns, half way up to their knees in order that they may display vari-tinted vaudeville boots, but long ago when appearing on the street, ladies dressed so quietly they were not apt to attract attention. When I see gaudy styles advertised as, "Made in Paris," I always suppose they were especially designed for the American market—just as a merchant trading with savages might use trinkets made in New York, but virtually valueless there."

The Paris Lillian remembered, the Paris of the late 1800s, was an exciting place but considered slightly wicked. Probably this is why she wanted to live there. It was the unrestricted environment teenagers of any era crave. She talked long and hard, but to no avail. The Westons wouldn't let her go by herself and live in a boardinghouse.

Perhaps they had read the comments by the editor of *The Pictorial World,* who, on March 10, 1883, wrote, "The curse of France is Paris. . . . Everything in Paris is false and over-wrought. It may be the most beautiful city . . . but I'm certain Paris is a fester upon France."

A definite decision, however, had to be made about Lillian's schooling, because the Westons wouldn't be returning to the United States for another two years. From November 21, 1883, to March 15, 1884, Weston had a contract with the British Temperate Society to walk fifty miles per day, except Sundays, for one hundred days and each night deliver a lecture on the evils of overdrinking. Because he believed in temperance in all aspects of life, he would never walk for prohibition.

Finally, although they couldn't afford it, they enrolled Lillian in a Catholic convent school in the center of Paris. Later, when she became a reporter, she wrote about the experience, saying she wondered if she had made a mistake, "as the outer gates of the French convent clanged shut behind me shutting me in bare white walls adorned with crucifixes and frightening pictures of suffering Christs."

Each time she left the convent, even for an hour, the same chill would creep over her when she returned and heard the outer gate shut. The whole building, tenanted by black funereal figures, was cold as a tomb. Even the smallest children were dressed in black, and she learned, to her dismay, she too must wear the same gloomy uniform. But she soon realized it was

Three

a welcome change from worrying about having the right clothes. Uniforms did away with snobbery and social competition.

She often attended the dimly lit chapel but dreaded the communion services, when the nuns lowered their veils and not even their white faces showed. Lillian thought entering a nunnery similar to "committing suicide," where nuns must take the three vows of personal poverty, obedience, and celibacy.

Because she couldn't afford a room of her own, she shared one with nineteen other students and two nuns. Twenty-two narrow beds filled the room. The windows above the beds were so high one couldn't see anything but the sky, and the girls weren't allowed to have a mirror. Each morning, the other students said their prayers out loud as they made their beds and dressed. The chanting always woke Lillian, who wasn't Catholic and so was exempt from prayers. She thought they could have whispered sometimes.

"They said enough prayers in that convent to save this sinful world if praying would do it."

Often at mealtime, nuns read extracts from St. Joseph's life. Lillian found it unpleasant trying to digest body and mental food at the same time. Right after breakfast the older pupils, including Lillian, usually took a walk in the park, passing by the school's playground, which was a barren dirt yard surrounded by a rough board fence fifteen feet high.

In the convent, there was no privacy, never a chance to be alone. Years later, she told how frightening it was to be sitting quietly in the library when a nun would seem to materialize from thin air as she slipped silently from a secret passageway or a movable panel.

Lillian, who seemed able to adjust to any situation, often found herself homesick. When letters from her parents arrived, the Mother Superior censored them and brought them to her. Once she gazed into Lillian's face and then kissed her, saying, "I kiss you for your mother."

At first, Lillian enjoyed the serene routine—study all day and to bed at 8 P.M.—but then the strict regimen and lack of freedom began to irritate her. About that time, she made new American friends, Fidella and Maud. The three became known as the American colony in the Rue Monceau. Fidella was the oldest and a boarder at the convent, considered a "young lady grown." Madame Viare was teaching her to sing. Fidella also had her own room, and so the three girls hung out together, chattering in

English. They always agreed they must speak French but always lapsed into English.

"With so much to say, how could we stop to convert it into French?"

They discussed every subject—laughed, joked, and quarreled. Fidella was a friend of the American writer Ella Wheeler Wilcox, and Maud and Lillian urged her to tell the slightest details of Wilcox's life. Because Fidella was older, she was allowed to take the other two girls out of the convent with her on weekends.

Lillian wrote, "Those were gala days."

One of their favorite trips was sailing down the Seine. How thrilled they were to leave the convent for the day! For a time, they were all free. Sometimes they hired a cab and drove to the Bois de Boulogne and would haggle over who would pay the extra sou if the fare couldn't be divided into three equal parts.

Once the three set out to hear High Mass at Notre Dame on Easter morning. They got up early, but when they descended to the refectory for breakfast, they found a "fast" in progress that couldn't be broken until noon, and so they ate their rolls without butter and drank their coffee without milk.

On Easter vacation, several nuns took Lillian and Maud to the country house connected with the convent, just outside Paris. Lillian remembered pansies and forget-me-nots growing in profusion and a lake surrounded by trees. It was said that at one time, the place had belonged to one of Louis XIV's favorite mistresses. Maud told Lillian the estate also had been owned by the Mother Superior, who held the rank of countess in the real world. She gave both up when she entered the cloister.

Much later in life, Lillian told us the sisters were kind to her, but they couldn't compensate for lack of "home joys and love." One sister, in particular, was so good to her Lillian often thought of her sweet, patient face. She was the nun who did most of the cooking. Once when Lillian went to the dining room, she rushed up to the sister and threw her arms around her. She told the nun she reminded her of her grandmother. The nun, because she was low in rank, didn't dare return her affection but pressed two chocolate cakes into her hand. Lillian felt so sorry and thought it went against all love and human tenderness to be locked up in a convent.

Fidella left the school first, saying she wouldn't board in a place where the gates were locked at 8 P.M. and everyone was expected to go to bed. Maud left soon after that. All three girls corresponded for a while but then finally lost track of each other. Lillian often wondered if their "air castles" built by the side of hers were ever realized.

Despondent at being left alone, she caught a cold she couldn't seem to cure. She was so unhappy she pleaded with her mother and father to let her board in the city. Even though she was eighteen years old by this time, Ed and Maria didn't think she was old enough to live alone in Paris. They agreed with her moving out of the convent on one condition— that she would stay in a family acquaintance's boardinghouse.

After much discussion, Ed finally crossed the channel and helped Lillian move.

She wrote, "My heart leaped for joy when I heard the gates shut behind me, and I left the cold prison-like place for the last time."

But in her handwritten unpublished novel *The Golden Cord: The Story of a Young Girl's Adventures in Paris*, she described her apprehension as the cab pulled up in front of the shabby row house on a grimy street that she would call home for the next year. Miss Bridgely, the landlady, had stepped around the corner to the grocer's, and so the other boarders pointed Lillian to her room.

As she climbed ahead of the cabdriver, who struggled up the narrow stairway with her trunk on his shoulders, her misgivings turned to total dismay. Her room's windows were small and faced the north, so there was little sunlight. The paint was peeling in one corner, and a worn, dirty rug covered the floor in front of the sagging bed. A feeling of homesickness swept over Lillian. Had she made another mistake?

"Doubts crept into my thoughts but I ruefully pushed them aside."

She knew her parents had made more sacrifices to let her stay in Paris to study at the College of France and the Sorbonne. She couldn't change her mind at this point. Just as the driver deposited the trunk in the middle of the floor, Miss Bridgely arrived. She was an ex-schoolteacher, tall and angular. Lillian wrote that she moved like she had a rod up her back. She had cold blue eyes fringed with light lashes. She thrust a large bony hand at an uneasy Ed Weston.

He wasn't often responsible for Lillian's welfare and so didn't know what to do when he saw the troubled frown on his daughter's face. He didn't like the landlady or Lillian's room either, but his cab was waiting, so he reluctantly departed after trying to reassure her with a firm hug.

Lillian knew she had to live with her decision to stay in Paris by herself. This was a long-term mistake if it was, indeed, a mistake, but she had to make it work, had to make the most of it. After her father left, Lillian threw herself on the bed with a sigh but jumped up immediately to see if it was clean. Though the sheets and rough blankets had a grimy look, they smelled of a strong soap. It was obvious they had been washed recently. It's surprising Lillian even worried about dirt. After living in Paris for several months, she should have been used to it. People didn't bathe much. Streets, air, food, homes, people, breath, clothes, and buildings smelled. A man could look perfectly groomed until one saw his shirt cuffs were as black as his fingernails.

Lillian unpacked and put her few belongings in the small chest next to her bed and hung her few dresses and coat on the hooks along one side of the room. By that time, it was twilight and she went down the narrow stairs hoping to find tea. She joined her new landlady and the other boarders at the dining room table and found them as "drab as their surroundings."

Mrs. Browne was a small, fragile-looking New Englander. Ill health had lined her face with wrinkles and given her an unhappy expression.

In her novel, Lillian wrote, "When she was young, she must have been prettier than her daughter who, although barely 25 years old, looked and acted 45."

At the end of her first twenty-four hours in the boardinghouse, Lillian decided the landlady was the most unpleasant person she'd ever met. She, in fact, called her a "she critter" in her private thoughts and writings. Miss Bridgely's long career as a schoolteacher had given her a know-it-all manner, which Lillian resented. And Miss Bridgely wasn't too tactful about the fact that she found the American the most conceited girl she had met in a long time.

Unfortunately, because Lillian was so young and new to Paris, she had to have Miss Bridgely help her find her way around. The older woman insisted they walk everywhere they went. Although Lillian liked to walk, she thought they might have taken a bus once in a while. They covered a lot of territory as Lillian set out to enroll in the National Art School, engage a music teacher, and decide what courses of lectures she would follow at the Sorbonne and the College of France. She was relieved when she finished setting up all her classes and could dispense with Miss Bridgely's company. Soon she was too busy to dwell on her landlady's unpleasant personality.

Within a month Lillian adjusted to her surroundings, enjoyed her studies, and was into a routine. She wrote her parents that the food wasn't as good as her mother's, but she ate enough, slept soundly, and was almost happy.

In 1884, France was full of energy, change, and prosperity. The Eiffel Tower was being built and was completed in 1889. The "Marseillaise" was designated the national anthem, and July 14 had been celebrated as a national holiday for the first time in 1881. At the time, Paris was considered the cultural capital of the world. Artists, writers, and musicians were busy laying the foundation of the modern twentieth-century consciousness to come. Writers Hugo, Taine, Renan, Flaubert, and Zola were hard at work.

Although Lillian found it "an atmosphere most conducive to the study of art," she probably didn't realize a revolution was taking place. The Impressionists had emerged as a major force on the Paris art scene after decades of struggle. Many now famous artists like Rodin, Monet, and van Gogh worked in the Paris of the 1880s, bringing French art out of the mid-nineteenth-century style of large-scale oil paintings of scenes from the Bible, classical antiquity, and French history.

Lillian found that art students were welcome to visit the art galleries and museums, where they could study and copy the world's greatest masterpieces. Eminent artists visited the young students' studios and criticized and offered suggestions on their work. These services were free; consequently, as Lillian wrote later, "These criticisms were unbiased and honest, a priceless service for the beginner in any art."

In U.S. private schools, she often saw the drawing teacher prejudiced by a pupil's money or social position and thus not giving the student honest criticism. A slightly negative aspect to all this enthusiasm may have been that many of these successful artists cruised the young artists' studios looking for fresh new ideas. Probably Lillian never thought of this.

She found that the Paris of the 1880s abounded in other educational advantages. There were free libraries and free band concerts. At the College of France, Lillian listened to the greatest French minds lecture on all subjects. She had to go early to get a seat, because only the enrolled students could reserve seats. Rich and poor took the same chance of standing.

Although she found the French had "exquisite taste and an outstanding sense of harmony," she complained most Parisians seemed to prefer "singers of doggerel rhyme while watching semi-nude dancers" to hearing the lectures of the most learned men of the century.

Barely existing in the boardinghouse for several months, she studied hard, tried to avoid her landlady, and rarely saw the other boarders except at dinner. She was beginning to feel like a hermit when, according to her story *The Golden Cord*, she met Dick Randolph, a handsome, rich young American living in Paris. He was Miss Bridgely's special pet, and the older woman didn't like it at all when he flirted with Lillian on his first visit. In her novel, Lillian said Miss Bridgely had memorized a long list of women married to men young enough to be their sons.

The next day, the landlady warned her Dick had lots of money and status and Lillian shouldn't take his attentions too seriously.

In no uncertain terms, Lillian told her, "I want you to know I consider myself just as good—in fact, a great deal better than he is."

One thing she wasn't about to admit to Miss Bridgely was she found Dick attractive. He was fun to be with in romantic nineteenth-century Paris, because he knew every nook and cranny of the city and took her exciting places. He was also welcome in the city's many fashionable salons and knew all the latest gossip.

She admitted, "It would be so easy to fall in love with him."

On bright spring mornings, they roamed the streets on the top of an omnibus because she wanted the best view. Besides, it cost half as much as riding inside, and she did pay her own way.

"How we enjoyed those days in the warm sunshine, which sifted through the spike-shaped, creamy blossoms of the horse chestnut trees that bordered the street on either side."

In the late 1800s, Paris had parks everywhere, from the great Bois de Boulogne, frequented by beautiful, fashionable women, to the "little patches of green, scarce bigger than a block where the children of the poor could enjoy sunshine and fresh air."

But Dick and Lillian's favorite entertainment was conversation over coffee at a small café. Lillian wrote, "I revealed all my ambitions and dreams," including the one of being a concert pianist, "as freely as I would have to a brother."

At that time, developing a career in music was paramount in Lillian's life. Here *The Golden Cord* records a painful true event. When it was almost time for her to leave France, Dick asked a famous American musician, teaching in Paris, to audition her.

Lillian described the poignant scene. "After the teacher heard and watched me play, she said, 'Ah! Very well done,' and she continued to sit, silent as if in deep thought. Then she took my hand and looked me straight in the eyes. She said, 'You're musical—in fact, talented.' She turned my hand over, 'but you can never hope to be a great pianist with such small hands.'"

Probably Lillian knew the verdict before she visited the teacher, but from this point on, she speaks of "my sadness."

In her novel, the hero proposes. Whether this really happened is anybody's guess. She has the heroine refuse his offer.

"Marrying anyone is very far from my thoughts; I wish to reap the reward of my studies—some way . . . not to be tied down to domestic life. I don't want to be an old maid, but I think 25 or 30 years of age is soon enough to settle down to domestic life."

Neither would she give him any hope for the future. She told him, "I don't have a vocation, as the nuns say, for married life. . . . I doubt if I could make you happy anyway. I can be very disagreeable and hard to get along with sometimes. You had better choose some nice, domesticated, good-tempered pretty girl for a wife, who would be a good housekeeper and make you comfortable. You are an uncommonly nice man and deserve a good woman which is something that can't be said for many young men now-a-days."

FOUR

In Old New York

Whenever I hear a buoy bell, I feel like crying. . . . I never forgot standing at the rail looking at land but not being allowed to put a foot on it.

"Lillian's Letter"
September 20, 1888

Lillian sailed for New York City with her parents in the summer of 1885. Unfortunately, when their ship arrived in American waters, it was forced to lay at anchor waiting for a clean bill of health. There were two cases of smallpox in the steerage with the crowded immigrants. This caused Lillian's already unhappy mood to deepen as she along with everyone else feared "being imprisoned on the ship with the dread disease."

Depression plagued her the whole trip as she realized her school days were over and her adult life was about to begin. Her failed hopes to become a concert pianist probably caused most of her sadness. After all, she had worked toward this goal all her young life. Now what could she do? She worried she would fail, would not find a job.

Even though she seemed to have accepted the idea she might become a teacher, she still had dreams of fame and fortune. She couldn't help it. It was her nature. The feeling that she had to succeed was so strong sometimes that she peered into her mirror and felt despair. She was her own severest critic. She thought her mouth weak and would say to herself, "If my mouth were different, I should have no fear of missing the 'crown of glory,' but I will not fail."

On this trip, the Westons met a southern senator, who followed them everywhere. Although he was thirty years older than Lillian, she found him attractive. His brown hair was sprinkled with gray, and he was youthful looking with an air of authority and opulence. He was also a bachelor.

Her mother loved it as he overwhelmed her daughter with attention. This irritated Lillian, even though she liked the man. She detested match-making mothers. There is some evidence in her writings that her sister, Maude, thought she was crazy not to encourage his interest.

"I'd rather be an old man's darling," Maude said, "than a young man's slave."

Lillian, however, meant it when she said she wasn't ready to get married. As far as she was concerned, at age twenty she was just beginning her life.

When the Westons finally landed, they settled in an apartment in Brooklyn and Lillian began her job search. She started with the classified ads, but they rarely listed a need for a music teacher, tutor, or writer, the professions she felt qualified to pursue. She hadn't taught before, but restrictions on teaching were much more lenient in an era when few women had an education. The truth was, Lillian really didn't know what she wanted to do. She had been so focused on becoming a pianist, she hadn't given any other career a thought.

Many of the classified advertisers were looking for skilled seam-stresses: "Gentlewomen wanted . . . professional females—expert tuck and puffed scarf makers, bookkeepers, dressmakers, fitters, models [in the New York City garment district], milliners." All her life, Lillian avoided any kind of sewing. She even botched attaching buttons or hemming skirts.

Finally she applied for a few teaching jobs and, later, wrote about them: "If there is one thing more provoking than another for a teacher, it is to carefully answer an advertisement, and receive a day or two later a prospectus for some teachers' agency."

Then she had to pay two dollars to keep her name on the agency's books for one year. If she did find a job, the agency would take five percent of the first year's salary whether she kept her position a month or a year.

"When board is included it is reckoned at $200 a year, and the commission on this must also be paid in advance," quite a sum of money in 1885.

Headlines like the following one appearing in the January 10, 1888, *New York Herald* were common in Lillian's day: "Mary Vanorden killed herself with prussic acid because she couldn't make a go of her boarding house."

It seems a drastic solution to the woman's problems, but in the 1800s if an uneducated middle-class woman found herself without a man—husband, brother, or father—to take care of her, about the only way to make money was renting rooms or crocheting scarves. Lillian was luckier than some middle-class women because she did have a father who would support her to a point, but because he had given her the best education he could afford, he expected her to earn her own living eventually. Did her father know about her dreams to be a pianist? Lillian never mentions telling him. When she was studying piano, he thought she was studying to become a teacher.

Lillian was shocked when she first began roaming New York City, looking for a job. It was an industrial center with clouds of noxious gases and unpleasant odors hanging low over Manhattan. Everyone—rich and poor, powerful and powerless—breathed this bad air, the result of no regulation of bone mills, refineries, and tanneries at Hunter's Point on the rim of the Bronx.

The city was also crowded. Tinderbox tenements bulged with thousands of inhabitants. Because New York was the principal American entry port, most of the thousands of immigrants who swept into the country between 1880 and 1900 remained in the city right off the boats. They provided the garment district with cheap labor for at least a generation and filled sections like Mulberry Bend, Ludlow Street, and Hester Street to overflowing. Immigration was at its height, and so many of these people were living poverty-stricken lives with barely enough to eat or a decent place to sleep.

Most New York residents tried to ignore the situation, but not Lillian. When she began her column, she occasionally wrote about the misery she saw on the streets, although her editors actively discouraged this type of "heavy" story.

On October 22, 1888, she wrote: "My attention was called the other day to the white slaves in New York; or in other words, girls and women who work hour after hour and day after day in close, malodorous rooms, and receive from thirty to eighty cents (a day) as the reward of their labors."

She said she knew her readers didn't want to read such a gloomy letter about oppressed people, but she told them she had to write about it, because she didn't have the influence to change things. She said she would rather not live in a world where she saw "the pinched faces, shrunken forms and exhausted, hopeless looking human beings one saw every day in our great city."

She wrote of businessmen in New York City's garment district exploiting their workers, mostly women, who were forced to work in decrepit buildings with many a life destroyed by fire like the one described in *The New York Herald* on August 4, 1888.

The story was called "In a Death Trap" and described how seventeen men, women, and children lost their lives "horribly" in a burning factory on the Bowery. The building had six floors, five of which were used for clothing manufacture. Workers were crowded together on every floor. A kerosene oil stove exploded in the first-floor apartment, and flaming oil spread over everything. It literally flew up the elevator shaft to the floor where over one hundred men, women, and children were working. The place had been a death trap, one of a thousand just like it all over the city.

No crowds gathered to watch the disaster. They were so used to these garment district factories burning, they didn't even stop going to the saloon that remained open for business in front of the building.

Lillian wrote about one friend who struggled to establish a mission to help the people in the tenements in an area less than a mile long and a quarter of a mile wide. The woman went from house to house, talking with families. It was slow, hard work.

"If they could have a meeting place, it would be a great help."

Her friend couldn't bear the sight of children dying of starvation or disease or of several families sleeping in a room only large enough for one person. The rooms weren't ventilated, the sanitary arrangements nil, and "the odors so vile that often the missionaries are sick after remaining half an hour in one of these buildings crowded with human beings."

Everyone, including Lillian, struggled with the problems of this rapidly expanding population. She, like every other pedestrian, scrambled over mountains of trash covering the streets. Kitchen slops, cinders, broken cobblestones, and discarded bits of merchandise were all piled on the sidewalks. Even in downtown Manhattan, one had to climb over heaps of rubbish or, in the rain, wade through slime.

New York City's 150,000 horses also added to the filth by each producing twenty to twenty-five pounds of manure a day. City carts attempted to clear the streets of manure, but too often it was smashed by the heavy traffic. Then during the dry spells, the manure was pounded to dust, and the wind whisked the particles into homes and businesses and up pedestrians' nostrils. Add this to a stable on each block filled with urine-soaked straw attracting swarms of flies and radiating a powerful stench.

Lillian, literally, had to force herself out of the house each day to interview for work. Her father tried to help by making an appointment for her with one of his editor contacts from his days as a reporter for *The New York Herald.* Later, Lillian wrote about visiting the man's office.

He seemed all business as he scanned her writing portfolio, but when he suggested they discuss her possibilities over dinner so they could get better acquainted, she pulled herself up to her full five-foot-two height and sailed out of his office. Disheartened, she found an empty bench in Central Park and sat down to figure out how she could earn her living. She had really counted on the contact paying off.

Lillian hadn't been walking the New York City streets long before she realized she was sick. For a week, her throat was sore, and she was so tired she could hardly drag herself out of bed each day. She thought she was depressed about her failure to find a job and so tried to ignore her symptoms.

Finally came a day when she couldn't get up and her mother called the doctor.

He looked serious as he examined her.

"It isn't diphtheria is it, Doctor?" Lillian asked.

Four

"Yes, I'm afraid it is."

". . . Some way I thought so. Will I die?"

"Die? Oh! No, no. We'll have you about again in a few days."

Lillian thought, "He doesn't believe a word he's saying."

For days, hour in and hour out, she lay in bed, too weak to care about living or dying. At times, she would listen as her heart beat "slower and slower, so long between its pulsations my life seemed to ebb away." If the next beat didn't come, she would be gone.

One time her mother came in and thought her daughter was dead. She leaned against the wall and cried, "Oh! Lillian, what shall I do?"

Lillian opened her eyes and, later, said her mother's voice brought her back to life. She had been sinking so quietly, so peacefully. It was easier to die than to try to swallow.

It was about this time that she had a strange experience. There's no proof as to whether it was an illusion or a vision, because in various stories, she wrote different versions of the same event. One evening, a bright image entering her dark room awakened her. A radiant angel stood before her and told her he was Gabriel.

She assumed he had come for her: "I don't want to go with you."

"I haven't come for you. I have come to give you a message from the Lord."

"Yes, yes. I know. I know what it is."

Lillian said she actually didn't know, but because she feared the angel would change his mind and take her, she wished him to depart at once.

The angel looked at her for a moment and said, "Remember—love one another," and then he was gone.

While recuperating from diphtheria, she had plenty of time to think about her life. Her vision or dream—she was never sure what to call it—forced her to analyze her attitude toward God and religion. Before this, there had been little emphasis on the spiritual side of her life. Her father and mother weren't churchgoers, and so her maternal grandparents had been her only religious influence.

From the first time she heard the Ten Commandments, Lillian tried to follow their rules. She, however, saw her pride as an obstacle to "proper humility." She wanted to live a good life but was well aware that at times she was overbearing and opinionated even as she tried to temper the trait.

By her stringent standards or anyone else's standards, for that matter, she would be considered a kind, decent human being.

In casting around to fit her newfound spirituality into a category, she became an admirer of the Russian Madam Elena Petrovna Blavatsky, a leader in spiritualism and the occult sciences, who, in the 1870s, settled in New York City and established the Theosophical Society.

Lillian quietly adopted its creed, based on the "ancient wisdom of India . . . stressing the universal brotherhood of man . . . seeking to investigate the unexplained laws of nature and the powers latent in man."

Theosophy's specific teachings state, "Man has, or may have, seven bodies, one on each of the seven planes of which the physical is the lowest. Developing his bodies on the higher and astral planes is the secret of latent powers."

Lillian's search for spiritual knowledge and comforting assurances concerning life after death was not unique, especially in the late nineteenth century. Unusual beliefs flourished. Lillian discussed some in her November 15, 1887, column in the *Richmond* (Virginia) *Star:* "Spiritualists, mental scientists, mental healers, and mental humbugs generally infest the country and reap a harvest from credulous dupes. The newspapers devote many columns to palmistry, fortune telling, astrology, and all kinds of Charlatanism."

In church one Sunday, her minister's sermon commented on the number of fortune-tellers' signs to be seen everywhere. Lillian allowed as how superstition was rampant in the nineteenth century. She mentioned a first-class weekly that devoted two pages each week to printing the horoscopes of its readers and identified a certain Turkish bath in the city that advertised a lucky stone upon which its patrons might wish without extra charge.

She wrote, "The number of people who object to breaking a looking glass, going under a ladder, spilling salt, or starting anything on Friday, may be counted by the thousands."

Lillian didn't admit to being one of these superstitious people, but she was. She avoided black cats, always tossed salt over her left shoulder if she spilled it, and never walked under a ladder. She also read tealeaves and claims to have predicted her brother's death through "reading" her own cup, something she never practiced again after he died.

She also believed in a mysterious world, and probably the only thing that kept her from delving into the occult and supernatural was her belief in God. In one story she said it was out-of-date to believe in Bible visions and dreams, but she found most people had wonderful experiences to relate about such things. She often said there was an unseen world, an unseen force, and a mysterious connection between the natural and supernatural that scientists had never yet fathomed.

FIVE

Out and About

Broadway surface cars still run merrily—over people. It is a real trick to get on a car because it is so hard to get them to stop. One waves a parasol and handkerchief in vain. Then one has to dodge trucks and run under horses' heads to get out of the street. . . . One day I lost the car and my parcels.

"Lillian's Letter." November 9, 1888

Lillian recovered from diphtheria, but it was weeks before she regained her energy or could speak above a whisper. In fact, for the rest of her life she was plagued with a hoarse voice whenever she was overtired. As she gained strength, she fretted and worried and was, understandably, anxious to get on with her life. Finding a job was paramount, on her mind all the time. The forced bed rest gave her time to evaluate what she might do. Chances are she began her "Lillian's Letter," an instant hit with editors, during her long convalescence.

Her column seems to be the same style and "flavor" as the "Fashions and Fancies" column in one of her well-thumbed books, *The Pictorial Review*, a compilation of the 1882 issues of a London newspaper. Her father probably realized her writing samples were better than average and gave them to a newspaper contact.

Although there's no record of how she broke into print, it was a good time to become a writer. As with every other phase of business in the late 1800s, publishing was on the upswing. Magazines, newspapers, and books were easy and cheap to produce, and the average nineteenth-century household spent more on reading materials than ever before.

Women's magazines were coming into their own. *The Ladies' Home Journal* had 270,000 subscribers in 1886. In 1889, a new editor, Edward Bok, took over. He was a bachelor who adored his mother and had no sisters or woman confidants. Although no man knew less about women, he was confident he knew what was best for his female readers. He saw his *Journal* as "the monthly bible of the American home."

Bok and his magazine certainly didn't do anything for women's liberation. Its monthly column, "Ideas of a Plain Country Woman," was full of homely platitudes like, "If we could only remember when we are doing for the family, we are at work on the human race. We often hear women lament the lack of time for reading. I'm convinced much harm has been done by women having too much time to read."

Nevertheless, circulation expanded each year to 440,000 by 1889. The average nineteenth-century woman, in most cases, couldn't, and wouldn't if she could, change her role in life and didn't want unconventional advice. She wanted understanding and guidance in dealing with her real world, and that did not include hints on rebelling against nineteenth-century traditions and her husband.

Lillian might have read the *Journal* as a possible market for freelance articles, but Bok's domestic agenda didn't interest her at all and never would. She was living at home with her family, and evidently her mother did all the housework. In one column, Lillian said, "I do not keep house." This probably accounts for her lack of housekeeping skills later in life. Most of it was done for her in her formative years.

By the time she was completely well, her writing career was under way and her column was appearing in newspapers like the *Richmond* (Virginia) *Star*, the *Stamford* (Connecticut) *Herald*, and some western papers.

Facing a regular deadline, she found herself struggling to keep up with column ideas. She also realized if she were going to write intelligent stories about New York City, she needed to know it from east to west

Lillian, a young reporter in New York City in 1887, covering city news and writing her column "Lillian's Letter."

and north to south. Toward the end of August 1887 on a hot summer day, she and a male friend set out to explore the streets in a horse-drawn cab. She described each step of the way in "Lillian's Letter."

They "proceeded along St. Nicholas Avenue," where she discovered "elegant houses lining the street, a most aristocratic neighborhood, one of many." In the late 1800s, wealthy financiers, landlords, and merchants

Five

built "palaces" in New York City. It was an age of great and sudden fortunes, and just as people today like to read about the rich and famous, the Victorians liked to read about them, too. Lillian also liked to write about the city's important people—the Goulds, the Vanderbilts, and the "400" leaders of American society hierarchy who could fit into and would be invited to Mrs. William Astor's ballroom.

Even entrepreneurs whose profits were made elsewhere built houses for their families in New York City. Ostentatious spending and an expensive home covered with ornate columns and sculptures determined one's place in New York society. Sometimes every style from Greek through Gothic through Turkish and Egyptian was combined in the architecture of one of these large homes.

These rich were very rich, and they lived rich. Diamond Jim Brady said it all: "Hell! I'm rich. It's time I had some fun."

Mark Twain blasted the era by calling it "the Gilded Age," while William James sneered at the American worship of the bitch goddess "Success."

On that summer's day in 1887, Lillian and her friend finally ended up at the Seventy-second Street entrance to Central Park, which was one of Lillian's favorite places. She crossed the park at least twice a week in pursuit of stories. How she enjoyed that walk! Each time there was something new to see.

"The monument of Daniel Webster seemed to wear a different expression every mood in which I saw it; the statue of the Falconer recalled to my mind numberless stories of the days of chivalry."

Later in the summer, she passed the place where Cappa's Seventh Regiment band played every Wednesday and Saturday afternoon, surrounded by a crowd of people. And then there was the lake on her left with its glide boats and swans in summer and skaters in winter, "whose merry shouts I heard ringing in my ears long after I had passed them by."

She talked of a Central Park resident: "Mr. Crowley was an old Liberian Chimpanzee, who had resided in Central Park for many years and lived like a prince."

He was no ordinary monkey. He ate soup with a spoon and managed knife and fork with great skill. He thought the napkin unnecessary and would make a dab or two at his mouth and throw it on the floor, upset the table, and take a swing on the trapeze. Like Louis XIV, he ate in state with many onlookers at each meal. In fact, the crowd was so great Lillian feared being crushed.

The newspapers carried banner headlines when Mr. Crowley died.

Casting around for new experiences to write about in the summer of 1888, Lillian and her sister, Maude, went to Glen Island one Saturday on a "glorious day." They timed their arrival for one of the band concerts of John Philip Sousa's marches, much in vogue at the time.

In her "Letter" she wrote, "It is not a very aristocratic resort, Nellie, but I enjoy mingling with the common herd occasionally, and it is such a delightful place."

August 1888 was a hot one. Lillian told her readers she refused to look at a thermometer because that only made her feel worse. She said it was too hot to write, but she seemed to be turning out a lot of columns. With no air conditioning and the Victorian dresses with both long sleeves and skirts, one wonders how Lillian raced around New York City each day.

In one column, she wished people wouldn't make love on the elevated road.

It isn't the proper place and it is very annoying to all of the right-minded passengers, although the wrong-minded ones have a wild desire to laugh. The other day I was quietly sitting in the car when a man and woman came in and took up a position opposite to me. Well, he hugged her and petted her and whispered and I expected any minute would kiss her.

Then I heard him say, "It is good to be where I can see you all the time again." I realized he was her husband and she had been away from him this summer. Now, I like a man to be fond of his wife, in fact, I fairly adore a loving husband, and I expect my better-half (when I get one) will just idolize me but I expect him to worship me privately as public demonstrations of affections are essentially vulgar.

When Lillian could afford it, she went away for a couple of weeks each summer to places like Bethlehem, New Hampshire. She always joined the annual parade of coaches from the different resort hotels, which rolled slowly over the Bethlehem Road from the Maplewood to the Centennial and back again.

Five

In 1889, this item appeared in the *Stamford* (Connecticut) *Herald:* "The next vehicle in the pageant was a nobby little private buckboard, which was elegantly decorated with golden rod. The buckboard was occupied by two handsome young maidens, Miss Ketchum and Miss Weston of New York. Miss Ketchum handled the ribbons with rare skill. A man servant in full livery was in attendance."

As a young reporter, Lillian was everywhere—so much to see, so much to say. After writing "Lillian's Letter" for a year, her editors evidently encouraged her to branch out into all aspects of the cultural scene. She, of course, had opinions on everything, and she couldn't believe she was being paid to express them. She was onstage, really strutting her stuff, and she did her best.

She called the nineteenth century a "century of disbelief," when the latest theories were that Bacon wrote Shakespeare's plays and a French monk wrote Bunyan's *Pilgrim's Progress.* She said she expected next year to hear that Byron's valet was the author of *Childe Harold's Pilgrimage* and Washington's overseer led the American armies to victory dressed in his master's clothes.

Lillian seemed to know lots of people and organized parties to the various events she needed to cover, and New York City did host the top-notch performers of the day. Her real bonus was being paid to attend and review these performances, and she was having fun. If she couldn't wow concertgoers as a virtuoso pianist, she would wow her readers with her scintillating analyses of others' performances.

Music was, and always would be, the "honey of life" for Lillian. She regarded it as the highest art form. "All the others have something material about them. Music alone is unearthly. It is a language of feeling; a language without words, but in which the innermost emotions of the soul may be expressed, delicately, yet with a power not found in words."

In November 1888, she attended the second symphony concert at the Metropolitan Opera House. Dr. Leopold Damrosch, who was the conductor for decades, had died. After searching for a replacement, the symphony society's directors decided that the best person to fill the spot was Dr. Damrosch's twenty-three-year-old son. He was conductor the night Lillian attended.

"I was enthralled with watching the young man take his father's place."

In this same story, she angrily denounced the $1-a-seat price for concerts. She thought those who could afford it should pay $2.50 for the best seats and leave the poorer seats for students for 25 cents.

In another column the same year, she voiced her disapproval of a popular musical playing in New York. In a special correspondence to the *Richmond* (Virginia) *Star*, November 29, 1888, she wrote:

> This is the last week of Shenandoah at the Academy of Music. If everyone shared my sentiments relative to war, it would not pay to stage that style of drama. Fighting is barbarous.

> *"Ez fur war, I call it murder,*
> *There you have it, plain and flat,*
> *I want to go no furder than my Testyment for that.*
> *If you take a sword and draw it and go stick a feller thru'—*
> *Government ain't to answer for it, God will send the bill to you."*

> James R. Lowell expressed my ideas when he penned those lines. I see no glory in war—only misery, pestilence, famine, weeping women, and dying men. But, judging from the success of Shenandoah and other war dramas, the majority of my countrymen and women do not agree with me.

In December 1888, she saw the play *She*, which opened in Brooklyn. It was not a success in London and Lillian admitted it was not very literary, but it was funny: "I laughed and laughed until I was ashamed of myself, and the people in front of me turned around to see what was the matter."

Lillian's love of the theater ranked second only to music. Broadway was on her beat, and she loved to come up with a bit of gossip in addition to reviews. When Monsieur Coquelin of the Theater Français and Madame Hading of the Gymnase of Paris were in a local play, she mentioned they were not the best of friends. She wondered how they could act so loving in their parts but went on to say, "Sometimes people off the stage have to do that, too."

She wrote in one column about having E. A. Sothern, a prominent young nineteenth-century actor, to tea. Probably she met him through his father, who was a friend of her father.

Five

"Mr. Sothern on the stage is very different from Mr. Sothern off the stage. . . . He is a very solemn young man."

In August of 1888, she reviewed his play, *Lord Chumley*, and said she was not impressed by Belasco and De Mille's production, but she praised Sothern's portrayal of Lord Chumley. She said he was going to be as great an actor as his father. He got his start by taking small parts and working his way up to bigger and better parts. Unfortunately, *Lord Chumley* opened in the worst of seasons, August 1888 in New York City. The people who could afford to attend Broadway plays were all out of town.

Decades later, writing to an editor, she criticized a 1920s movie production called *The Lights of Old Broadway*. She wrote that although the production's picture of gaslit Broadway, with its horses and carriages, brought more or less pleasant memories to the old and middle-aged, it was a "still life" picture of those earlier days.

"Author, actors, and director must have been imbued with the idea the Victorian Age was slow and firmly resolved to sacrifice everything to atmosphere."

She wished there had been "one in the bunch" old enough to have depicted life on Broadway as it really was—a busy congested street, a vital cultural center of drama and music in the Victorian age.

Another favorite stop for any New Yorker, including Lillian, was Tiffany's. Long after her city tour, Christmas of 1888 found Lillian trying to shop there and lamenting its high prices. She did find a beautiful silver pencil for a dollar that was at least two dollars everywhere else. Hereafter she decided to patronize Tiffany's, and since "my jewelry expense runs all of ten dollars a year, I know they will be delighted at my decision."

She described Christmas that year as a "time of let down and sorrow," a classic psychiatric description for holiday depression. Lillian said she felt Christmas without children was not much of a Christmas. Maude gave her Edward Hale's *Man Without a Country* for Christmas. She thought it a very sad story but found *Airy Fairy Lillian* good reading for a cold rainy day. Lillian said she liked it because the author "never harrows up one's feelings."

— SIX —

The Female Condition

> *My dear Nellie, it is the style to wear your dresses long enough to touch the ground. Did you ever hear of anything so absurd? You sweep the street, as it were, are in imminent danger of tripping yourself up and do not improve your appearance in the slightest degree. . . . It seems a pity no one is smart enough to invent a style for the 19th century.*
>
> "Lillian's Letter." August 8, 1888

Maude and Lillian were walking through Fleetwood Park with their father when they passed the new steep toboggan ride that had just opened in late 1888. Lillian had been yearning to ride it and tried to insist Weston ride with her, but he refused.

"I can't, Lillian. I feel my family needs me on this earth a while longer." He admitted he was a coward and used his family as an excuse.

A moment later, she spotted her church's handsome young minister and talked him into taking the ride with her. Although Lillian wasn't afraid of many things, when she got to the top of the slide, she wondered if she had made a mistake. She also had another problem.

"What can I do with my feet?"

Because of her long skirt, she couldn't sit behind anyone. This meant she had to sit in front and hold the rope, "a position not generally given to novices in the noble art of tobogganing."

But she'd come that far and so wasn't about to turn back. She ignored the attendant's doubtful look and sat down in the front position, gathered up the rope, and announced, "Ready."

Off they went, speeding down the steep hill.

She admitted to Maude, who was waiting for her, "It scared me to death."

"Serves you right," Maude said, "for being so unladylike."

Her comment irritated Lillian. Not being allowed to join in the fun of an exciting sport was just one more example of discrimination against women as far as she was concerned. Restrictions, however, were loosening, or Lillian would not have dared mention the plight of the Victorian woman in her "Letters" the way she did. Her editors would have censored her comments. Many, especially professional women, were questioning their traditional roles just as Lillian was. She was riding the crest of change when she became a reporter and freelance writer.

At first, her editors wanted her to cover the New York City fashion scene, in detail. This was a bit ironic, because she spent less time thinking about clothes than most women. In typical Lillian fashion, she saw it as an opportunity to criticize yet another frustrating aspect of being a Victorian woman. She knew her female readers also found Victorian fashions hot and heavy. In fact, they were downright unhealthy.

Lillian also craved liberation from such torture as the tight corset used to achieve the tiny wasp waists and soft rounded contours so popular in the late 1800s. At the time, it was the style to have the dress stand out at the hips, probably to emphasize the small waists created by the corsets. She said her dressmaker told her only poor people bought bustles to do this. Rich ladies had bustles formed in their dresses by six or seven steels placed close together.

"It is so much more comfortable than having a separate contrivance to make your dress set out, and I advise you to try it if you have not already done so."

On March 13, 1888, she went shopping with a friend for a hat, who wore out Lillian's shoes and her patience. They started at Macy's and shopped along Fourteenth to Broadway while her friend looked at every hat, trimmed and untrimmed, and imported (expensive). When Lillian asked her if she would pay $20 to $30 for a hat, the friend said, "Why no, Goosey, but I want to see how hats are trimmed this fall and which of the prevailing styles is most becoming on me."

As they wandered around, Lillian also asked her if the clerks didn't all know her by now, and her friend said, "I don't care if they do."

They found the competition keen on Sixth Avenue, as the stores offered wonderful bargains. They bought fabric at 69 cents a yard at a two-hour sale and saw imported dresses at half price for the end of the season. Her friend finally found a defective hat at a bargain price. She told Lillian she could disguise the flaw with a ribbon and grumbled because ostrich feathers were fashionable but expensive.

Lillian said her friend dressed twice as well on half as much clothes budget as anyone else she knew, but now she knew why because they had walked at least ten miles to find the bargain hat. Lillian thought it too much effort to try to be fashionable.

Although she knew quality clothes and how to dress for any occasion, she was sometimes absentminded and often looked a bit untidy. She always had a difficult time controlling her wispy blond hair. It added to her charm, but she didn't see it that way. She was distressed when she couldn't make her hair do what everyone else's was doing. She advised her readers to spend all their spare money on false curls to add to their real curls in order to build the huge top-heavy hairdos favored by the late 1800s woman. These, undoubtedly, were the cause of many a headache.

But even with false curls, Lillian couldn't get the hang of it. "I have only confused ideas concerning the way I ought to comb my hair to be fashionable."

On the other hand, she complained women were "like sheep," rushing to adopt the newest fad. She was right, for there was no room for creative fashions or "creative" behavior in the Victorian era. American society, at the time, was as uptight about the smallest details of social behavior and status as the women were drawn up tight in their boned corsets.

The book of etiquette was second only to the Bible as the most important book in any household. It was a guide to everything from the proper party menu to proper dress for every occasion. James D. McCabe, in his *National Encyclopedia of Business and Social Forms: The Laws of Etiquette,* published in 1879, explained the need for his book because it contained "plain and simple instructions in the art of appearing to the best advantage on all occasions."

These etiquette rules also restricted women's actions, something Lillian abhorred. Just as she longed for comfortable clothes, she longed for other freedoms, most of which she took when she dared. Some restrictions she couldn't control. It was a time when six rooms and a bath, completely furnished, rented for $60 a month, but even if a working single woman could afford such a princely sum, a landlord wouldn't rent to her. Women also had to pay taxes, but they couldn't vote.

Actually, it was a time of great change for women's status in society, but it was a battle all the way. On August 19, 1888, a male reporter decried the bad manners he saw at Bar Harbor that summer. Men actually smoked as they talked to women, but even worse, the men kept their hats on as they talked to the opposite sex.

With this subtle but gradual change of men's attitudes toward women came, of course, a gradual change in everyone's attitude toward marriage. From *The New York Herald*, April 7, 1889, "Massachusetts has the most lax divorce law. One marriage in 30 ends in divorce in Massachusetts. There is no divorce in South Carolina." Although divorce cases often made front-page headlines in this era, divorce was gaining acceptance.

Lillian didn't follow many nineteenth-century social rules. Her parents appeared to trust her to do the right thing. Take chaperones—they never chaperoned her or objected to her roaming New York City, often alone, as a reporter. Fifty years later, she told us, her grandchildren, she was sure she could take care of herself, for she always carried a can of red pepper in her muff to ward off would-be attackers. Although she lived at home, she more or less did as she pleased. This was probably her father's doing. Her mother would have been more traditional, given a choice. Lillian, however, would have fought Victorian restrictions.

She wrote, "This system of espionage is bad; it takes away the sense of personal responsibility. . . . Are we really going to bring our bright, free, independent American girls down to the level of the social slavery carried on abroad?"

Everyone would profit, she thought, if mothers identified the principles of the men who called on their daughters instead of the size of their bank accounts. It would be a much more sensible way of guarding them than sitting in the next room with the door open.

Lillian saw examples of this overprotectiveness everywhere. She was disgusted with one mother who "lost" her grown daughter on a sight-seeing tour boat in 1888. For more than an hour everyone hunted for her and her boyfriend. It seemed as if every nook and cranny of the boat had been searched. Finally everyone came to the conclusion they must have been left behind. Then the mother thought of the upper deck.

She asked the stewardess if there was any way of getting up there and was told there was only a little passageway to let the captain and sailors squeeze through. The stewardess sent someone up, and the lost couple was found. They were sitting on camp stools, with their backs against the wheelhouse, enjoying the summer evening and the pale light of the stars, far from the "meddling crowd." Lillian hoped the mother didn't scold her daughter.

She let her female readers know she didn't follow the chaperone rule by writing about her own dating days and ways. One summer, while vacationing in upstate New York, she went out with a country boy. "If you make yourself too agreeable, the man will walk his horse most of the way. . . . He will always have a box of candy along for refreshments."

She wrote, "I had the urge to take the whip and try to speed the horse up," but she admitted this wasn't the wisest move because some "country boys have a penchant for fine, nervous horses thus the whip business could prove disastrous."

Most Victorian parents were glad when their daughters married. It relieved them of emotional and financial responsibility. Lillian resented the fact that many women she knew were forced into marriage by economic necessity.

"Women's parents should be advanced enough to give them a professional education so they might compete with their husbands, brothers, and fathers rather than depending on them."

At the time, even though seven out of ten colleges were coeducational and, by 1900, graduated 7,000 women doctors, 3,000 female ministers, and 1,000 women lawyers, this was still a tiny percentage of middle-class women. Lillian knew the uneducated middle-class woman found it almost impossible to take care of herself if she didn't have a profession or a husband. Although Lillian still lived at home, she contributed to household expenses and knew how much it cost to live.

> Our down trodden sex can make money and, at the same time, retain a semblance of gentility only by teaching school or taking boarders which are not remunerative employments. The prejudice against women earning their own living makes the female sex virtually the economic slaves of men. . . . A woman should have all the help, all encouragement in the difficult task of earning her own living, and, for such women, all professions and business should be open. There is no reason they should be handicapped in the race of life by calling any honorable occupation unwomanly.

In one column, she wrote, "The efforts of the ordinary gentlewoman to earn a livelihood would seem comic if it were not so pathetic. It seems easy, judging from the alluring advertisements in the newspapers, and the novice answers them with hope, ignorant of the trials that lie before her. . . . Crocheting seems a favorite way of earning money, probably because it is such ladylike work and so entirely 'within the sphere.'" It was, however, about the only skill some women had in the nineteenth century.

Lillian followed the misadventures of a friend, who, desperate for work, answered a classified ad in a New York City paper. She found the advertiser in a small room on a crowded street. The job was crocheting hoods, and the applicant had to remain the whole day to learn the stitch. Her employer paid $4 a dozen, but one hood took one hard day's work. She went home with a raging headache and enough yarn to make a dozen hoods. A dozen days later, she presented a dozen hoods to her employer, expecting payment. Instead, he scolded her and said he ought to make her pay for the worsted she had spoiled. He didn't pay her a cent.

Lillian, however, applauded some changes she saw in the work world: "John Smith & Son is a familiar sign, but John Smith & Daughter is something of an innovation. The latter sign is now to be seen in this city, and marks progression in civilization in the opinion of some people."

She realized most Victorians thought this was just another step toward general disorder and chaos "and are looking forward with horror to the time when the sign will read, Jane Smith & Daughter, while John

& Son remain at home and attend to their household duties. But those who believe in the eternal fitness of things and the survival of the fittest are not at all alarmed."

But like so many women before and since, Lillian had ambivalent feelings about male and female roles, marriage, and women's rights. She heard a friend, a physician, once remark she was so interested in her work she sometimes forgot to go into her kitchen and give the day's order to her cook. Lillian thought she was trying to display proof of her intellectual superiority and felt sorry for the doctor's husband and family. She wondered, in her column, how a woman with a good husband to support her could neglect her home duties in favor of her profession.

Although Lillian wrote a sincere feminist line, it's obvious, from some of her writings, that deep down, she went along with the Victorian idea that the perfect marriage was one where the husband's daily life revolved around his business and his club. The wife stayed home, tending the hearth and children. If they were poor, she worked hard, but if they were well off, she had certain prescribed ways to fill her days, like making formal calls on friends and acquaintances.

Lillian also had the same mixed feelings concerning women's character—or lack of it. She did admit that if women were more deceitful than men, it was the fault of their training. She reminded her readers that higher education for women and mental discipline for female brains were something recent. She felt the majority was still in a state of dependence, "one might almost say 'servitude.'

"And think of the fondness for dress and pretty things manifested by most women and the niggardly meanness of a great many men, and is it any wonder the weaker sex fall into the habit of scheming and contriving and deceiving to outwit their lords and masters, and so become very subtle?"

She did admit that she saw many of her friends and acquaintances using their female status to their advantage. She wrote of Brooklyn girls from first-class families boasting of never paying carfare, young women with plenty of spending money. They had many friends and almost always met men, who paid their fares, whenever they rode a streetcar.

Lillian saw it as correct for a man to pay a lady's fare when he was escorting her to and from someplace, but she thought it outrageous for him to feel called upon to do it if he chanced to meet a female acquaintance in a public vehicle.

"What would a self-respecting girl think if a man offered her five cents every time they met?"

Lillian asked, "What is the difference between giving her the money and paying her fare on all occasions?"

Much later in her career, she criticized the "taxing" life of the more affluent married Victorian women. "These hard-working women, who so rarely receive sympathy," she wrote in her February 21, 1895, column for the *Richmond* (Virginia) *Star.* "I speak of those ladies who labor to be beautiful and who often work harder than their breadwinners."

She described a woman, probably her sister, Maude, spending many hours every day trying to beautify herself. She steamed her face, greased it, and powdered and painted it. Maude pushed Lillian for compliments on her "beautiful" complexion until Lillian said she had the urge to say, "It is so long since we have seen your real complexion it would be impossible for me to offer an opinion on it.

"But," Lillian said, "such a remark would raise a tempest in the family."

She then tempered her sarcasm with, "It is not only the right but the duty of everyone to look as beautiful as possible, but the worst complexion and the homeliest features can be illuminated by a kind spirit and good heart until they far outshine physical perfection—for true beauty like the kingdom of heaven is within."

In her investigative mode, she also saw women mistreating each other. It was a poor home in the late 1800s that couldn't afford at least one maid. Lillian found that her married women friends displayed the most callous attitudes toward their employees. She thought it was a real shame "men and women will not apply the Golden Rule."

She reported on the travails of a working woman she interviewed, who accepted what she thought was an easy job in a newlywed's home. The poor maid then learned the couple ate in the back parlor and expected to have a course dinner every evening. She had to set the table, then go downstairs, put the soup on the dumbwaiter, go up and serve it, then go down again and repeat the performance with the roast, dessert— the whole dinner. She stayed one night.

The Female Condition

One of Lillian's acquaintances had only one household helper, but she wouldn't even help the woman by clearing the table and washing the breakfast dishes on washday although there were eleven in the family.

The poor overworked maid complained and her employer told her, "Why don't you get up at 2 o'clock in the morning and get the clothes on the line before I come down to breakfast? That is what my other girl did."

Needless to say, the woman soon found other work. Her employer then told friends, "It's so hard to keep a girl these days."

Lillian said, "The idea of expecting anyone to work twenty hours out of the twenty-four!"

Another of Lillian's friends said she wouldn't be bothered with a servant. They were careless, unclean, and impertinent. That particular woman made her workers pay for every dish they broke and she set the price. These Victorian ladies thought they had a sympathetic ear in Lillian, but she "held her tongue" and used them as fodder for her column. She reminded her readers: "Do unto others as you would they should do unto you."

Six

— SEVEN —

In Search Of . . .

They say they have the original Deadwood Stage Coach in the show and they invited outsiders to take a ride in it at every performance. . . . But being a girl, it would not have been proper for me to do it. I had to sit quietly and watch a man mount the box seat, the place I desired to occupy myself.

"Lillian's Letter." August 15, 1889

Each year, she reserved a front-row seat at Buffalo Bill's Wild West Show in Madison Square Garden and reported its details to her readers. It was one of her favorite events and fueled her desire to head west herself.

"I want to see cowboys, Buffalo herds, and Indians before they are a thing of the past."

By this time, *The Helena* (Montana) *Record* carried her column. Frontier women liked "Lillian's Letter." They enjoyed the fact that Lillian ridiculed the old codes of conduct, ones western citizens often ignored. From the beginning, women had more freedom in the West than their eastern sisters even in fashions. If a ranch woman had some hard riding to do, she wasn't above borrowing a pair of her husband's pants.

Not only did Lillian voice their opinions, but she also added sophistication to their daily paper by giving them inside news on big-city happenings. If she went west, she thought she could find more markets for her "Letter." At the time, she was growing restless with her life and career. She also thought she might find a good man, something she didn't admit to anyone. Although she needed a new challenge and new adventures, the subconscious search for a husband was probably the biggest part of her decision to go to Montana.

In 1890, "Lillian's Letter" bemoaned the shortage of single males on the eastern seaboard. Statistics and her social life, or lack of it, told Lillian this was true, and everyone knew there was a shortage of women in the West.

When she began thinking of something she wanted to do, she usually did it. By 1890, train travel west was reliable and speedy. The new coast-to-coast railroad made it possible to go from New York City to San Francisco in seven days. Before the railroad was built, it took a full month by rail and stagecoach across country, or five months by wagon through Missouri, or six months by windjammer around the "horn," the southern tip of South America.

Lillian watched for her chance and negotiated several writing assignments to pay her way to Montana. These gave her and a woman friend a reason to go. It was still not quite common for two young Victorian women to travel alone, but they did exactly that in late summer of 1891.

One night in August, they boarded the 6:25 train in New York City. It was warm and muggy, but they knew that would pass as they moved ever northward. They soon fell asleep in their berths but woke up the next morning to a "horribly cooked breakfast in the Montreal train station." The alternative had been breakfast in St. Albans between 6 A.M. and 8 A.M., but no one wanted to get up so early. Obviously, there was no dining car on the Montreal Express.

Lillian found the scenery from Montreal to Minnesota boring—nothing but trees, log cabins, and an occasional cow or horse.

They found St. Paul, however, to be a flourishing city, "its air clean and the people cordial and courteous and there were many beautiful homes like Mr. Hill's, the president of the Great Northern Railroad, whose mansion cost a million or more dollars."

Residents of St. Paul proudly pointed it out to her, saying it was the finest house in the United States.

Seven

Lillian met Frank, seated on the right, on a train to Great Falls, Montana, 1891.

When they left Minnesota, only six passengers remained on board as the train headed for Montana. All anticipated the last, most interesting part of their trip as the festive, intimate air drew them together. Frank Hazen was one of them. He was going west to visit his former college roommate, O. S. Warden, who was managing editor of the *Great Falls Tribune.* He and Lillian soon formed a pair for the rest of the trip as they chugged across the northern flatlands.

"The weather was cool," Lillian reported in her column, "and the trip comfortable, but the scenery through Minnesota and Dakota was, again, monotonous—flat prairie land sprinkled with a few cattle farms . . . astonished prairie dogs peeking out of their holes."

The train conductor enjoyed being the center of attention and gave them a running commentary on each region they passed through. The name of Devil's Lake City intrigued the travelers, and when they asked him its origin, he didn't need much persuasion to sit down and tell them the legend:

> Long ago, before a railroad crossed Dacotah, an Indian chief with his braves was pursuing a retreating enemy over those waters, when a great storm arose in which he and his followers perished.
>
> Since then no Indian has ever launched a canoe on that lake, as they believe they can still hear the spirits of the dead warriors moaning over their untimely end.

Lillian explained to her readers that the Indian name Minnewauken means Spirit of the Water, and white people, as usual, associated earth-loving spirits with the "author of evil" and called it Devil's Lake.

"His Satan Majesty must be paramount in the region—as the Devil's Heart and the Devil's Backbone can likewise be seen from the train window."

Unfortunately, Lillian had waited too long to go west to see live buffalo and was appalled at the sight of "the ravages of civilization" on the prairie. The last big buffalo slaughter had taken place in 1882, and in 1891, bleached buffalo skulls still littered the plains. At Minot, North Dakota, where they stopped for a half an hour, there was a huge pile of buffalo bones.

"Alas! Those dried bleached bones are about all that remains of the distinctly American beast. I am told the Indians pick the bones up and sell them for $6 or $8 a ton to someone who disposes of them to sugar refiners. How sad that these once mighty Indian warriors who used to hunt the great buffalo have been reduced to the state of collecting bones!"

Lillian had long been concerned with the plight of the Indians. As early as November 9, 1888, her "Letter" reported the Indians in the

Dakota Territory were starving to death. She followed the progress of the Sioux Delegation in Washington and felt they had been wronged.

"I know you will say, 'Lillian is like the rest of the eastern girls, sentimental on the subject of Indians, and probably has never seen half a dozen of them in her life; that she reads Fenimore Cooper's novels and then prates about the noble red man!'"

She knew many westerners had known people tortured and killed by the Indians and so could understand their attitudes. She, however, could comprehend the Indians' anxiety as they saw settlers pouring into the western states and territories, crowding the Indians out in every area, their land being taken from them, little by little.

Sometimes their people were killed one by one, or, more frightening, the white man's disease, smallpox, sometimes wiped out whole tribes. Big game, the Indians' food source, was almost extinct. New settlers flooding in with the railroad were not only destroying the buffalo herds but were killing everything else that roamed the lush grasslands—the pronghorn antelope and the whitetail and blacktail deer.

Although many Indians were on reservations by 1891, being taught to "walk the white man's road," often they were starved by dishonest Indian agents, who stole the beef meant to feed the tribes. Not only were they victimized by those in charge, they were urged to farm—something totally alien to the former warriors' culture, a plan doomed to failure.

Lillian was well aware of the unsolvable problems as the frontier was fast disappearing, but she thought the whole question had been mismanaged.

"William Penn had not trouble with the Indians. He treated them like brothers, and the red men did not betray the trust he put in them . . . . Not so many years ago this country's soil was saturated with the blood of her sons wherefore? That the slaves might have their rights. Have the Indians no rights?"

Their train stopped at Williston, North Dakota, "a primitive place where three or four ranchers came down to meet the train on untamed broncos. . . . They wore the regulation slouch hats and top boots and looked fierce enough to undertake the wildest kind of adventures."

Soon after leaving the town, their train crossed the state line into Montana, the newest state in the United States. Although it had been part of the Louisiana Purchase, it was not named the forty-first state until 1889, when it was also dubbed the "Treasure State" because of its rich gold, silver, and copper deposits.

Pierre Gaultier, Sieur de la Vérendrye, first explored the territory in 1742–43. Then in 1807, the Lewis and Clark expedition built a fort and trading post at the mouth of the Big Horn River. More posts, serving the trappers and traders, appeared along the Yellowstone River between 1809 and 1829. Still, few settlers braved the wilds of Montana, because of the area's isolation and lack of good transportation.

When gold was discovered in 1852 near Hell Gate River in western Montana, gold seekers crowded in along with the usual shop- and saloonkeepers, con men, and rough wanderers. When the new railroad made it easy for settlers to migrate to Montana, civilization began arriving with families.

Lillian and the other eastern passengers expected to find Great Falls a primitive western town, but it surprised them. Before she left New York, her "comforting" city friends told her, "Western towns generally exist in the imagination of property owners, and doubtless you will find a few tents and two or three shanties when you reach your destination."

The train conductor realized they were worried about living conditions, so he sat down and gave them a glowing account of a civilized town. Lillian and her friend decided he was a big liar. He said the hotel was near the depot, and they didn't need a cab because there were sidewalks.

"Sidewalks!" They couldn't believe it.

It was pouring rain as they pulled into the train station, but they found, "He spoke the truth, the whole truth, and nothing but the truth," wrote Lillian.

Sure enough, there were the cabs and Lillian began to feel quite at home.

She wrote, "Luckily, we did not take one for one must have a bank account like the Rothchilds' or the Goulds' to pay the charges."

Their hotel was comfortable and "wonder of wonders, it was lighted by electricity. . . . The table and service were also good."

After lunch, the weather cleared, and as Lillian and her friend rambled around town, they were surprised to see brick and stone buildings.

There were banks, churches, libraries, schools, and all kinds of stores. Far from roughing it, they found all eastern conveniences and luxuries—if they didn't mind paying a high price.

The next day, some local ladies called on them. Again Lillian and her friend were amazed. The visitors were dressed in the latest New York fashions; even their calling cards were "high" style.

In Lillian's story "Life in a Growing Western Town," published by the *Stamford* (Connecticut) *Standard*, August 20, 1891, she wrote: "Great Falls is the third city in size in Montana. The climate is dry and would be delightful were it not for the high winds blowing the sand in clouds through the streets."

She went on to say that residents talked about everything from the climate to real estate in exaggerated, enthusiastic terms.

"Great Falls women," Lillian wrote, "talked about a newcomer's pedigree like their select circle had been established for centuries whereas the town was only five years old.

"If the stranger dresses well and has a respectable bank account, his or her father and grandfather may have been hung for horse stealing for all these westerners care."

Lillian and her friend longed to sightsee outside the city, but they couldn't decide whether they could handle their own horse and buggy. All the rest of the drivers seemed reckless to them. They had just about decided to do it when they witnessed a runaway. That did it. They would see the sights within walking distance.

That's why Lillian was delighted when, later in the week, Frank and his friend left word at the hotel that they would like to take them to Rainbow Falls, one of the city's famous sights. Frank, because he was a skilled horseman, did the driving. They headed out of town moving fast, the fresh breeze blowing in their faces, "bolstering our sense of adventure." As they sped over the prairie, there were no landmarks, no houses, no trees.

When they finally reached the edge of a canyon at the top of a long flight of steps descending to the bottom of Rainbow Falls, Lillian later wrote that the scene was so "awesome" she, for one, couldn't say anything. The wind died down and the stillness was broken only by the sound of water falling over the massive rocks. The sun was just setting as they descended to the level of the river. As it grew dark, they looked up and saw a crescent moon that appeared to be resting on the canyon edge.

"It seemed to be the only link that connected us with the rest of creation," Lillian wrote later.

EIGHT

A Pause for Consideration

A very wise young man gave it as his opinion that a girl who would not marry on twelve or fifteen dollars a week is not worth having. I am afraid a number of girls are worthless according to his standard as few pose as financiers, and it would certainly take one to support a family in this city on that salary.

"Lillian's Letter," February 14, 1889

After they returned from their trip, Frank started a rather formal relationship, not really to Lillian's liking, but she knew better than to push him for anything more intimate. They wrote each other polite letters, and, occasionally, he came to New York City from Boston on business and always stopped to see her.

When Lillian first met him, she thought he might be the right man for her, and he appeared to have money. It's sure she pursued Frank as openly as she dared. As for him, he was as enthralled with Lillian as he could let himself be about any woman, but he was a cautious man who was to keep her waiting four years before he proposed. Because he took so long to decide, she must have had some misgivings about marrying him, even though she eventually convinced herself he was her Prince Charming.

After her return from Montana, Lillian threw herself into her work, but matrimony was on her mind when she wrote about various American women marrying English noblemen.

"No one can say the two girls bought their titles with money. Miss Terega, the Duke of Newcastle's fiancée, has little or no fortune and the Duke of Norfolk is the wealthiest nobleman in England and doesn't need Miss McFarish's gold."

Lillian mused whether or not she would marry an English duke—if she had the chance, that is. "You see the trouble is my acquaintance among them is limited. I do not know how fascinating they are, and it does take such a remarkable man to make an impression on me."

How to find that special man was the subject of endless discussions by Lillian and her many women friends. They spent hours analyzing the men—or the lack of men—in their lives as they empathized with each other's setbacks and disappointments. Sometimes they played parlor games in search of the names of future husbands.

"Peel an apple in one strip and toss the peeling over your shoulder. It is supposed to fall to the ground in the shape of the initial of the man's name." Or, "Take a hard boiled egg, halve it, remove the yolk, fill the hollow with salt, eat it, and never speak again that evening, else the charm will be broken. Retire immediately to the bedroom, take 13 pieces of paper, put names on 12 of them, the word, 'unknown,' on the 13th, undress yourself, pin the papers on your robe, turn out the gas, take 12 of them off in the dark and then lie down and try to sleep." The remaining paper on the robe would be the name of the woman's future husband.

Even as they played these games, several of the women, including Lillian, admitted they were not sure they wanted to marry at all.

When asked what her objections were to matrimony, she said, "I don't know that I should have any if I could find a man I could really love. I hate the idea of giving up my freedom. I should not like to ask a man for money. I dread the cares and responsibilities of married life. Marriage to me seems the end of things."

Lillian and most of her friends were wise enough to realize it was the most important life decision a woman ever makes. These were ambitious young women, who, like Lillian, had careers, were out and about more than most Victorian women and not sitting home doing needlepoint waiting for the right man to come along.

Although Lillian did not admit she was worried about finding a husband, she watched her friends play the mating game and tried to learn from their mistakes. It was also a good subject for her column. She wrote she found it a sorry state of affairs that smart women seemed devoid of all common sense as they tricked themselves into believing they had fallen in love when, in reality, many gave themselves to the highest bidder in exchange for room and board. Sometimes one of her friends found herself in worse circumstances than if she had been on her own.

Lillian certainly didn't agree with many female Victorian writers, who said, "Even an unloved husband, assuming he was at least not cruel, is preferable to none at all."

But still, she couldn't bring herself to ignore such Victorian advice found in an 1880s marriage manual called *The Mystery of Lovemaking Solved:* "For a woman to live through life unmarried is to be worse than dead. A woman's whole life is a history of the affections. . . . If she, indeed, escape a part of the snares that best the path of the man unmarried, she encounters others of even a more deadly tendency. Some fall, others save themselves—to a prolongation of misery. The career of the old bachelor is bad enough in the name of all that is sensible, but his case is a paradise compared to the ancient maiden."

In her stories, Lillian often described old maids in a disparaging way: "tall, angular . . . stiff in her movements." She herself was thirty by the time she married and, in the Victorian age, was considered an old maid, but she was determined not to make do with any man. She vowed she would never marry unless she found the right man. She also had definite ideas on the forming of the male-female relationship. She thought a man and woman should first be chums and then lovers. At the very least, Lillian was determined that if she did marry, it would be to a kind man with an education, money, pedigree, and moral standards.

"Any gentleman who can make this world, this topsy, turvy, greatly misunderstood world a far better place, because he chanced to pass along this way . . . who doesn't swear, get drunk, tell dirty stories, or go to low places. He won't kick a dog, abuse a horse, misuse a child, laugh at another man's mistakes, or gloat over another man's failures . . . isn't cynical, sour, or pessimistic . . ."

Although Lillian abhorred dishonesty and the use of manipulation, she knew what a nineteenth-century woman had to do to attract such a man. Throughout her stories and articles, she emphasized the fact that women had to appear passive to attract men—that openly aggressive women turned men off. In the same era, women's magazines and self-help books also discouraged women from asserting themselves in a straightforward manner.

Sarah Josepha Hale, who was the *Ladies' Home Journal*'s editor until 1889, when male editor Bok took over, urged readers to emphasize grooming, indirect speech, and proper etiquette. She urged them to use roundabout, ladylike methods in controlling their destinies: "flirt a little, cry a little but always be charming." In extreme cases of manipulation, women actually took to their beds with various ailments like "dyspepsia," indigestion. This fortunately, or unfortunately, was not Lillian's style.

Although she told women they had to be quiet and ladylike to attract a good husband, she struggled with these attitudes all her life. She found it difficult to follow her own advice and probably unnerved many young men in her day. Lillian appeared to be well aware of the Victorian woman's double bind. In one of her unpublished short stories, two male characters, one of them a minister, discuss women.

"For many generations the majority of women have been dependent on men, and have often been obliged to get what they wanted by cunning and cajolery. Naturally, they learned to flatter and fawn and pretend until dissembling was bred into their very natures. I hope and believe we shall see a great change in them now so many are earning their own livings."

Her female readers liked her "Lillian's Letter" because she tried to write about their problems in an honest way. They felt her empathy, and they needed sympathetic words to validate their own feelings. They wanted to know how other women viewed life. It was a revelation to discover many felt the same as they did, helpless, unable to control their own lives.

Lillian knew there had been smart, attractive women who, since the beginning of civilization, decided on a man and used subtle—and sometimes not so subtle—means to attract him. She had given the subject a lot of thought and decided she would not wait to be chosen. She would do the choosing. A woman who waited passively to be chosen for marriage, as far as Lillian was concerned, deserved what she got.

She wrote in an 1889 column: "God made man first and woman after him, and—she has been after him ever since."

That "man goes about like a roaring lion with woman as his victim," Lillian saw as a popular fallacy. "We are all to act and talk as though we really believed Cleopatra, Catherine of Russia and Nino de L. Enclos were freaks, instead of normal women, who cast aside conventions and lived according to their inclinations."

As her columns explored more controversial subjects in depth, things were falling apart in the Weston household, where she still lived. In 1893, her father left her mother. The final argument, according to Lillian's son, Richard, was over Ellsworth. Ed Weston never got along with his only son and finally ordered him out of the house. He, of course, was old enough to leave, in his twenties, but Maria objected.

With that, Ed turned on his heel and left. He had found the excuse he thought he needed. Their separation was no surprise to those who knew them. It was simply the culmination of much marital strife, obvious to their children for a long time. Lillian described their marriage as "the shackles they both hated."

Family rumor also suggests Ed was a bit of a womanizer. Because he was good-looking, a definite charmer, and a famous sports figure, women often pursued him.

Sad to say, Lillian never saw him again. One wonders why both of them let this happen. The only way she kept track of him was through the newspapers, following his career, which lasted into the 1920s, as he "walked" almost until the day he died. She didn't even see him age, because she always talked of remembering a man in the prime of life. Later, when she wrote an article about him, she said the things she missed the most were "his enthusiasm, his hearty enjoyment of all the pleasures of life, his capacity for work or for entire relaxation when a task was done, and his old firm handshake and the twinkle in his eyes."

Although Lillian knew their separation was best for both her parents, she was heartbroken and, at first, angry. She loved her father. Ed continued to take care of the household bills until three years later, when he approached Maria about a divorce so he could marry Annie O'Hagan, the woman he lived with for the rest of his life. In a thinly disguised unpublished short story called "The Other Woman," Lillian described what happened next.

Maria told Weston, "I couldn't stop you from leaving, but I'll never give you a divorce."

Ed said, "So be it. You'll never get another cent of support from me."

Lillian sympathized with her father.

In later years, after Lillian had been married herself for some time, she recounted a conversation with her mother. Even in that, Lillian was unconventional by Victorian standards. When her mother began ranting about Annie O'Hagan, Lillian told her, "She didn't steal your husband. She didn't even meet Dad until you and he had been separated three years. That was twenty years ago and all this time she has lived with him and made him happy without sacred vows or legal bonds. I'll tell the world I take my hat off to her."

Maria was angry. "What did I ever do to have such an immoral daughter? You are just like your father."

Lillian tried to ignore her mother, who railed away in an effort to make their children loathe and despise the other woman in Weston's life. As their daughter, Lillian knew there were two sides to their story.

She realized her father was a self-centered man who always did as he pleased. Of course, Lillian's mother appeared to be a nag as she struggled to assert herself in things that mattered to her. She was a very conventional person, and Ed Weston was as far from conventional as a person could get. That alone created a great deal of strife.

As for Annie O'Hagan, Lillian was right about his relationship with her. She was "the woman who gave everything she had to my father and stood by him through thick and thin."

"They aren't even married—just living together unlawfully," her mother would tell Lillian over and over.

Lillian always answered, "And whose fault is that?"

She felt Annie O'Hagan had to love Ed Weston, because she came from a respectable family and gave up home and reputation for him in a day when people just didn't live together unmarried. In various published newspaper stories over the years, she is described as Weston's secretary or housekeeper.

Eight

Even as Lillian's home life was falling apart, her column was gaining readers, and her career was on the upswing. The Montana trip seemed to add a new dimension to her writing. She began to cover more controversial subjects. First, she did some investigative reporting for her column. She set out to see if it was just as difficult to find a job in 1892 as it was in 1886. She applied for a position as a book salesperson.

The publisher asked her, "Have you ever sold books before?"

"No."

"Have you ever had a job before?"

"Yes. I was a teacher."

"Good! I'll send you to schools."

Lillian gave him a phony name and paid 50 cents for the prospectus. The book's price was $7.50. Then she "sallied" forth with her list of schools.

The first principal was a kind little old maid who peered at the book but said she had two or three thousand volumes and didn't need any more at the moment.

She also said, "Book agenting is the worst business a woman can undertake. . . . You ought to try being a store clerk."

That day, Lillian didn't sell a book.

The next day, she went to homes but found this an uncomfortable ordeal. Sometimes a maid would let her in and when the "woman of the house" appeared, she would be most irritated to find a book salesperson sitting in her living room. Sometimes she ordered Lillian to leave.

Later that day, Lillian returned to tell the publisher of her "non-success."

He was angry and said, "You didn't present it right."

It was obvious to her the job market hadn't changed much since 1886, when she spent those miserable months searching for work.

For the *Richmond Star*, December 28, 1894, Lillian wrote:

Much has been said and written about woman's sphere by the anti-suffragists, while the advanced woman has been loud in praise of those who have been instrumental in opening up all trades and professions to women, and prates about the glorious future of the sex and compares it with what she calls the slavery of the past; aye, the past and the future. Too many of us live in one or the other. Meanwhile, in the present . . . what are they to do now before the glorious future comes?

— NINE —

Resolution

How old are children when they begin to think of love and marriage? A little girl of five told her mother, "I'm going to marry Harry when I grow up."... It never seemed to occur to the child she might possibly make other acquaintances in the years to come. Sometimes grownup girls forget this, too.

"Lillian's Letter," July 5, 1895

The real turning point in Frank and Lillian's relationship came in 1895, when he invited her to Boston to meet his parents. She spent the whole month of June sight-seeing with Frank and wrote her column from there. It was the first time they were together more than a few hours since the Montana trip, and Frank charmed her in every way that month.

They visited Franklin Park, the Arnold Arboretum, and the new $2.5 million public library. As they drove around town, she saw the old elm "under whose branches George Washington took command of the American forces in 1775 . . . Longfellow's house on Brattle Street in Cambridge where Lowell also lived."

She found Boston more distinctively American than New York City, more homelike and not so cosmopolitan. She could see why Bostonians thought there was no place like their city. "It is so beautiful and surrounded by picturesque suburbs, of which Brookline is the most aristocratic."

Frank impressed her in every way that month, with his apparent status and money. His family belonged to the Brookline Country Club, where he wined and dined her, and Lillian reveled in socializing with Boston's "elite society" as they watched the club horse races one summer day. They then interrupted their whirl around the city to attend a polo match—again at the country club. She mentioned one of the players was a young Harvard student who had an income of $100,000 a year.

Because Frank socialized with these people, was well dressed, well spoken, well educated, and lived in a nice house, she surmised he probably had that kind of money, too.

Although Lillian returned to Brooklyn at the end of June with marriage on her mind, she was at a crossroads in her life. After so much hard work, she had a successful career. Her column was popular.

> We cannot refrain from expressing our gratitude to some of the correspondents of *The Star* who have so kindly contributed to the success of the paper. There are few syndicate letters that will compare with the papers that have been regularly furnished to *The Star* by L. M. Weston from Brooklyn and Boston. From a literary standpoint, these letters are alone worth more than the subscription price of the paper.
>
> Editor
> *The Richmond* (Virginia) *Star.* June 19, 1895

As the months went by, sometimes Lillian despaired Frank would ever make up his mind to marry her. Early in their relationship, however, she learned she couldn't hurry him into anything. And so she waited. She knew that more than most Victorian men, he required a subtle approach.

She didn't exactly put on a false face for Frank, but she didn't reveal much of her true self either. She knew Frank wanted a typical Victorian wife, who made a good appearance, was quiet, and would defer to him. She was well aware her intellect would not win him; thus she knew she had better play the "game," and so she consciously tempered her actions and words.

Nine

Late in the summer of 1895, Frank visited her in New York City on a cloudy Sunday afternoon. While she and her mother waited for him to arrive, her mother told her to be careful and not lose her heart until she was sure she had won one. She reminded Lillian that she was used to European ways, that men and women in America were on an entirely different footing.

She told her daughter an American man will court a girl for weeks, be as loving as she will let him, pay her all kinds of compliments, say all the sweet, tender words in his vocabulary. Then the man might think it was perfectly honorable to lift his hat and ride away when another girl caught his fancy.

When Frank finally arrived that day, Lillian noticed he seemed depressed and asked, "Why so gloomy? You look as though melancholy had marked you for her own."

He put his arm around her. She protested, "You mustn't. You have no right to hold me like that."

"Would God I could ask you to give me that right!" he said, but immediately dropped his arm.

Lillian was disappointed. She later wrote in some unpublished fiction she understood the temptation that induces a woman to forget honor, duty, and reputation to follow the man she loves: "The revelation of my weakness appalled me for I feared—I almost know anything Frank had asked I would have given." But he made no overtures at all.

She wrote in her journal, "A certain innate fastidiousness had always prevented me from billing and cooing with the opposite sex until I met the man who was to be my husband."

When she asked why he couldn't ask her to marry him, he said, "Because I've always depended on my father for my bread and salt. I've been in business with him for five years, and, if I should marry against his wishes, my wife and I would be beggars."

Frank didn't have to explain this remark. Lillian knew the Hazens didn't want her to be their daughter-in-law. After all, her father was a pedestrian, a professional sportsman. This conversation disturbed Lillian. She wasn't sure Frank would ever propose. She, of course, had other suitors and continued to see them. One was a local minister. Lillian's mother begged her not to even consider marrying him although he was "young and good looking and all the girls in the parish are crazy about him."

Lillian mentioned this same minister in several of her columns and described dating him in an essay: "We sat on the broad porch, side by side, in wicker rocking chairs, shielded from observation on the street side by clinging rose vines in full bloom. No one was in the house.

"He was inclined to be sentimental as the warm, sweet scented air enveloped us both in a kind of sensual aura, and he talked lightly of parish affairs and ridiculed, casually, all the odd characters amongst our mutual acquaintances."

He laughed too much at her clever comments. Then he turned serious.

"You are very attractive Miss Lillian," he said when she stopped talking long enough for him to speak without interrupting her. "You have a great deal of power over men and will probably have more as you grow older, but I don't know that you would make a suitable wife for a clergyman. I don't suppose you would marry a minister though, would you?"

Although it probably wasn't on his mind, Lillian thought he was remembering her father's profession and her lack of dowry when he asked this question.

Almost before he finished talking, she said, "No, I wouldn't."

"I noted his little breath of relief, but I didn't betray I had read his wizened little mind correctly."

She went on to say,

"I wouldn't marry a minister, butcher, doctor, or an undertaker. A minister's wife has to keep on good terms with her husband and his congregation besides and that would be too much of a job for me." . . . A little more scorn crept into my smile as my eyes rested on the man's complacent face. I went on calmly, "I am a vegetarian and love all animals and a man whose business it is to slay them could have no attractions for me." . . .

"I have a very jealous disposition, and I should suffer torture every time my husband locked himself into his office with a charming female patient so doctors are taboo for me, and I certainly could never warm up to any man who was always handling stiff, cold corpses."

Nine

There was another man, however, who appeared to linger on the edge of her consciousness for the rest of her life. According to several of her short stories, he was a soldier stationed at West Point and was probably the cherished "lost love" often mentioned in her poetry:

Of all sad words of tongue and pen
The saddest are these,
"It might have been. . . ."

"I remember the hush that precedes the noises of the night—the hour between daylight and dark never passes that I don't think of a twilight long ago, when happiness was within my reach and I failed to grasp it."

Her unfinished story describes this meeting at West Point, where a certain regiment of the National Guard was camped. The heroine was in love with a soldier and he with her.

"He was poor and humbly waited for some sign of encouragement from her. His face glowed with hope and joy as they met in the tent-lined street. But he was busy then and couldn't stop to talk."

At sunset, Lillian sat on the cliff, overlooking the parade ground, as she watched the regiment's maneuvers. Her friend, off duty for a few minutes, came up quietly and sat down beside her. She wrote of the few words that passed between them, how they were content to be with each other. The music of the band softened by distance added to the enchantment of those wonderful moments as the setting sun colored the parade ground but didn't penetrate the trees' shadows where they sat.

His hand closed over hers as the sunset gun boomed. The soldiers saluted the colors as they were hauled down. Lillian wondered if he felt the diamond ring placed on her finger by "a rich man" the night before, but then he was gone.

Lillian wrote, "The spectre of poverty so near him frightened me."

There's no record of how Lillian and Frank resolved the conflict over family, but resolve it they did. The following handwritten note was delivered to Reverend Charles Thompson in the last days of September 1895:

Dear Sir:

Although I am not a member of your church, I have attended service there, and so feel emboldened to ask if you would officiate at my marriage next Wednesday, October 2, at nine o'clock in the morning. If you would do this favor for the stranger within your gates, please let me know.

Lillian M. Weston
110 East 45th Street
New York City

— TEN —

After Marriage Arrives a Reaction

*Take romance—romance gilds the grayest hours and makes
life worth living. . . . Nothing can take the place of, or take
away from you, the memory of the ecstatic joy of those first
few days of belonging to a man whose charms you know,
but whose faults you have not yet discovered.*

"Mildred's Mannequin." 1897

Lillian was soon to find, to her sorrow, her dreams of happiness and
wedded bliss, mostly based on romantic nineteenth-century literature and
her own wishful thinking, did not culminate in the perfect marriage. At
first, neither of them realized they were worlds apart in what each considered important in life. Even their approach to the mundane details of
maintaining a family was poles apart. Because Lillian had approached
marriage with so much care, it was hard for her to admit theirs was far
from ideal. Although Frank seemed to fit her perfect-mate profile, Lillian
was to find out how true were the philosopher John Stuart Mill's words
written in the mid-1800s:

> Marriage is really, what it has been sometimes called, a lottery. . . . Those
> who marry after taking great pains about the matter, generally do but
> buy their disappointment dearer.

73

Lillian's number-one mistake was ignoring what she knew of the Hazen family's style. She and Frank might have been compatible if they had been the average Victorian couple, who grew up in the same neighborhood and had known each other all their lives, as was the case of so many couples in the late 1800s. This would mean they belonged to the same ethnic group in American society, whether Italian, Jewish, or northern European, and they would have inherited the same belief systems and cultural attitudes.

When families knew each other, they also knew all the gossip. Was there mental illness, physical disease, or a criminal tendency in the family?

Frank and Lillian's families, although both English, were about as different as one could find—differentiated by the subtle internal systems that governed each family, its values, and its approved behavior. The most serious difference was how each expressed feelings.

No subject was taboo in the Weston family and loud voices, sometimes raised in verbal combat, were considered normal and healthy. Frank, though, was the product of a Yankee-style discipline, something Lillian had never experienced. In fact, a favorite Hazen family saying was, "Children should be seen and not heard," and they meant it. Little wonder Frank was a silent man.

Add these contrasts to the fact that Frank's upper-middle-class family didn't want their son to marry a professional athlete's daughter no matter how pretty or intelligent she was. It made no difference that Weston was considered a world-class pedestrian.

It was unfortunate Lillian found this family to marry into. They intimidated her. She was an unusually confident person in most situations, but as a result of the discrimination she suffered because of her father's profession, she was very class conscious, a dichotomy of superior feelings and attitudes, proud of her intellect and ashamed of her family's lack of money and status. Much later in life, she recalled how she felt that "wives and daughters of gamblers and saloon keepers were about the only females who didn't look down upon my mother and me from the heights of their social eminence," because her father was a pedestrian. She never quite discarded her awe of the Hazens' supposedly impressive pedigree from pre-*Mayflower* days in England.

Another aspect of marrying across class lines was the two would never understand each other's motives for their words and actions. It was an era when most Americans were completely bound by the social system they were born into, and prior generations' traditions and attitudes ruled the home. Many families were first generation in America and followed old-country customs and different approaches to life.

Today American society is much more homogenous than ever before, because most Americans watch the same television programs, have access to the same films, go to the same schools, and are concerned with the same issues.

Frank J. Hazen was born on May 24, 1866, in New York City, the first of five children—two sisters, Francis and Grace, a brother John, and one brother who died soon after birth. He graduated from St. Johnsbury Academy in 1885 and Dartmouth in 1889. He was not as active in college affairs as his cousin Charles Downer Hazen, who attended Dartmouth at the same time. The *Aegis* '89 lists Frank as secretary and treasurer of the Football Association, his only affiliation, and he belonged to the Phi Delta Theta fraternity. Sixty years later, he still kept in touch with the other members of the class of '89 and was keeper of the traditional peace pipe trophy of his graduating class.

The Hazen family once owned the Oxbow Ranch in Vermont, but they sold it and bought uncleared timberland in Whitefield, New Hampshire, near Mount Washington. Frank's father was a wealthy farmer, dairyman, and lumber merchant who, through the years, cleared and sold the timber, planted grass, and began raising cattle and horses.

While Frank was in college and later after he graduated, he and his father made regular trips to South Dakota to buy wild range horses. They brought them back to New Hampshire, where Frank "broke" them out for carriage horses. Then they sold them in Boston.

Years later, Frank's son said, "My dad—I can honestly say—was the best horse trainer for driving I ever knew in my life. He wasn't afraid of any horse no matter how big or how mean it was. He could hitch it up and drive it," an unusual feat because Frank was a small man.

He worked for his father until 1890 and then became his business partner. At that time, Frank's mother, tired of country living, talked her husband into selling the ranch. Then Frank and his father bought as many apartment houses in Boston as they could finance with minimum down payments and planned to pay them out from the rents. The Hazen family moved to Boston.

With their move to the city, Frank's mother became even more determined that all the family members would live up to her notion of their family standards. When she caught Frank helping the gardener, she scolded him for stooping to do manual labor. That was probably one reason he loved gardening in his later years.

Although Frank's mother liked to think the Hazens were a cut above "the common herd," she was perpetuating a myth. The family did not descend from nobility. A little genealogy research shows that even though a few famous people like James Russell Lowell lurk on the family fringes, the Hazens were simply well-to-do English farmers who were among the first to come to the New World and settled in New England to make their fortune.

It was difficult to tell if Frank inherited his mother's snobbery. People liked him, so it was covert if it existed at all. Years later, although his diaries didn't reveal much more than the current weather, one could sometimes get a peek into his attitude toward other people. Once, when he and Lillian finished a bridge session, he wrote, "Enjoyed the evening . . . topnotch people."

In reality, the only traits Lillian and Frank shared were their good looks and a mutual need to find a mate. During their engagement, each saw what he or she wanted to see in the other, and each played the expected role. Neither stopped to realize endearing idiosyncrasies observed during courtship eventually might irritate each other beyond endurance.

Even their personal habits created a major conflict in their marriage. Lillian was an untidy person, a fact that galled Frank from the beginning. She impatiently neglected the mundane details of life, both about her person and around the house, whereas Frank was neat to the point of compulsive as he went about life's ordinary tasks.

Everything had to be done in a precise manner. He ate his food with impeccable manners, always moving the same direction around his plate. His grooming and clothes were flawless. In later years, he even wore an old suit, complete with tie and frayed dress shirt, to tend his garden and furnace.

At first, Lillian wanted to believe Frank's silent ways masked great intelligence, but soon after their marriage, she decided he didn't talk because he had nothing to say. Little wonder his stoic face and quiet reserve soon began to irritate her. He was a careful, conservative man who didn't make up his mind quickly or easily, a trait that caused him much trouble all his life.

Probably because she loved to talk and he liked to listen, she hadn't noticed his silence earlier, but she had to have noticed that Frank, although he sometimes smiled, rarely laughed out loud.

Lillian complained that Frank behaved like a querulous old maid even as she tried to adapt to his "mind and taste . . . study to please," as nineteenth-century marriage experts counseled good wives to do. Because at first she dubbed him a superior man and treated him accordingly, catered to his every whim, this set the tone of their relationship for the rest of their lives.

She could not help catering to her man. She grew up trying to please her father. Although Weston urged her to excel in all things in a time when women had little such encouragement, she still had to deal with his giant ego. The Weston household revolved around this charming man and his wishes; thus Lillian's attitude toward the opposite sex was determined early in life.

Frank was raised and educated to be what Lillian thought she admired—a gentleman, but she didn't understand what this meant. By Victorian standards, her father had been anything but a gentleman. Although Frank could read Latin and Greek, he knew nothing about real life and earning a living. He rarely said what he thought, whereas no one ever had to guess what Weston thought about anything. Lillian soon grew frustrated trying to figure out this silent man she had married.

Over the first months of their marriage, as Frank and Lillian each struggled with a private set of standards, she yearned for a way to complement each other, to maintain a "live and let live" attitude. She hoped the characteristics one lacked the other had, and they might combine their talents to make "the perfect whole." In fact, a popular nineteenth-century nursery rhyme voiced this common Victorian myth:

Jack Spratt could eat no fat;
his wife could eat no lean
and so betwixt them both
they licked the platter clean.

Frank and Lillian might have been a winning team if they could have reached a compromise, but Frank ignored the fact he had married a competent, intelligent woman. She was to have no voice in running their life. He wanted her to defer to him in all matters. On the surface, she seemed to do her best in order to maintain a peaceful household, but one can only guess at how she played out her resentments in covert ways.

Lillian had a sharp wit and sometimes tongue to match, and she was outspoken to the point of tactlessness. In fact, Frank was no match for her. He never "bit" with words, never raised his voice in anger. The most extreme statement he ever made was, "Damn you!" One wonders what he did with his inevitable angry feelings over the years. Because Lillian knew Frank didn't consider her sharp words ladylike, she reacted with even more anger when he criticized her behavior. When she first met Frank, it's sure she censored her comments, knowing full well he wouldn't be attracted to an outspoken woman.

Elizabeth Cady Stanton, first president of the National American Woman Suffrage Association, spoke for all Victorian women like Lillian when she addressed a women's rights convention in 1890:

> Some men tell us we must be patient and persuasive; that we must be womanly. My friends, what is man's idea of womanliness? It is to have a manner that pleases him—quiet, deferential, submissive, approaching him as a subject does a master.

ELEVEN

A Rude Awakening

My air castles, created out of imagination and desire,
tumbled, and I lay in their ruins, gasping with despair and
distrust.

Lillian's journal. 1897

Lillian put her misgivings on hold after Barbara was born on August 12, 1896. She wrote, "The tiny clinging fingers had enough power to keep me in the nursery much of the time. . . . The first time the baby shook a rattle it was a household event."

Lillian wrote, "My cup runneth over."

Frank and his father were making a great deal of money when he first met Lillian, but by 1895, when Lillian and Frank married, the Hazens had lost almost everything after the 1893 recession. Lillian didn't know this. In 1897, after moving to Boston, they had barely settled into their large rented house in a good section of Brookline, Massachusetts, when their financial condition went from bad to worse. Lillian didn't know they were bankrupt until everything was gone and their creditors were at the door. Frank, as did most Victorian men, took care of the finances and didn't share his problems with his wife. It was a total surprise to Lillian— a most traumatic event, because she didn't see it coming.

Realizing they were bankrupt was bad enough, but Lillian was horrified at what she saw as her husband's "stark weakness and naked cowardice." She didn't seem to realize, as his son did years later, that although Frank was a Dartmouth graduate, he majored in the "art of being a gentleman." He was not equipped to deal with the real world. His was a most impractical background when faced with the reality of feeding a growing family.

At the time, Lillian's anger spewed out in an unpublished short story called "The Mannikin":

> By age 25, she detested her father, disliked her brother, and despised her husband. . . . She was not old enough to comprehend the good and evil in human nature is so inextricably mixed that it takes a long refining process to extract the priceless ore.
>
> She was shocked at an early age to learn her father was unfaithful to her mother and, from that time, could not discern his good qualities, his generosity and unselfish, genuine love for his fellow men—as well as women. . . . Her brother's wife deserted him and he became a drunkard, a weakling.
>
> Then she married—a man who was unusually good looking and rarely talked. She had a wonderful imagination, so invested her admirer with all kinds of knowledge on every subject, and expected to be electrified by his wisdom every time he opened his mouth.

As usual, Frank was silent. Angrily Lillian denounced him as "slow witted and almost incapable of acting on his own initiative." Much to her disgust, Frank appeared to give up: "Adversity usually strips a man of superfluous padding and borrowed graces. In vain, I struggled to imbue him with my courage and ambition, but I felt like one trying to imbue a wax image with life."

Frank also developed an "irritability that was peculiarly exasperating." She wrote that although her father and brother had not been devoid of temper, "their explosions of rage were usually followed by decent intervals of peace and quiet, but Frank whined, complained, and fretted continually."

In Lillian's eyes, Frank's behavior proved he was incapable of solving life's major problems. When, however, she suggested solutions, he turned belligerent. For the rest of their married life, Frank was to insist on making all decisions, for better or for worse, and if Lillian saw they were approaching a crisis situation, she had to sit by, helplessly, and let calamity strike.

He was having trouble meeting their expenses even as they began married life living on his small savings in New York City. If he had told Lillian his financial problems, they could have cut expenses. Why did he move his family into a new house in Boston when he was on the verge of bankruptcy? It was sure Frank didn't want to admit to Lillian that he had lost all his money for several reasons. He probably understood part of his charm was his money. He also hated confrontation and couldn't face Lillian with the truth about their finances.

The banks called in the Hazen loans on the Boston apartment houses, loans they couldn't pay, and credit dried up. It's amazing Frank managed to hold things together until 1897. To the end, he thought he and his father could recoup some of their losses, but they never did. It would appear Frank did what he would continue to do all his life. He could never admit to a bad decision and would cut his losses and run no matter what the situation was.

He was not alone in thinking it was only a brief dip in the economy. He, as well as the financial experts, thought the country was in a temporary recession, but the 1893 financial panic ushered in America's first full-scale depression. Banks failed, and the Philadelphia and Reading Railroad went bankrupt. The New York Stock Exchange was shaken by the first great selling spree in its history, and the market collapsed.

The year 1894 was the most brutal of the depression. Between 2.5 and 3 million, one out of five, workers were unemployed, but no one really knew how many.

"Mills, factories, furnaces, mines, nearly everywhere," reported the *New York Commercial and Financial Chronicle* in August, "shut down in large numbers."

The Hazens moved out of the large house they had rented. Lillian never forgot how sick she felt as Frank ushered her and baby Barbara into a shabby apartment hung with dirty wallpaper, its carpet worn by the feet of many renters, sparsely furnished with a rickety table and a sagging bed. It was, however, a bargain at $3 a week. Lillian knew Frank's "cup of bitterness overflowed."

Later, when Frank lay down on the bed, he immediately jumped up.

"I can never sleep on that thing," he said. "I shall simply sit up all night."

He, of course, soon came to bed, where Lillian said she was "vainly trying to adjust my body to the numerous hillocks and hollows of our anything-but down couch."

The next day, after Frank sold everything at auction, including Lillian's cherished wedding gifts of fine china and silver, he returned that evening in a depressed mood. Their household goods had not brought as much as he expected. Five hundred dollars was all they had left after settling their debts. Lillian wrote of their troubles in an unpublished story where they both appear brave as they faced their problems head-on. In reality it was an anxiety-charged existence full of arguments and fear.

Lillian finally knew what she had to do to help. She must save money any way she could and worked out a budget to stay within a $10-a-week limit. She also began writing again, a revealing new version of her column called "The Lackaman Club," first appearing on May 17, 1897, in the *Bridgeport* (Connecticut) *Standard* with her byline, L. M. Hazen:

> Owing to the preponderance of the female element in Boston society, it was extremely improbable that all of us would find a consort, consequently we considered it wise and prudent to establish a club, where single women could congregate, and comfort each other, unrestrained by the presence of their married sisters.

It was lighthearted modern satire on women and marriage in Victorian society. It doesn't condemn marriage, but it does raise questions about the universal idea that all women should marry, regardless of situation or wishes, and if they don't, they are doomed to a life of misery.

The column followed a unique format, ahead of its time, because it portrayed a woman's consciousness-raising group in an era when they rarely voiced the truth about any of their facts of life.

Lillian described the club's beginning: "The president and three members of the Lackaman Club were assembled for the weekly chit-chat meeting. These gatherings were very informal, entertaining, and usually well attended. Anyone was free to express an opinion on any subject, and many of the ideas put forth were calculated to shock people who were not accustomed to the advanced notions of some members of the Lackaman Club."

Club members had such descriptive names as Miss Wavering and Miss Strong, who was a longtime member of the club and said she hoped Miss Wavering wouldn't be blackballed when her name was introduced for membership at the next monthly meeting. Only single women could belong. Actually, Miss Wavering thought the club a kind of "nunnery" because it had no male annex. No man was allowed in the club rooms except on "Gentlemen's Night," once a month.

"Did you tell her we give a big reception to members on their marriage, on the same principle nuns have a grand ceremony before renouncing the joys of life?" asked Miss Haightman.

"And that we present them with two hundred dollars worth of solid silver so they will have something to fall back upon in case times are hard?" added Miss Prudence.

Allegories were a favorite mode of expression for Lillian, and over the years, she published many such essays. She needed money and developed the "Club" column because she was sure that she could sell the idea, that the subject would interest editors and readers. She knew women outnumbered men in Boston; thus they could relate to fictional women who hadn't found mates. In keeping with the times, she had her club members say they were ready and willing to marry if they could find the right man.

Lillian's Miss Haightman had a strong opinion on the subject of men. "You may have expressed your sentiments and those of Miss Loveman, but, for my part, I wouldn't marry the best man that ever walked the earth."

Then Miss Loveman said, "Probably not; he wouldn't have her."

In that column, there followed a short description of a long boring reading by Miss Bookly about "a day's ride" through the suburbs of New York City. (Could this be Lillian's ride through New York in 1887?) Miss Loveman thought, but didn't say, the ride would have been much improved by a few companions of the opposite sex.

Lillian wrote, "Miss Loveman took no stock in an Adamless Eden, and was quite willing to forego the privileges of the Lackaman Club at the first opportunity."

By this time, the other members had moved on to a fierce discussion of the Greek War and the Cuban Revolution.

Miss Loveman's only contribution was, "In my opinion, war is a fearful thing, as it kills off all the men, and makes Lackaman Clubs altogether too common."

Lillian's next version of "The Lackaman Club" was printed in *The (Winchester, Massachusetts) Star* on September 24, 1897. The column is pasted in her scrapbook next to a photo of a two-story Victorian house and the notice "Mr. F. J. Hazen of Brookline has rented the Roswell House on Highland Avenue."

On October 22, 1897, Lillian wrote "The Lackaman Club" under the name of L. M. Weston. It's not clear why the switch back to her maiden name. Perhaps Frank was embarrassed that his wife was writing such forthright columns and probably thought it didn't speak well of their marriage.

At that meeting, Lillian had her characters develop a spirited discussion on women going into the plumbing profession. Her Miss Haightman said, "I am sure it needs the elevating and refining influence of our sex."

Next Miss Liveasy gave her opinion. "Well, perhaps you want to spend your days with your nose over defective drainage pipes, but, as far as I am concerned men can monopolize that money-making occupation. There are too many disagreeables connected with it to suit me." All agreed women would never lie like male plumbers did about when they would come to make the repairs.

Just then, Miss Cheering entered the room and said, "Now, hold on a minute. Men are not half bad; in fact, I just dropped by to announce my engagement to marry a man."

All the members started to talk at once until Miss Cheering said, "Shh! I'll tell you all about it."

She was going to marry Harry Ellersie, who was going to the Klondyke gold fields. When she told him she would like to go with him, he proposed. They were going the next spring.

"I suppose the club had better make a new departure and present you with a mining outfit, instead of the usual gift of silver," said Miss Haightman, rather sarcastically. "But to go back to my first subject," she continued, "I do not see why the fact of your marrying need alter my opinion of the masculine sex, which you will probably share after a few years of wedded bliss. Even if your beloved finds gold in the Klondyke, which is exceedingly doubtful, he will probably ask what you do with every nickel he gives you. Positively, girls," she continued, getting somewhat excited, "I once, actually, heard a well-to-do man ask what his wife did with the five cents he gave her the day before."

Frank might have been the "well-to-do man" in the last sentence. Right after she married Frank, she thought he was merely stingy when he questioned her about every cent she spent, but too soon she learned the sorry truth. At this point, she was writing the column so they could eat. They were lucky she had a way to earn money.

As she watched Frank futilely search for work every day, she worried. She went to bed anxious, tossed and turned with dreams, and woke up anxious. Every morning, Frank would set forth determined to find a way to support his wife and child, and every evening he returned, discouragement settled in the lines of his face, his feet dragging. She saw "hope dead within him."

One night, late in October 1897, Frank broached a new plan. He wanted to buy a periodical-and-variety store nearby.

He told her, "The owner is asking $400, but he won't refuse $350. The stock doesn't amount to much now, but if we succeed in the business, we can build up an inventory. The present owners have few ideas and no taste."

"That's a good plan," said Lillian. "I'll help."

Frank said, "You'll have to because the store will be open 16 hours a day."

And so he became the "paper man." In the magazines he sold, there were articles and stories about polo and golf matches and other country club diversions, illustrated with pictures of his old friends, also lengthy descriptions of houses and people with whom he was far better acquainted than the writers. He let his beard grow so friends wouldn't recognize him if they wandered into the neighborhood. Because Lillian and he avoided everyone, even their families, they were alone and isolated in Boston.

Before a week had passed, however, Frank was tired of selling newspapers. He regretted putting all their cash in the business instead of living on it and continuing his job search.

It was a hard life. Lillian rose at 5 A.M., stoked up the fire in the range for warmth, and cooked a frugal breakfast on the gas stove. Frank then left for the store to receive the morning papers. After breakfast, Lillian gave Barbara her bath in the kitchen. Then she washed the dishes, tidied the rooms, got dressed, and the two set out for the store.

While Frank, with his daughter, went for a walk or ride on the electrics—anywhere away from the dingy little shop—Lillian would take her turn selling magazines and papers. At 10 A.M., Frank would return Barbara and then Lillian did her day's marketing and the two returned to their rooms, where she fixed dinner and put Barbara to bed for a nap. Then she went back to the store to relieve her husband so he could eat and take a nap. Sometimes Lillian stayed to talk with Frank when he came back to the store with Barbara, but the little girl was into everything.

Later, Lillian and Barbara would return to their apartment to eat supper and then back to the store while Frank ate his supper. Lillian and Barbara were always in bed by 8 P.M. Frank didn't come home until the store closed at 10:30 P.M. The days were long and Frank never complained of insomnia or the lumpy bed again.

Christmastime that year didn't bring good cheer to the Hazen household. For the first time since their marriage, they didn't have gifts for each other.

Lillian wrote, "This thought made our poverty harder to bear than anything that had gone before."

She told Frank, "I think we can afford a dime for Barbara."

And so, on Christmas Eve, Frank brought home a lopsided canton flannel dog and a box of blocks from the dime store.

As if they didn't have enough troubles, by Christmas, Lillian was sure she was pregnant. The news shocked them both out of their lethargy—the store wasn't making enough money to live on, and the bit left had to be used to find Frank another job. After Christmas, they sold the business at a loss and returned to stay with Lillian's mother in Brooklyn, where Richard was born on July 13, 1898.

Frank put pride aside and contacted everyone he knew in search of a job. In the meantime, he worked in a men's shop selling suits, a position he felt beneath him—one that galled him each day he set out for work. Although his silent ways didn't make him a successful salesman and most customers sensed his attitude, his appearance seemed to outweigh his liabilities. He realized he was lucky to have a job.

Six months later, in January 1899, the father of one of his college friends asked him to Chicago to interview for a bookkeeping job with the Great Northern Mining and Development Company. When Frank boarded the train to Chicago, he assured Lillian he would send for her and the children as soon as he was settled. Unfortunately, he found the work was not in Chicago but in Gilt Edge, in the heart of Montana's Snowy Mountains.

There was nothing for him to do but go west alone. If he didn't, the company wouldn't hire him. After arriving at the mining camp the last week in January 1899, he realized Lillian and the children couldn't make the trip until spring. The only transportation into the mountains was a stage line, a rough trip in any weather but almost impossible when temperatures dropped to minus forty degrees and snow covered the trail.

Later Lillian wrote, "My husband, like many others, decided to seek his fortune in the great Northwest, but, because we had two little children, he dared not take his family until he established himself somewhere so he set forth alone, while I waited with what patience I could command until he sent for me."

Lillian was thrilled at the thought of moving to Montana. To her, it was a great adventure, and she wasn't at all upset at the prospect of leaving New York City. Although she thought she knew the isolation she was facing, the breaking of "old ties, old pursuits, and old habits," she was sure anything would be better than their last two years.

She wrote Frank, "I look forward to being far from the madding crowd, and, anyway, it sounds as if every man has a chance to strike it rich."

TWELVE

The Road to Gilt Edge

The sun's rays struck the glittering white expanse, burning our faces. My eyes ached with the glare that nothing relieved—not a house, a tree, a man nor an animal in sight. Only mountains in the distance, but they, too, were covered with snow.

"One Hundred Miles in a Blizzard." 1899

A faded snapshot of Lillian taken right after she arrived in Gilt Edge says more than all the words she wrote. It is hard to see the beautiful, vibrant girl reporter in the face of the haggard-looking woman standing in front of an unpainted wooden building holding baby Richard with Barbara clutching her skirt. She must have wondered how she wandered so far from her early dreams and plans.

In her story "One Hundred Miles in a Blizzard," she wrote, "By the time I reached central Montana after three days and nights on the train with two tiny children, I was sure traveling the prairie in a covered wagon would have been easier."

The train trip had been almost more than she could bear by herself. Barbara was well behaved and quiet, but Richard was a cranky, noisy baby. A compartment would have made things so much easier, but as it was, Lillian had to borrow money from her mother to afford a berth.

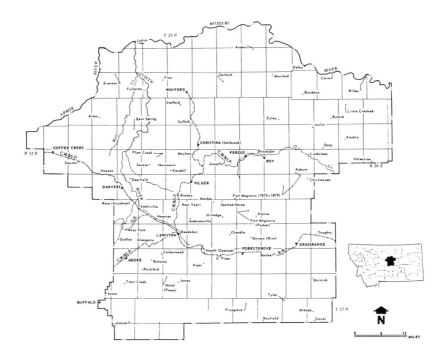

Fergus County

The thermometer in the sleeper registered ninety degrees from New York City to Chicago, but when she stepped off the train in Fort Benton, Montana, large snowflakes swirled around her and she found herself ankle deep in snow. Shocked and dismayed, she tried to bolster her courage by telling herself, "It's the last day of May and the storm won't last. It's nothing more than a flurry."

Lillian knew they still had to finish the hardest part of their journey the next day by stage, one hundred miles south to Gilt Edge. It was a good thing she didn't know late May blizzards are common in Montana and 1899's was a fierce one.

Their first night in Fort Benton, they stayed in something she later laughingly called a "hotel" but always hastened to say, "I was so thankful for a wide, still bed."

A haggard-looking Lillian with Richard and Barbara, 1899, right after they arrived in Gilt Edge.

She was lucky to find a room because the town, once a booming trade center on the Missouri River but by 1899 a quiet, isolated village past its prime, had few travelers' accommodations. Lillian awoke the next morning feeling happy and refreshed until she looked out the window and saw it was still snowing. They were eating breakfast when the desk clerk hurried in to tell her the stage was ready to pull out. She quickly gathered her belongings for the clerk to carry and followed him, carrying Richard and holding Barbara's hand as they walked through softly falling snow. She thought they would finish the last hundred miles of their journey in a regular closed stagecoach. What she found, however, was the Montana version—a double-seated open buckboard wagon pulled by two horses.

Twelve

"Haven't you an umbrella?" she asked the driver.

"Nah! You couldn't hold one up if you had one. Here—here's a coat that's got to go back to camp."

With numb hands, Lillian pulled on the fur coat, three sizes too large, and thanked the driver. Then she boosted Barbara into the back-seat and handed Richard to the driver so she could scramble up beside her daughter, "—the front seat being already occupied by an old China man."

After lifting Richard up to her, the driver tied Barbara to the seat. Then he started the horses off at a fast pace, jouncing along the rutted dirt track. Each mile seemed rougher than the last until they left the trail to drive on the ditch banks, the wagon tipped at a sharp angle, needle-sharp sleet stinging their faces. Even though Barbara was tied in, Lillian didn't trust the rope and her arm was soon numb from cling-ing to her daughter.

What a relief it was when they reached the first stop for lunch. They waded through foot-deep snow for a meal of soggy potatoes, limp bacon, and boiled cabbage, but Lillian found herself too tired and worried to eat. When the driver asked her to wait for the next stage, she refused. She knew she was the only woman for miles.

When they started out again in the snow and cold, she and the chil-dren sat next to the driver. Her tenderfoot's eye saw no road at all, only prairie—broad, white, and bleak. They climbed a steep hill for three miles. At the summit, the driver gathered up the reins and called to the horses, who ran down "the other side at breakneck speed." Lillian shut her eyes, expecting the worst. When the man beside her laughed, she peeked out and again saw a level, snow-covered prairie.

As night closed in, Lillian was sure they were lost, but just before total darkness, they reached the next station. Relief filled Lillian as she saw a woman standing in the doorway. The cabin's interior was warm and welcoming with good food smells, and there was a tiny room and large bed for Lillian and her children, so welcome after the daylong jouncing in the wagon. The dirty sheets on the bed, however, made Lillian think "cleanliness was at a discount" in the West. When it was time to go to bed, what to do? She finally spread her own shawl over the pillows, removed her and the children's shoes, and they all climbed into the bed with their clothes on. They, however, slept soundly until daylight, when they discovered snow had drifted in around the window and was a foot deep on the floor.

The next morning, the driver left her and the children to wait for the next stage, and he drove off through the heavy snowfall, intending to deliver the U.S. mail. Later, her only complaint was the total lack of reading material—no books, no magazines, no newspapers, and the owners of the stage stop were not conversationalists, to say the least.

An hour later, the driver was back. The horses had refused to cross the first stream.

Lillian wrote, "The next day dawned fair and clear—glittering icicles hanging from the eaves, brilliant snow drifted man-high. The driver dug the buckboard out of a drift, and we set out to finish our journey which was far from done."

Some ranchers with ten horses pulling two loads of hay had broken six miles of road through the drifts, so they reached the next station in fairly good time, but dinner wasn't ready because the crew wasn't expecting them. The driver said he didn't dare wait, and so the station attendant pushed some hastily made sandwiches and a bottle of milk into Lillian's hands for Barbara. She doesn't say in any of her writings, but she was probably still nursing Richard.

They were thirty miles from Gilt Edge, and it was already 11:30 A.M. A mile past the station, snow was a foot deep on the level. The horses tugged and strained, dragging the wagon slowly through the soft clinging stuff. It took four hours to go fifteen miles. At mid-afternoon, they reached a station, where they changed teams. The stock tender wasn't sure they could make Gilt Edge by night, but he reluctantly hitched some big, strong, fresh horses to the wagon and they started off, moving fast.

Lillian wrote, "It seemed as if they would take us to town in a couple of hours, but their enthusiasm didn't last a mile," when the team settled down to slow, hard pulling.

Finally the driver said, "I'll drive along the bench [a small hill] and maybe I can find a shallower place to cross the coulee."

This faced them into the north wind, which whipped them with light drifting snow until the children cried with the "hurt of it."

Lillian kept thinking, "Just a little farther—".

Twelve

Turn-of-the-century Gilt Edge, 1900, huddled at the foot of a rugged mountain, was to be Lillian's home for the next three years. Courtesy of the Montana Historical Society, photo by W. H. Culver.

They came to another deep coulee filled with snow, but on the other side, they could see a bare trail. The driver jumped out and shoveled for twenty minutes. Then he made the old man get out and walk, and he took the horses by their bridles.

"With whip and voice, he urged them through the drift."

The driver and the old man climbed back into their seats and the horses, revitalized with the near prospect of food, rest, and shelter, trotted briskly along the snowless road. Lillian let herself sit back with relief to enjoy the scenery.

"The sun had set, but the peaks of the mountains were still glowing with shafts of light, white and dazzling, and just below the summit a delicate pink with opal tints gradually merged with the purple shadows of the valley."

Just as Lillian began to relax, to think the dangerous trip was over, the driver said, "I wish it was lighter. There's an awful bad place in the road about a mile from camp."

In her story, Lillian wrote, "His words wiped out the beauty of the scene."

A few minutes later, he yelled, "Hold on tight."

"I thought the wagon was turning upside down. The horses seemed to disappear under it—a groan, a creak, a struggle, and a terrible lurch—then the horses reappeared and the driver gave a sigh of relief."

"I didn't know whether we'd make it or not," he shouted.

For just a moment, the town of Gilt Edge lay before her—a collection of bare-board shacks and log cabins huddled together at the foot of a mountain. Lillian, however, was still so frightened she could hardly breathe.

They drew up in front of an unpainted building identified with a rough board sign, "The Hotel," where an anxious Frank stood on the porch. He had been waiting for two days. Everyone told him the stage would never make it that night. They ate supper in the dining room, and then Frank drove her and the children in his own buckboard to their new home, perched on a side hill at the entrance to the gulch, overlooking the town.

THIRTEEN

Far from the Madding Crowd

*It's sad that in such a beautiful country of birds and cas-
cading waterfalls, most people hear only the clink of metal
and see only the diggings.*

Golden Gulch. 1900

Gilt Edge was past its peak as a boomtown when Lillian rode in that cold,
snowy day in June 1899. At its most prosperous, the town claimed a population of 1,500. Many of its buildings were barracks moved from Fort
Maginnis after it closed. By the time the Hazens arrived, the population
had shrunk to 350, but the town still boasted two streets, one hotel, a post
office, a jail, a schoolhouse, two large general stores, and several small spe-
cialty shops. There was also an oversupply of saloons and dance halls,
including the Palace, where the prostitutes lived.

The mine doctor ran a clinic in a stone hospital built by the miners,
and a traveling dentist stopped by and set up shop for a week on a regular basis before moving on to the next town.

Gilt Edge began growing on the southwest edge of Judith Basin in
the early 1880s, when homesteaders first moved into the Montana area
and the government sent soldiers to Fort Maginnis. About the same time,
miners roaming the mountains nearby discovered gold. Then in 1884 and

1885, the Great Northern Mining Company dug the mine in Whiskey Gulch and built a three-hundred-ton cyanide mill, one of the first in the United States to use the cyanide process for extracting gold from ore. It was a state-of-the-art operation with all equipment pulled into the area by oxen, horse, or sixteen-mule teams.

Lillian wrote, "Steam drills, electric lights, and every other labor saving device known to man could be found in Gilt Edge."

When she first saw her new home, Lillian was surprised. She didn't expect anything so grand. First of all, it perched on a side hill overlooking the gulch. Wild climbing roses covered one side. She could look up the canyon, which narrowed until the mountains towered over it, to the mine and smelter, and she could look down the gulch to where it broadened out into flat, grass-covered plains.

It was obvious Frank had done his best to make them comfortable. He told Lillian a miner told him, "One room is a cabin; two rooms a shack; and three rooms, a house," and so he built a house with a living room and kitchen combined and two bedrooms.

Lacking water or indoor plumbing, it was not much by modern-day standards, but to Lillian, anything would have been better than their last home in Massachusetts. Later she realized she had it better than most of the women in town. Frank had gathered together all the bare necessities for housekeeping, a real feat when one considers how difficult it must have been to find simple household items like two beds, a crib, six chairs, a cookstove, a table, and two lamps. They also had two saucepans, a frying pan, and a limited supply of dishes and flatware.

Lillian wrote, "Housekeeping was carried on in a most primitive way."

The kitchen sink was an oak chest with an enameled washbasin for hand washing and a larger pan for dishwashing. These were emptied into a pail on the floor that, when full, was emptied down the side of the gully. Several times a day, Frank carried two pails of water up from the well at the bottom of the hill. He joked that his arms soon stretched two inches. Although Lillian never mentions it in her writings, there must have been a privy close by.

Her first morning in Gilt Edge, Lillian dithered about trying to prepare dinner for Frank. She knew he would arrive soon after the mine's noon whistle sounded. Then he wouldn't have long to eat. She tried to hurry but found herself anxious and confused in the strange kitchen, still weary from her grueling trip. Barbara was outdoors making mud pies with some neighborhood children, something she had never been allowed to do before.

When Richard woke from his morning nap and started crying, a sense of utter desolation overcame Lillian. She gathered her son up in her arms and sat down on the edge of the bed and cried, too.

Just then, she heard a commotion out front. She rushed to the door and saw a sobbing Barbara running toward the house.

"They threw mud on me."

Lillian was upset and shouted, "You go home," as she pulled Barbara in and slammed the front door.

Just then Frank rode up for dinner, but Lillian was too upset to eat.

He said, "I'm afraid this is going to be too hard for you."

Lillian said, "I'll be all right. I'm just not used to the stove."

Frank said, "Don't let Barbara out of the house to play unless you can go with her."

"It seems a shame to shut her in when the weather is so fine. I wonder if I speak to the parents if they'll stop teasing her."

"I think those children will be more quickly influenced by a horse-whip than by their parents," Frank said. "But we'll see."

Barbara was a gentle, quiet child who had never played with other children. Lillian never mentions trouble with the neighborhood children again, so, in time, their daughter probably adjusted to the situation.

As for Lillian—she soon found herself so busy she couldn't dwell on trivial problems. She was working harder than she had ever worked in her life just to maintain their home. It was such a change from city life, the only kind of life she had ever known. The one thing that saved her from depression was the fact that Frank was the happiest she had ever seen him. He liked the people he worked with, and he liked the country. He also tried to help her in every way to make her life good, too. She was surprised at the understanding he displayed and reacted in kind.

A month after she arrived, she met most of the people in town as they all celebrated the area's biggest holiday of the year—Union Day. Lillian wrote about the early morning parade, which launched the day's festivities, in her unpublished novel *Golden Gulch*.

"The Gilt Edge band headed the procession" and floats, advertising the different merchants, had "all been arranged with care" as the town's small businesses tried to outdo each other in producing the cleverest one. The Assay Office float, with its roaring furnace, gigantic scales, and mammoth gold bar, took first prize. The barbers' float pleased the children, "who shrieked with delight at the sight of a well-lathered pig sitting in a chair, while two men shaved him." A prospector with pick and shovel, riding an old horse and leading another laden with a camping outfit, was an appropriate end to the parade.

Later in the afternoon, everyone headed for the grandstand a half-mile below the town to watch the various competitions—pulling contests, races. Frank bought ice cream and lemonade from an entrepreneur who sang in a monotone:

Ice cold lemonade,
Made by an old maid,
Stirred with a dirty old spade,
Ice cold lemonade.

Lillian wrote, "Notwithstanding his doubtful recommendation, he was well patronized as were the peanut and candy vendors.

"Without intermission, the merry-making continued into the night as we adjourned to the ball in the Miners' Hall," where the walls were draped with red, white, and blue bunting, the floor covered with wax flakes. Small children slid from one end to the other, having a great time as they formed a slick surface just right for dancing. A piano, a cornet, and a fiddle began blasting away from a rickety small platform at the end of the hall.

When earlier Lillian asked one of her new friends what to wear to the dance, she was told, "They wear everything here at social functions like the 'beggars that came to town. Some are in rags, and some are in velvet gowns.'"

"If you waltzed with one you must waltz with all," Lillian complained.

Because some of the men were drunk, she didn't care to get any closer to them than a round dance made necessary, but because they were her neighbors, she didn't want to insult them either.

"Everyone, including the older children, danced energetically stomping the well-waxed floor as they circled the room—the Lancer, Two Steps, waltzes, the Quadrille—while the town's babies and small children slumbered peacefully on a pile of quilts in the cloak room."

Frank knew everyone in town and introduced Lillian to various people, later filling her in on histories and gossip as they sat on the sidelines. Lillian had many questions.

"Who was the lively lady in white muslin, dancing in our set just now?"

"That's Mrs. Riggs, the assayer's wife. Her manners are a little rough, but she's only twenty-one."

"Only twenty-one—she looks thirty-five at least."

"Most of the women in this camp look older than they are. They marry young and work hard like Mrs. Smith."

Frank nodded in the direction of a sandy-haired, freckle-faced woman who was struggling to comfort a six-month-old child with a piece of candy. The baby was busy smearing her mother's dress.

"She's only twenty years old."

Soon Lillian and Frank were invited everywhere. They entertained, too. In a letter to her sister, Lillian wrote about her first dinner party.

"All the male guests ate with their knives and called their wives, 'the old woman.'"

When Frank passed out after-dinner cigars, the men bit the ends off, and, because they needed to spit them somewhere, one man opened the stove's door and fired away. And they weren't always good shots. After the last guest left, Lillian made Frank clean up.

He complained to a friend later, "I told Lillian it would be fairer if we pitched pennies for the job, but she didn't agree." So Frank, not one to fight custom, bought a cuspidor before their next dinner party.

As the weeks went by, Lillian began to settle into her new life with her usual flexible attitude. There were too many problems to be solved for her to sit and feel sorry for herself. A first and foremost worry for her and her family was food. It was scarce in Gilt Edge. People paid top prices for inferior products. Many a Gilt Edge store made its owner rich, like the Emporium, run by Nathalie Belanger, who saw that one didn't need to pan gold to make money. Although her store carried everything from canned and dried food to shoelaces and toothpicks as well as a disorganized array of millinery supplies and other dry goods, she carried no perishable food. People paid top prices for inferior food, because it was all hauled in by oxen, horse, or mule teams.

Bob and Jim Murray were two of these early freighters in Judith Basin, hauling both dry goods and ore. Their outfit was unique because they used Montana range-bred horses to pull their wagons, sometimes carrying as much as 2,500 pounds in five wagons. They found the horses had more endurance than oxen or mules, could travel faster, and their hooves gave them better footing than the cloven-hoofed oxen. The Murrays never used the small-hoofed mules, because they didn't function well on muddy ground. They also were champions with the ten-foot-long blacksnake whip and could pop out the flame of a standing candle.

At first the Hazens ate what they could buy at the store, like canned goods, beans, and oatmeal. Lillian soon realized, although it was late in the growing season, they had to plant a garden. She also learned to bake her own bread, something she had never done before.

She saw a few ambitious women raising chickens, cows, and gardens and "reaping a golden harvest" when they sold eggs, butter, chickens, and milk to the rest of the Gilt Edge population. But they didn't do it on a large scale, and so everyone was as "deprived of decent food as if they were on a whaling vessel. . . . All thought of one thing—gold, gold, gold. Men dreamed of great wealth and luxuries in the future and ignored the necessities of the present."

Although most men worked for the mine, all searched for gold in their off-hours. The mountains were dotted with prospect holes. Lillian was a bit of a hypocrite when she complained about their obsession with gold, because she also dreamed of making a lucky strike—she more than Frank, for she was a gambler at heart just like her father. The thought of all the wealth being dug out of the mountainside intrigued her. Several times Lillian dreamed of staking a claim on a certain plot. When she urged Frank to heed her dream, he scoffed at her. For years, she claimed a strike was made on the very spot of her dreams.

Gilt Edge: A Law Unto Itself

*The saloons flourished and men lay full length on their
floors, dead drunk, but the liquor dealers were too humane
to take a man's money and then kick him into the street.*

Golden Gulch. 1900

Each Gilt Edge saloon had its own scale and accepted gold dust at $18 an ounce, and all found a way to take the miners' money. Gambling was a recognized profession and the gambler plied his smooth trade twenty-four hours a day. Sometimes a thousand dollars was lost on the turn of a card. Many a miner was fleeced out of his precious paycheck hard earned at $4 a day, seven days a week.

Although the western frontier was shrinking and civilization was coming in with people like the Hazens, it was still a rough, frontier atmosphere. Prosperous new mining towns like Gilt Edge attracted every hustler in the West, and some Gilt Edge residents, unlike the Hazens, had shady pasts. They were "wanted" somewhere by their families, their creditors, or the law. Many years later in Lewistown, when one of Frank and Lillian's good friends died, it caused quite a stir when the man's undivorced first wife showed up for the funeral to stand by the second wife.

In Montana at the time, a man's past was strictly his own business. If one listened to speech, one could hear every kind of American dialect from southern to Bostonian, but one learned not to ask questions unless "invited." It was one of America's last frontiers, where vigilantes still lynched men for stealing horses but a man, or a woman, could commit murder and never be brought to trial.

A few years before Frank and Lillian arrived in Gilt Edge, a famous local mystery involved a beautiful woman who came to nearby Fort Maginnis as the army doctor's wife. The fort's commander, a colonel, fell in love with her, and her husband didn't seem to mind. When the colonel bought a ranch near the fort, the doctor's wife spent her weekends there with him. He then made out a will leaving the ranch to her in case of his death.

One Sunday afternoon, she returned from the ranch without the colonel. She said she didn't know where he had gone. Army investigators searched the ranch for him but didn't find any clues. There had been a good hundred-foot-deep well on the ranch. It had been filled with rock. Community gossips were all sure the colonel had gotten drunk and some-one had dumped him down the well. Because the doctor's wife was the colonel's only heir, she and her husband moved to the ranch.

Soon after the Hazens moved into their cottage on the hill, Slippery Tom held up the whole town one summer afternoon for over two hours. The local sheriff merely talked him out of his gun and fined him $10. It turned out he was a tenderfoot, who was trying to act like his version of a real westerner according to eastern books.

He was a young mine mucker who worked for $3 a day and com-plained, "There ain't nothing around here for a guy to do on his off-hours except drink and gamble." He said he couldn't even find a woman to date.

Single women were a scarce commodity in Gilt Edge in the early days, and many of the first ones into the territory were dance hall girls and pros-titutes. Although drinks were only a quarter, the girls charged the miners $1.50 to twirl through a waltz, schottische, or quadrille as their partners. Most of these women soon married. In fact, some well-known Montana families started with the combination of a miner and a "lady of pleasure."

When an occasional single schoolteacher arrived in town, she was courted by all the single men in camp and didn't stay single long.

Male white settlers also married Indian women, usually according to Native American tradition by giving the bride's father a gift of such items as blankets. This gift was a metaphoric compensation for the loss of their daughter from their household and meant the new husband would be responsible for his in-laws' welfare in addition to his wife's and future children's. They in turn would give him and his new wife protection and aid.

Unfortunately, when more single white women arrived in the area, some of these men sent their Indian wives back to the reservations and married white women. Others, who made their fortunes in gold or cattle and could afford it, went east and found brides to import and then informally divorced their Indian wives.

This wasn't always the case. Granville Stuart, a famous early pioneer, married a beautiful Shoshone woman when she was only fourteen years old. They had eight children and stayed married until she died. Stuart, however, was not the usual frontier man. He, Reese Anderson, A. J. Davis, and Sam Hauser were some of Montana's first great cattlemen. They started the DHS ranch in the Judith Basin, where they sold their beef to the army's Fort Maginnis.

Granville Stuart was also a bit of an intellectual, whose first book about the new territory was published in New York in 1865 under the title *Montana as It Is.* That same year he helped found the Historical Society of Montana and served as its first secretary.

Most citizens did not go to such extremes as Slippery Tom and the doctor's lovely wife. Many were like the Hazens—educated, middle-class people who had somehow failed in their former lives and sought to hide themselves with their humiliations and their disappointments in obscure Gilt Edge as they looked for a way to make a new financial start.

Calamity Jane was an elderly single woman who was leading a lonely life in Gilt Edge those last months of the nineteenth century. Richard said Frank told him that although her language was a bit "vivid," she was never loud, never made a nuisance of herself or flirted with the men. She spent a lot of time in the local saloons and was always the first up to the bar when drinks were "on the house." She fascinated Lillian, who often saw her on the street smoking a cigar and dressed in coveralls like a man.

She asked Frank, "Why do they call her Calamity Jane?"

"There're a lot of stories—the most glamorous one is that she was with the army fighting the Indians when her captain's horse was shot out from under him. When she dared go back to rescue him, he told her he hoped she would always be around when calamity struck."

When later Lillian heard some of the town's wives criticizing Calamity Jane, she stuck up for her: "I hear the woman was courageous."

The sheriff's wife snorted and said, "Why shouldn't she be? She ran away from home real young. She grew up in the army, fighting. She drinks and swears like a man. She's a disreputable old thing without modesty, manners, or morals."

Her comment infuriated Lillian: "There's never a miner who gets sick or in trouble that she isn't on hand to help him out."

"Oh! I know she's always been a favorite with the men, but that isn't saying much for her."

"All the same, I'd rather have her in camp than the fine doctor's wife."

Lillian found the mine doctor and his wife "both wanting." The miners didn't like him, either. He played poker for high stakes during his off-hours, took money from them, and displayed few medical skills. When the mine owners hired the doctor to examine the prostitutes, the women reported he was rude to them and demanded free favors. Then he charged them for their checkups.

Lillian had good reason to think the doctor was inept. Their first Montana winter, just as Lillian was getting to know the other women in Gilt Edge, the whole camp was quarantined for smallpox and everyone was isolated for several months. She wasn't surprised to learn the schoolteacher was the first to contract smallpox, and the doctor let him go on teaching. He diagnosed the teacher's rash as ringworm. Even though the Hazen family had been vaccinated, Lillian was frightened.

Because she followed the latest advances in medicine as best she could, right after she arrived in Montana, she ordered smallpox vaccine from New York City. She broke the vial, scratched each person's arm, and rubbed the serum in. Frank did the same for her. Although this left large scars, the Hazens didn't catch smallpox either.

Lillian also used homeopathic medicines, her vials stored in a small, compact, round metal box, as a sensible alternative to traditional medicine. Homeopathy treatment proceeds on the assumption that diseases or symptoms can be cured by drugs given in minute quantities to produce effects on the body similar to those from the disease being treated. Although modern physicians still prescribe syrup of ipecac to induce vomiting after the ingestion of poisonous substances, homeopathy practitioners use it in minute quantities to treat nausea and vomiting.

Even before moving to Gilt Edge, Lillian doubted modern medicine and learned early not to depend on the medical profession, with good reason. Nineteenth-century doctors often caused more symptoms than they cured with their harsh practices of bleeding and purging.

When Lillian learned they were in the middle of an epidemic, she even worried about sending her clothes to the local laundress. The next Saturday morning as she stuffed their dirty clothes into a gunnysack for Frank to deliver on his way to the mill, she begged him to ask the woman if her family had the disease. He didn't want to.

She fretted until Frank returned that evening to report the woman had asked him carefully, "All well over at your house?"

When he said, "Yes," he said she looked relieved.

Then she told Frank, "I have three going to school. When my oldest came home and described how Brinker was broken out, I said, 'You'd better stay home until I'm sure what ails that teacher!'"

Lillian later wrote: "Wasn't she wise? She has twelve children and nobody knows how many grandchildren, and she said if one of them got it, probably they would all come down with it, and she knew what that meant as she had been through smallpox epidemics before."

Most people in Gilt Edge continued to send their children to school until most, who hadn't been vaccinated, were sick.

Lillian said, "The whole camp was like a pest house."

FIFTEEN

The Bewitching Mrs. Gay

*The assayer reminded me of a wizard when he turned over
the cooled trough and took the pure gold bar out of the deep
end from under the black slag.*

Golden Gulch. 1901

Sometime during the Hazens' first year in Gilt Edge, Ellsworth, Lillian's
brother, came looking for a job. Frank found him one shoveling coal
into the mine furnace, dangerous and unpleasant work. He soon left
for California.

John Hazen, Frank's only brother, a tall, handsome, mustached version of Frank with the same proper speech and education, also stopped
off for a visit on his way to hunt in northern Montana. In the following
years he often visited them. He was a music teacher and so had plenty of
leisure time each summer. One year, he would tour Europe, and the next
he would head west to hunt big game.

Frank and Lillian looked forward to his first visit to Gilt Edge and
planned to show him all the tiny town had to offer—hiking, horseback
riding, picnicking, and Lillian's favorite tour, one she never tired of—a
visit to the mine, the cave in the mine, and the smelter. She said the tour
always gave her goose bumps as they passed through the tunnel where

miners were drilling and the muckers were shoveling the blast-loosened ore into the cars running on rails pulled by a horse or mules.

She wrote, describing the scene, "The drivers wore small lamps in their caps that even in broad daylight gleamed and flashed like great yellow eyes."

To reach the cave, one followed a path through a damp tunnel and then down a ladder, all done by the light of candles that kept going out. Frank relighted them with matches. At first, Lillian said she found the cave frightening because it was so dark and quiet. But when her eyes became accustomed to the dim candlelight, she was struck by the beauty that surrounded her.

"Thousands of stalactites hung from the roof, all shapes and sizes, graduating in color from reddish brown to pure white, each tipped with a drop of water, glistening like a diamond in the candlelight."

After exploring the cave, they again passed through the mine's tunnel and on to view the cyanide solution tanks, where the ore was dumped. A vacuum pump sucked up the cyanide solution and poured it on zinc shavings to attract the gold in the solution. This soaked for ten days, and then the zinc was cut with dilute sulfuric acid and the product was delivered to the assayer, "the solution man."

Lillian always made sure they stopped to watch him form the gold bricks. Adding a small amount of the "product" to some other ingredients in a crucible, he returned it to the furnace and turned on the heat. When it was time, he put on asbestos mittens and, with tongs, lifted the red-hot crucible out of the furnace. He poured the contents into a trough about two feet long, four inches wide, and an inch or so deeper at one end than the other. The heat of the burning, molten mass of metal was almost intolerable and its fumes, stifling. After it cooled, he dumped a gold bar out on the table.

Sometimes John and Lillian did things together with the children while Frank was at work. It was about this time that she started writing her *Golden Gulch* novel—not a very good novel but one revealing a great deal about her inner life. Dreams were cheap and legal, so Lillian dreamt of romance and began writing a story that seemed to grow out of these yearnings. This is when her "bewitching Mrs. Gay" emerged as a central character in her stories, a sophisticated, attractive, and wealthy woman from the East. She appeared in Lillian's fiction, in one form or another, for years. Mrs. Gay always found romance and respect. She was also a bit adventurous for the times, doing things Lillian would never dare do.

In fact, one might guess John was the romantic male lead in the *Golden Gulch* novel, about "unrequited love among the pines," as Lillian described the story to an editor years later. It's doubtful her or John's conscience would have allowed them to carry on a full-fledged affair. The extent of her feelings for him is something Lillian didn't reveal unless one tries to read between the lines of her novel and her diaries. After all, she wouldn't find many men to fantasize about in Gilt Edge. Actually, John was a safe person to center her dreams on because he lived in the East and they only saw him, at the most, every two years. He never married and continued to visit until his death in 1925.

Although Frank and Lillian were happier in Gilt Edge than at any time in their marriage, Lillian was definitely yearning for something more than she had with him. How bad it was, what the problems were, again, one can only try to read between the lines of some of Lillian's writings. She never spells them out except in an oblique fashion.

She continued to struggle with the fact that Frank never talked, never revealed much of what he was thinking or feeling. Lillian talked a lot and revealed more about her feelings and thoughts than Frank wanted to know. Although she should have seen this, it appears she didn't. And she did want to please him, but she could never figure out where she stood with him. She really couldn't change her approach to life any more than he could.

When, during discussions of friends' or relatives' marriages, someone might say, "Oh! Her husband seems so nice . . ." Lillian would counter with, "Well, perhaps he's a devil at home and an angel abroad."

Her poem "Saint and Sinner," published in the *Great Falls Tribune*, probably defines her marriage as she saw it:

Tom said he was a saint on earth,
But thought his wife a sinner,
And while he did increase in girth
She, steadily, grew thinner.

He never tired of telling o'er,
His virtues and her failings;
She listened with true wifely awe,
To his conceited railings.
"I do not swear," he said, "nor smoke,
And do but little drinking;
You're luckier than most folk,
Is what I'm always thinking. . . ."

Obviously, swearing—or the lack of swearing—was no longer at the top of Lillian's "wish" list describing the perfect mate. Now she dreamed of a cheerful man who knew how to smile, who might look on the bright side of life and make the best of things. Lillian, however, struggled to make the best of what she saw as her bad bargain and saw no alternative to her marriage, even though she had been earning her living when she married Frank.

It's true there wasn't much for the Hazens to be happy about in 1900. While Frank was out of work, they had borrowed money from everyone, including John, and were still struggling to pay off those debts and put their life back together. It took all the strength Lillian could muster to overcome the depression that threatened to engulf her daily.

She knew when things seemed the worst, there had to be a point where they "bottomed out" and started to improve. She was luckier than most because writing was her therapy. It was a perfect time to write, and Lillian took full advantage of it. Her poetry found a ready market in the *Great Falls Tribune*, where she published under the name M. D. Gaines, the pseudonym her novelist grandmother used decades before. Besides, O. S. Warden, Frank's good friend and old Dartmouth roommate, was managing editor. Because there weren't that many local writers in the early 1900s, he used all she submitted.

How distant her early dreams must have seemed as she sat in her wee cottage overlooking Gilt Edge and tried to convince herself motherhood is the most important job in the world. She worked hard at being a good one, a difficult task because she was so isolated, with no family and no friends for support. For months, she and the children took walks down the gulch away from town. How quiet the Montana wilderness, as she didn't even dare have a cup of tea with a neighbor to pass the time of day until the smallpox scare was past!

Frank told her the mountains roared when there was to be a winter storm. Sometimes the pine-covered hills did seem like great monsters, still and watchful, waiting, ready to pounce. Often the cabin's windows were covered with a quarter inch of frost and the ground covered with hip-deep snow. The Hazens' only contact with the outside world was the mail, which included some magazines and a newspaper that came in each day on the stage.

There was no other intellectual stimulation—no libraries, museums, or theaters. There were few diversions and much spare time. This brought out a serenity and sharpness of thought Lillian had never found before and would never know again. Her new environment sparked creativity. From the beginning, Lillian liked the western-style informal, no-nonsense approach to life.

One of the first things she did during the long cold winter was organize her scrapbooks with clippings of her "Lillian's Letter" interspersed with the many poems she had sold to the *Great Falls Tribune.* Her saved columns indicate the parts of her career she was most proud of, but for some reason, she never talked about her earlier life once she left it. No one, perhaps not even Frank, knew how she had covered every aspect of New York City life in an era when women were seldom journalists.

Her New York life seemed so far away when she looked back and thought how trivial some of her concerns seemed after a year in Gilt Edge. She remembered the first summer when she began working as a reporter. Her friends asked where she intended to spend August. She wrote it took a lot of nerve to say, "In New York, most probably," and described how she cringed at their look of polite astonishment.

"It was the ruination of one's social status to stay in the city during the hottest weather," she wrote. "People thought I had no money, and what state of affairs in this world can be more awful than that?"

The truth was Lillian didn't have any money, but she remembered having a good time even if she didn't go to Bar Harbor or Newport or the White Mountains. Lillian had to have spent a lot of time thinking about the turn her life took to the mountainside in Montana as she read her old clippings. What a difference between her first eastern home and

Fifteen

her bare cabin and her neighbors' bare cabins! Interior decorating, Gilt Edge style, might consist of a new set of curtains or a vase filled with wildflowers. The Hazens lost most of their valuable possessions when they went bankrupt, but Lillian found she really didn't miss them. She liked her simple life and environment. Besides, fewer possessions meant fewer things to dust and clean.

Did Lillian wonder if she would ever see an art museum again when she read what she wrote in 1889, "Culture and refinement are a national need," decrying the fact that the government did not support art other than building museums? At the time, she also covered the alterations to the Metropolitan Museum of Art and thought it sad most paintings were produced by foreigners.

"Is it possible, in our population of 50 or 60 million souls, there are no artists?"

Another favorite chore as a roving reporter was reviewing concerts, one she really missed in Montana because, at the time, there weren't even radios. Later she never missed a concert when performers like Jascha Heifetz came to Lewistown, Montana. Lillian, however, was making do, putting her many talents to work in Gilt Edge by helping the local musicians present several concerts. Sometimes she played the piano.

She remembered the first time she attended a concert in Gilt Edge. Her neighbor took her to the long, low log building where the concerts were held, which townspeople had decorated with shabby red, white, and blue bunting. The rickety platform for musicians and performers bent and swayed with every footstep. A piano, considerably the worse for wear, stood on the floor below the platform. Planks supported by kegs were audience seats.

About half an hour after Lillian arrived, the band straggled in. They took their seats on the platform and at 8:30 P.M. began playing. To Lillian, each instrument seemed tuned in a different key or not tuned at all; no two played in unison and the effect of the whole was "a fearful and wonderful noise." By the time the band's first selection was ended, an audience of about a hundred had gathered, and Lillian wondered if they felt they were getting their 50-cent admission's worth.

They listened politely, but it was apparent to all the band had not practiced enough together. In fact, one band member stood up and explained that owing to a delay in getting their instruments, they had been unable to practice much. After the band, Lillian accompanied a local woman some called "the Mrs. Astor of Gilt Edge society," singing "Never, Never Fall in Love" in a high squeaky voice. She was the wife of the leading grocer in town and insisted on wearing her brand-new hat. Lillian described it as "a remarkable combination of yellow straw, yellow and red net, and big artificial cherries."

Lillian said, "She appeared to highly appreciate her own perform-ance, and betrayed no nervousness."

On the other hand, Lillian sounded a bit superior when she con-trasted her own good taste in dress—"dark blue cloth skirt and light blue silk waist finished at the neck with a real lace collar. A gold pin was my only ornament."

She played Weber's "Invitation to the Dance," and even though the piano was slightly out of tune, she wrote she made "the worn out old keys sing and thrill with life." Lillian was amazed to hear the burst of applause that followed her classical selection. To her, it demonstrated the rough-looking crowd knew much more about music than she had sup-posed. Everyone wanted an encore, and so she sat down and played Paderewski's "Minuet in G."

Sometimes she wished she had never offered her services to help the band. She complained in one story that the musicians rarely played together, but she admitted they did the best they could. "What more could one ask?"

Actually, they were lucky to have her knowledge and expertise, but probably no one recognized this. She had been practicing on the town's piano and yearned for one of her own. When John returned east after his first trip to Gilt Edge, he carried specifications for a new piano. Frank asked him to price one and the cost of freighting it into Gilt Edge, a definite financial sacrifice he was willing to make.

Lillian carefully pasted a December 11, 1901, letter from John in her scrapbook:

Dear Frank,

Yesterday, I asked a friend, a dealer in pianos, about the "Wing" and his reply was he would not advise me to sell one to any person whom I ever expected to see again, which I thought was enough said.

I am afraid I could not get any piano that I would want to recommend for less than $250.00. The freight to Chicago (from New York) would be $5.00. . . .

You must feel quite grand with a whole house, no-bunkers [boarders], and running water. Your arms will probably shrink to their normal length now.

I don't believe there is ever a day that I do not think of my visit to Gilt Edge and there is no part of my trip that I think of with more pleasure. I am glad to know the children remember me. Yesterday, I sent you a doll for Barbara and a Noah's Ark for Richard for Christmas. I hope they will arrive in good condition, will be enjoyed, and all the rest of the family will not send them the same things.

I was very pleased with the photograph you sent me some time ago. I have been too busy to thank you for it before. I think the likeness of Barbara is perfect but Richard's I don't like so well. He doesn't look half smart enough. It doesn't begin to do him justice.

John

Even though they were essentially broke, and Lillian knew they really couldn't afford it, they finally ordered the piano, one of the first freighted into the area.

Later Lillian wrote, "No one could ever know the joy of running my fingers over the keys that first time."

— SIXTEEN —

End of the Jawbone Line

Old Panhandle Jake had determined to
run
For some county office, and when he be-
gun
To campaign the country, I tell you we
stared
At the things that he did, and old folk
declared
That they never had seen a candidate
make
Such a hot time in town as Panhandle
Jake.

M. D. Gaines
From "Panhandle Jake's Campaign"
Great Falls Tribune. November 5, 1910

A Mr. Hilger placed Frank's name before the State Convention as Democratic nominee for clerk and recorder of Fergus County in Lewistown in 1902, while the Hazens still lived in Gilt Edge. He said Frank was the one man in the county who could make the present incumbent in the clerk and recorder office "slide, Kelly, slide."

At the mine, Frank was active in union affairs, was well liked, and, of course, made his usual good impression. He and Lillian both agreed they were ready for a change. Few who moved into Gilt Edge during those last months of the nineteenth century intended to stay. Most came to make their fortunes and move on. Frank took the bookkeeper job with the mines because he had to have work. It was pure happenstance the job was in the Far West. He was marking time until something better came along.

That fall the Hazens hit the rough Montana campaign trail. Lillian, however, was no stranger to politics. Often her "Lillian's Letter" had covered New York City's political scene.

In an October 1888 column, she wrote, "Last Saturday the Republicans paraded in the afternoon, and the Democrats in the evening—A Republican gentleman told a young lady with whom he wished to be on the best of terms that the Democrats paraded in the evening as, 'They love darkness better than light, their deeds being so evil.'"

Lillian was most likely the young lady. She wrote she surprised him with her angry reaction when she turned and said, "Thank you, Mr.___ for the fine character you have given me."

The poor man was crushed, and then made things worse by saying he had always looked upon her as a woman of such good sense that he supposed, of course, that she was a Republican. His condescending manner was more than Lillian could take. He forgot she had a handy weapon—her column. She relished sticking it to him. She, in fact, often managed to turn a put-down to her, and women's ideas, to advantage in her "Lillian's Letter."

In 1888, she also wrote, as far as she was concerned, elections were a farce, and she didn't think it mattered much who won—the Democrats or Republicans. It didn't make the slightest difference to her whether Harrison or Cleveland sat in the presidential chair.

Lillian said she believed in voting for the best man, for an "intelligent, honest, upright, god-fearing man." Then American interests would be safe in his hands, "be he Democrat or Republican," but she admitted a person had to be astute in determining who this "intelligent, honest, upright, god-fearing man might be."

Regardless of her and Frank's marital problems, Lillian knew he was an honest, organized man who would make a good clerk and recorder. Besides, she wanted to move back to civilization. She was willing to do almost anything to help Frank win the election but couldn't resist poking fun at the whole process:

The afternoon tea,
Between you and me,
Is a terrible bore and a sham,
You talk with a smile,
To strangers awhile,
Eat grub you don't like, and salaam.

It was a tough campaign: his opponent was a longtime incumbent. Frank needed all the help he could get, because Kelly ran a "dirty" operation from start to finish. He did sneaky, underhanded things like announcing meetings for the Hazen campaign that weren't scheduled, like in the following item, which appeared in the *Fergus County Democrat:*

The report given out that there would be a meeting at Rock Creek last Friday night, and that John Alexander would be present, must have been started by some of his opposition, as there was no intention of holding a meeting there on that date. The report that he and Mr. Hazen, who was accompanying him in the vicinity of Ubet, were too drunk to get to that place was the work of some lying tongue who wished to do both gentlemen harm.

Because there was no speedy mode of local transportation in 1902, voters and candidates had to make a real effort to reach meetings by wagon or on horseback, and the voters were mighty irritated when a meeting didn't take place. Voters also came expecting free handouts of some small luxury. It was traditional for the precinct committeeman and the president of the political club to accompany the candidate, one carrying a box of cigars and the other, a bottle of whiskey paid for by the candidate, of course. They even carried stick candy for the kids and plugs of tobacco for those who preferred to chew their nicotine.

A family portrait, 1903: Frank, Lillian, Barbara, and Richard in Lewistown just as Frank became clerk and recorder for Fergus County.

Lillian complained, "It took a lot of money to give every man in the county a drink of whiskey and a cigar."

Lewistown's *Fergus County Democrat* newspaper backed Frank Hazen and labeled Kelly a "blustering bully," who capped a long series of blunders and official mistakes by threatening a man who stopped at the office of the clerk and recorder to view a public document. Because Kelly had been on the official payroll since Fergus County was formed, the *Democrat* added, "The public service is never benefited by retaining a man in office until he becomes fossilized."

The editor saw Frank as a civil, courteous gentleman under all conditions and described Kelly as "arrogant, domineering, and insulting."

Needless to say, Frank won the election:

On the first day of January next [1903] Frank J. Hazen will assume charge of the Clerk and Recorder's office and then for the first time since the organization of Fergus County, the name of Kelly will fail to appear upon the official payroll.

And so the Hazens moved to Lewistown, Montana, the county seat of Fergus County, so designated by the state legislature in 1886. It was twenty miles southeast of Gilt Edge in Judith Basin, an important region for many reasons. Because it had once been covered by water, there were petrified fossils of oysters, clams, and fish preserved in clay banks, washed and polished by time. On the basin's north rim, the local Indians found white-bleached bones of prehistoric animals half buried in the broken badlands country on both sides of the wide Missouri River, which they called the "Big Muddy."

Just before the Hazens moved to Gilt Edge, there were few settlers in Judith Basin. Lillian wrote it had been more green and beautiful than any man-made park, a lush grassland swarming with buffalo, antelope, deer, bear, wolves, and grouse. Prairie dog towns covered the flats. Honker geese, mallards, and teal ducks nested along the lakes and creeks. Kit foxes prowled the night, and beavers built dams in every creek. In the foothills and mountains surrounding Judith Basin, there were whitetail and black-tail deer as well as grizzlies, black bear, brown cinnamon bear, mountain lions, and timber wolves. Eagles nested in the pinnacles and hawks were plentiful, as were magpies, blue jays, and crows.

This all began to change as, at the turn of the century, settlers poured into the area on the improved railroads. The last of the original mountain men and gold seekers were disappearing, and the beginning of a vast ranching industry was coming in with land-hungry settlers from the East. It was a significant era passing in Montana history. By the time the Hazens moved to Lewistown, Judith Basin was the home of several big cattle outfits backed by eastern and European capital. Longhorn cattle grazed the grass-covered flatlands, crowding out much of the wildlife.

Construction of the new county courthouse, begun in 1903, was due to be finished and "under roof" by December 1907. Professional people—doctors, dentists, and lawyers—were moving to town and advertising freely in the local paper. Although in 1900, politicians found more voters in Gilt Edge than in Lewistown, by 1902, that began to change. The Judith Basin area was booming, just as the whole U.S. economy was booming.

Sixteen

Teddy Roosevelt became president in 1901. He was the man of the decade, who was fond of saying, "I like to drain the wine of life with brandy in it."

He was a modern president who curbed the nation's huge trade monopolies and financial trusts. He was also aware of the great wave of settlers moving west and the need for environment protection. Roosevelt took a leading role, advocating restraint and foresight in the exploitation of natural resources. Through his initiative, the national forests were increased from 43 to 194 million acres, many in Montana, during his administration.

Even the U.S. Treasury showed a surplus of $46,380,000.

Lewistown's economy was prosperous, too. Besides being the center for cattle ranchers and gold mines, it was becoming a leading wool market. The sheep ranchers began bringing their wool into town to sell. Then they stayed to shop. Lewistown had better stores than Gilt Edge, and they stocked a wide variety of consumer goods to lure the people from the surrounding ranches and gold-mining centers. The prices at Power Mercantile, the only department store in town, seem low by today's standards but were probably more than that day's average, because everything was imported from the East.

Cotton stockings sold for 25 cents a pair, and fine all-wool cashmere flannel was 25 cents a yard. A woman could buy a fox scarf for $12.50.

Everything, however, is relative because the average weekly wage was $12, and men thought nothing of laboring ten hours a day, six days a week. Furnished rooms rented for $5 to $10 a month with board thrown in for $5 a week, not cheap when one considers the pay.

Improved transportation methods were helping the town grow. It was getting easier every year to get around the state and in and out of Montana. By 1900, Americans owned eight thousand cars, but few of these were in Lewistown, because they weren't practical. There were few gas stations in town and none outside the city limits, and if a driver "dared to venture outside the city, he soon found himself in an uncharted wilderness of rutted dirt roads and meandering country lanes."

In 1902, the Judith Stage Company was still advertising horse-drawn stages "leaving Great Falls at 7 A.M. daily from the Great Northern Express Office for Belt, Armington, Cora, Geyser, Stanford, Utica,

Philbrook, and Lewistown." It was also in 1902 when the *Fergus County Democrat* announced Lewistown was to have an "automobile line" that would connect with the railway at Harlowton. Unfortunately, when the car arrived, they found it wasn't tough enough for the primitive roads in the area. Then Thomas Wilson, who had the carrier's contract for the mail service to and from Harlowton, made a trip east to find an automobile able to function on central Montana's primitive roads:

> The automobile purchased by Mr. Wilson will use a gasoline engine and will be arranged to accommodate 12 passengers. He is very confident it can be operated successfully on these roads, and, as it will make the run from Lewistown to the railway in about half the time used by the stages, it will greatly facilitate travel in the only important sans railway section of the state that is left.

Finally, the town fathers talked the Montana Central Railway into extending its line from Harlowton to Lewistown. It was nicknamed "The Jawbone." With its completion in 1903, Lewistown joined the network springing up along the vast countrywide railway system. This made it much easier to ship local agricultural products to market and to bring in consumer goods.

Such progressive businesses as the Fergus County Creamery, run by Fred and William Dissly, sold frozen eggs to bakeries and shipped frozen turkeys in dry ice all over the United States.

From the first, Lillian liked Lewistown, "the biggest little city west of the Mississippi . . . ideally located on a swift flowing creek [Spring Creek]." Today Spring Creek is famous for having some of the best trout fishing in the United States, and anglers come from all over to try their luck.

Although the first town site of Lewistown was platted in 1882, the streets, in 1902, were still dirt and the sidewalks still wooden. Most buildings on Main Street housed saloons. Historians are not sure, but Lewistown may have been named after the Lewis and Clark expedition. There is an old log cabin said to have been a resting place for the party in town. Or then again, it might have been named for a military camp called Camp Lewis at one time, on the west bank of Spring Creek.

Lillian with their Boston terrier, Mike, in their backyard in Lewistown, 1905.

Life was good in Lewistown. In late 1902, the town built its new water system, fed by delicious artesian spring water, for less than $8,000, which is still used today. By 1905, the YMCA was open for members. The Lewistown-Billings telephone company wanted to establish a central phone system, and long-distance lines were going in. Some ranchers were putting in their own phone lines. Lewistown was similar to many towns of fewer than 2,500 people, where 60 percent of the U.S. population lived in the early 1900s.

Small news items in the *Fergus County Democrat* indicated civilization had arrived. Stray horses were no longer allowed to roam the streets and were picked up by the city pound and the animals' descriptions advertised in the local paper. Progress brought other problems and humorous incidents such as the following one, reported by the *Democrat:*

The freight train ran over a cow just above the Cook place as it came in last night. There were several of a herd laying on the track and all but one moved when the train whistled. The remains of the one which did not move were scattered promiscuously along the track.

Both Lillian and Frank decided Montana was to be their permanent home. Perhaps in the beginning they thought about returning east if their financial situation improved, but after two years, they never gave it another thought.

Something that may have contributed to Lillian's wish to stay away from the East was her family's situation. A February 7, 1902, letter from her sister, Maude, contained money she had borrowed earlier. Lillian pasted the note on the front cover of her last scrapbook. It appears that even though Frank and Lillian had little money at that point, were just getting on their feet, Maude had borrowed $35 from them (a lot of money in 1901) and had moved in with Lillian's mother.

She had a little girl and gushed on about how the child loved her grandmother, how living with her mother was more convenient than she and her husband trying to maintain their own apartment. Over the years, Maude was to take complete advantage of her mother, and Lillian was powerless to stop her.

SEVENTEEN

A Wish for Bliss without Alloy

A hedge of thorns has grown between us two;
It seemed so slight a thing, and yet, we knew
When it began to grow, t'would part us soon.
We should have plucked it down that afternoon
The first shoot started—without prickles then—
Alas! Too late we learn what might have been.

Lillian's journal. 1904

The Hazens' Gilt Edge stay had been the best time in their marriage, but after their move to Lewistown, their relationship began to deteriorate. Perhaps Frank was under more pressure as a new officeholder. Lillian nagged, trying to penetrate his quiet facade, to force him to be more of a companion. He must have yearned for tranquility as much as she but just couldn't express himself in a forthright manner. The more Lillian persisted in trying to make a connection with her husband, the more he withdrew.

She thought she saw constant disapproval in Frank's immobile face as she struggled to make him happy. She was totally in the dark trying to read his moods and thoughts. He never appeared happy. Perhaps he wasn't sure how he felt about many things.

One problem for him was their lives had been in a constant state of upheaval for several years, first with their bankruptcy and then with their move west. Because Lillian had been on the move all her life as she followed her father around and lived his hectic life with him, she didn't realize how hard it was for Frank to accept change as she did. Until he married her, he had never moved or traveled much.

Her barrage of words always left him speechless. He could not face confrontation in any form. When their son was eighty-five years old, he reminisced about being trapped on the battlefield of Frank and Lillian's marriage. At the first hint of unpleasantness, Frank would put on his hat and head for the door.

Each time, Lillian would say, "If you go out that door, don't bother to come back." Frank always reluctantly returned.

Some family gossip says Frank had an affair. Lillian would never forgive that kind of a blow to her ego. She was like an elephant. She never forgot or forgave a slight. She wanted Frank to care for her more than any other, and she did write the poem "Jealousy":

Our love should be a thing of light and joy,
But jealousy has tarnished its bright sheen,
Has crawled like some foul reptile in between
Our golden hours of bliss without alloy.

My heart is sodden with a nameless woe,
My feet have grown too weary for the dance,—
Because I caught the swift, admiring glance
You gave another girl you know.

In the community, Frank was seen as a good husband and a charming guy, while Lillian reported his shortcomings in various stories and poems (most unpublished). They were a good way to vent her anger without doing damage. She complained that one grumpy person could plunge a household into gloom while another's smile lit up the darkest, saddest hours. She thought a couple should strive to make the home a haven from the "tumults of the world."

Each failed to recognize the other's needs and worries. Lillian complained Frank was an "uncongenial, sordid soul, incapable of appreciating me," that he didn't understand her nature "in all its heights and depths." But as a moth is drawn to a flame, Frank was drawn to Lillian and her constant cheerful optimism, such a bright contrast to his own low-grade depression.

With no money of her own, and because Frank's clerk and recorder salary was small, Lillian often wrote how powerless she was to oppose her "petty tyrant's" will. She, however, thought there was some way to solve their conflicts even though she couldn't seem to accept herself as she was or Frank as he was. She thought she could learn to please this man if she could just crack the code—an exercise doomed to fail.

Lillian also noted that competition may be the life of trade, but it is fatal to marital happiness. She soon learned Frank was most sensitive when she disagreed with some course of action or opinion. Almost always, he would go against her suggestions even when they made sense. Over the years, she learned to pick her battles.

Although Lillian's writings most often seemed to blame Frank for their marital woes, deep down, she recognized and admitted she was at fault, too, and wrote the following "code" to remind herself to be constructive in her everyday life.

Refuse to use words that bite and tones that crush.

Practice patience at home lest my testy temper break through unexpectedly and disgrace me.

I will remember that my neighbors have troubles enough to carry without loading mine on them.

I will excuse others' faults and failures as often and fully as I expect others to be lenient with mine.

I will cure criticism with commendation, close up against gossip and build healthy loves by service.

I will wear everywhere a good-will face unchilled by aloofness.

I will gloat over gains never, I will love boys and girls, so that old age will not find me stiff and soured.

I will gladden my nature by smiling out loud on every fair occasion and by out-looking optimistically.

A Wish for Bliss without Alloy

I will pray frequently, think good things, believe men and do a full day's work without fear or favor.

Divorce was out of the question as far as Lillian was concerned. Now she had two small children, and she knew how hard it would be to earn a decent living on her own even though she had more credentials than most. Besides, she would rather be married than single and didn't want to give up her marriage. She was happy in Lewistown, liked living in a proper town with streets and stores and nice houses surrounded by grass and trees. She and Frank were making a good life for themselves. Also, Frank was a known quality. She knew he had a better attitude toward women than most men.

Early on, as she began her career as a writer and thinker, she realized many Victorian men had flawed attitudes toward women. In one of her last columns before she married, she wrote about the problem. The following remark, reprinted in her "Lillian's Letter" from one of her favorite magazines, infuriated her:

> As for men, I have studied them closely, and were I to live to fourscore could scarcely know them better than I do now; but, as for women, I have thought it useless they being so much more wicked and impenetrable.
>
> Prince Charles of England
> *Scribners.* April 1895

She wrote that Prince Charles's low opinion of women wouldn't be important except that it was shared by many good men as well as "dissipated, immoral" men.

By the time the Hazens moved to Lewistown in 1903, Lillian was only thirty-eight years old. She looked ten years younger than when she arrived in Gilt Edge on the cold snowy day in 1899. Her face softened with the easier life. The pretty girl had turned into a handsome woman. Although she was growing older more gracefully than most, she never acknowledged her birthdays and never told her age, even when she was in her eighties.

The family doctor once asked Richard, "How old is your mother?"

Richard, of course, repeated the conversation to Lillian and she exploded, "How dare he? It's none of his business."

Actually, one would think her age was her doctor's business, but her anger indicated one of her problems. She had strong opinions, not always rational, and wasn't bashful about voicing them. Because she at one time earned her living analyzing—and criticizing—various aspects of life and society, she found she had a tendency to do the same thing in her every-day life. She tried to be friendly and outgoing, even when she felt angry and wanted to speak her mind to acquaintances and friends. She wrote that a continually cranky attitude would lead to an unpleasant and sour old age.

— EIGHTEEN —

A Question of Attitude

The ripest fruit hangs now within my reach—
What evil can there be in touching—tasting, I beseech
Thee, Lord, to satisfy my fierce desire, my bitter need—
In sore distress, I come to Thee and plead.

M. D. Gaines
Great Falls Tribune. February 26, 1910

Not only did Lillian daydream about earlier loves, but at the same time, she appeared to be struggling with her own urge to be unfaithful to Frank, according to the above poem, titled "Forbidden," published long after she wrote it.

In an incomplete manuscript, she discussed the same subject: "A good woman is supposed to center her affections on her husband 'for they twain shall be one flesh'! I cannot think she would be guilty of such an awful sin as harboring a guilty love for another man—"

She, however, has the heroine say:

But suppose the twain are not one? Perhaps she married the man in good faith when too young to judge character. If, at first, she performed her wifely duties conscientiously and lovingly, only to have her affections repulsed, her sensibilities wounded, until her love was killed beyond any possibility of being resurrected, can the twain be one flesh then?

Clearly, these words indicate that different sex drives and attitudes were causing much of Lillian's dissatisfaction. Years later, Richard said she complained to him when he was a teenager that she had to beg for sex, not a healthy discussion for Lillian to have with her sixteen-year-old son.

One comment she wrote stands out because probably many Victorian women felt this way: "Life would be much less complicated if women could ignore their sexual natures."

The Mystery of Love Making Solved or an Easy Road to Marriage, copyright 1880, "guaranteed mailed in a plain brown wrapper," seemed to assume women weren't much interested in sex, that only men thought of sex. It gave oblique advice that could be interpreted any way the reader chose. One gets the idea, however, that anything but food is being discussed.

> Not the least useful piece of advice—namely though it be—that we can offer to newly married ladies, is to remind them that husbands are men, and that they must eat. We can tell them, moreover, that men attach no small importance to this very essential operation, and that a very effectual way to keep them in good humor, as well as in good condition, is for wives to study their husbands' peculiar likes and dislikes in this matter.

If a woman aspired, as Lillian did, to be a wife and lover, if a woman admitted, even to herself, sexual feelings as Lillian did, she was cautioned to keep her feelings to herself. Nineteenth-century advice literature—women's magazines, etiquette books, marriage manuals—urged all women to be ladylike and "good." It was an era when Victorian doctors called masturbation "self-abuse" and warned their patients they would go crazy if they "abused themselves." They also advised men not to have sex more than once a month, because ejaculation spent valuable energy.

In the late 1800s, Dr. William Acton appeared to be trying to reassure male readers that marriage was not beyond their physical powers when he wrote, "Women, happily for them, are not very much troubled with sexual feelings of any kind." "Good women" were supposed to subdue passions, not kindle them.

The true Victorian gentleman, and Frank was that, probably would have been appalled and, perhaps, rendered impotent by a healthy woman who happily jumped into the marriage bed. Did Lillian go so far as to pretend reluctance in approaching marital sex? Maybe at first modesty prevailed, but then if honesty eventually prevailed, their troubles began.

The Victorian male also had a difficult time dealing with his real sexual nature. After cheating his good Victorian wife of her role as lover and forcing her into her chaste wife role, he had nowhere to turn for uninhibited sex. It's not surprising he often hired a prostitute to satisfy his carnal cravings and little wonder that prostitution flourished in the late 1800s.

A year after Lillian and Frank married, she wrote a strange story about a prostitute.

> She rapped loudly with the sphinx head knocker until the door was opened by a Negro dressed as an Egyptian.
>
> "Madame Tua is not at home," he said.
>
> The woman showed him a fifty dollar bill. "This may persuade you to open her door for me."
>
> The servant hesitated and looked longingly at the money, murmured uncertainly, "Her orders were positive."
>
> The woman pulled out a revolver and forced her way in to see Tua, the Egyptian. The celebrated courtesan was lying on a couch dressed in barbaric splendor. She didn't rise when the woman burst in upon her, but merely said in a surprised tone, "Who are you and what do you want?"
>
> "My husband—where is he?"
>
> A ripple of amused, mocking laughter preceded the insolent answer to her question, which was, "Name, please. So many husbands call here, you know."

Lillian goes on to tell the whole story of the exotic courtesan. She wrote she had been a secretary in a married man's office and had an affair with him; thus her life was ruined. Therefore, she turned to prostitution to earn a living, because society saw her as a "tainted" woman after the scandal.

It was small consolation that other women wrestled with the same "demons," that other women were going through the same torment, each coping with it in her own way. Lillian and other Victorian women didn't find any sensible advice for dealing with sex.

Years later, Lillian admitted birth control was difficult. She and her friends used "a small sponge, attached to a silk string, dipped in boric acid and inserted into the vagina." Margaret Sanger didn't open her first birth control clinic in Brooklyn until 1916.

Some nineteenth-century women retreated into hypochondria and succumbed to a variety of ailments rather than acknowledge their unhappiness openly. To complain or to express anger or sexual desire simply was not acceptable. Rummage through the advice literature of the nineteenth century and you can readily see why the Victorian sexual mores produced impotent men, frigid women, and secret alcoholics and drug addicts. Eugene O'Neill's *Long Day's Journey into Night* is a poignant portrayal of an unhappy Victorian wife turned addict.

Magazines like the *Ladies' Home Journal,* with a circulation of 440,000 a month, carried great blocks of patent medicine vendors' ads:

Ladies—I have found a safe home remedy that will cure all ailments peculiar to the female sex. No physician required. I will send it free with full instructions to every suffering woman.

By 1889, these vendors were receiving thousands of sick women's letters, which were sold to brokers. One marketer said he had a million letters stacked in a warehouse, all broken down into certain categories: 55,000 female complaint letters, 44,000 bust developer letters, 40,000 regulator letters, 7,000 paralysis letters, 52,000 consumption letters, 3,000 cancer, and 65,000 deaf. The most startling statistic, however, was the 9,000 narcotic addiction letters.

No surveys were ever taken to determine how many women were hooked on unregulated patent medicines full of opium, morphine, or alcohol sold over the counter by drugstores and by mail. Although many women became addicts without even being aware of what was happening, everyone looked the other way. It was an acceptable, ladylike way of coping with life's secret realities.

Lillian never used any of these crutches to survive. She was not frail, pale, and sickly; she never retreated into drug or alcohol addiction, headaches, or hypochondria, manipulative tactics Frank would have accepted. She was extremely healthy, uncomplaining, and hardworking, but she met all opposition head-on, had strong opinions, and displayed an obstinacy in her makeup that Frank soon found unpleasant.

As for Frank—he manipulated Lillian with his silence, something he could not help and probably did not understand. In his quiet way, he often let her talk herself into a rage and when she erupted in anger, he was disapproving and she was dismayed, vowing to herself never to let it happen again.

— NINETEEN —

Urban Life

*No fear of prying eyes, and malicious tongues or the
rapacious demands of church and society—just freedom to
worship nature's God in awestruck thankful silence.*

"A Summer's Vacation." 1905

Helena (Montana) closed gambling activities and so did Great Falls. *The
Democrat* reported, on February 7, 1905, that Lewistown would follow the
trend by outlawing gambling on the first of the next month. All houses in
which there were games quietly boxed up their chips, covered up their lay-
outs, and prepared to wait for something to turn up before opening again.

At the same time, the town fathers decided Lewistown was too small
to support its twenty saloons. The *Democrat* editor applauded the town
fathers' effort to bring Lewistown up to early-1900 urban standards by
passing a new ordinance that raised the city license for saloons from an
annual fee of $60 to $300. City business leaders, however, were not as
concerned with the morals of the saloon patrons as they were with losing
the $200,000 the saloons' customers spent each year, money that might
be spent in local stores.

At the time, Lewistown businesses were struggling to survive a
drought that began in 1904. Because Frank was not a rancher or merchant,

the drought didn't affect the Hazens directly, but it devastated Lewistown businesses. When the ranchers' crops failed, they had little cash to spend on consumer goods.

Judith Basin is one of the richest farming areas in the United States, where the soil consists of a foot of black loam covering clay. This helps it retain moisture when it rains, but growing seasons without rain, droughts, are an inevitable part of Montana's weather cycle. When one arrives, ranchers peer into the sky day after day and wish to see clouds forming. But sometimes they peer in vain for weeks at a time.

The year 1904 was the kind Montana ranchers, from the beginning of dry farming (as opposed to irrigated farming), dread the most.

The *Democrat*, December 13, 1904, reported:

> Although many encomiums are passed everyday on the beautiful weather which has prevailed in this part of the country all fall, there are many who would like to see a little change for the worse.

Judith Basin needed snow. There had not been enough moisture to start the fall-sown grain growing or keep the freshwater springs spouting. The cattle couldn't roam far from the few water holes when there was no snow. The areas around the water sources soon were stripped of food.

The drought meant even less money coming into the town in the form of taxes at a time when the city fathers were looking for a broader tax base to pay for bare necessities and a few luxuries. The *Democrat*'s editor knew the growing town needed shape and form. He urged the city government to set aside land for small parks and playgrounds within the city's boundaries. Because Frank was one of the "town fathers," he was involved in deciding these local issues.

In 1904, he easily won a second term as clerk and recorder. *The Fergus Democrat News* reported he brought the same careful attention to the job he had displayed in his job as a mining company accountant. Frank's office filed original documents within forty-eight hours after they were returned by the attorneys. In fact, Frank found he needed less help and laid off one deputy, thus saving the city $1,000 a year.

The local paper called him a "gentleman," saying he treated everyone with utmost courtesy. Although Lillian insisted Frank thought himself superior to most, it wasn't apparent to other people. Most would have been surprised to find he was considered a grouch at home. Because Lillian was angry at Frank so much of the time, she seemed "cold" almost to the point of rudeness to the "masculine members of their social circle." She said Frank didn't like her aloof manners, because he valued his possessions by the value placed on them by others. He wanted his wife to be popular. This was an important consideration if he was going to make politics his profession.

He didn't seem to see that Lillian was popular, especially with other women. Open friendliness was her natural style, and because she couldn't maintain an indifferent attitude for long, she was an asset to Frank, in his political career and in the community, whether he realized it or not. She kept the same friends for years. The Lewistown people, who got to know her, liked and admired her in spite of the fact that she was straightforward, had the courage of her convictions, and usually voiced them.

Even though 1904 was not a good year for most of the area, it was good for the Hazens. They moved into their new $1,200 house on a large corner lot at 314 Seventh Avenue South—one of ten new residences built in Lewistown that year. Much later, in 1920, Lillian wrote her description of the perfect house in the perfect setting. It sounded much like theirs with its many windows. She wrote, "Sunlight and fresh air are God's medicine."

Their house faced east, so their front porch got the sun in the morning. The kitchen on the north was in the shade all day, and its pantry had a window. Lillian didn't have an icebox, and, of course, there were no refrigerators at the time.

At first, the house had a coal shed and outdoor privy in the back. Later they added a bathroom and a garage and dug out a basement for a coal furnace. It was similar to the first house they rented in Brookline, Massachusetts, a typical Victorian two-story house, with a front porch, or "piazza," as Lillian called it.

Right after they moved in, Frank started turning it into a green oasis. He planted several trees and put in grass and hedges. Although Lewistown blocks were small, he had enough garden space in the back to grow his many flowers and vegetables, where he spent many happy hours during the growing season. For years, the Fergus County Fair awarded him blue ribbons for his giant zinnias and squash. He, however, didn't grow roses, and this is interesting because roses were Lillian's favorite flower. He even planted current bushes, a labor-intensive crop from which she made wonderful jellies. Although the area constantly went through droughts, Lewistown had an abundance of good water for drinking and growing large gardens.

The house was wallpapered after the fashion of the day and furnished with a mixture of styles. Lillian had her great-grandmother's Hepplewhite chair. Frank contributed an antique Roman tax collector's chair that John brought back from Italy on one of his trips. There was, of course, the piano on one side of the living room. A large table, always cluttered with papers and magazines, dominated the dining room.

A large framed print of a Lawrence Alma-Tademas painting, *A Reading from Homer,* hung over the piano. Nostalgia was at work here, for the painter was at his peak of popularity when Lillian was in London in the late 1880s. In fact, Queen Victoria knighted the artist in 1885. Today his paintings are considered high Victorian kitsch even though they are technically perfect.

That first year in the house they didn't have money for a vacation, but Lillian thought they both needed one. She was "house worn," and Frank was "office worn." He borrowed a spring wagon, a tent, and another horse to go with the horse they owned and announced they would all go camping for a week.

At sunrise they started for the mountains thirty-five miles away.

"As we left the town behind us, small worries and vexations fled away too, and the peace and quietness in the great heart of nature enveloped us."

At noon, they were halfway to their destination. They stopped by a stream, where they ate their sandwiches, cake, and fruit Lillian had prepared the night before, making sure there would be enough for both the noon and evening meal, as she did not want to experiment with camp cooking before the next morning.

The scenery changed from prairie to forest as they neared the mountains and the shadows of evening fell around them. They pitched their tent in an ideal spot on a slight hill above a fast-moving stream. Richard and Barbara watched their sleeping preparations in amazement. All around were pine and fir trees, single and in clumps. Frank chopped off branches and laid them in the tent. When he thought their bed was thick enough, he put the raincoats over the boughs and a blanket on top of the coats.

After eating supper, they quenched their thirst at the mountain spring.

Lillian wrote, "The water was like a life giving elixir, never before or since have I tasted anything like it."

Then they lay down on their fragrant bed and slept soundly until morning. On awakening, Lillian took the children down to the natural stone basin formed by the stream, where they washed and drank. She showed the children the deer tracks and told them they had come down to drink, too. The stream was clear and, in some spots, deep and filled with trout. They could see the dark forms swimming lazily around the basin.

They were alone, no other people for miles in any direction. On every side, the mountains towered above them, the silence broken only by their own voices, the call of a bird, and the noise of the swiftly flowing water. Lillian found it so restful—no furniture to dust, no beds to make, no inane chatter, no sense of crowding or hurry, just absolute freedom.

Breakfast was the next exercise. Frank placed two stones parallel to another two with a space between for a wood fire below a metal rack. Soon the coffee was boiling and the bacon sizzling in the pan, and Lillian stirred up some pancakes. By that time, they were all hungry.

After breakfast, Frank took the fishing rod to catch some trout for dinner. Lillian and the children watched him land the speckled beauties, and after they were cleaned, sprinkled with Indian (corn) meal, and cooked in the frying pan, they were a dinner "fit for a king."

After dinner, they picked blackberries for dessert, read their books, or idly lay on their backs, looking up at the pine-covered mountains. The children paddled with bare feet in the brook, played with pebbles and pinecones, and dimly wondered at the silence and freedom, which surrounded them.

"Seven happy peaceful days we spent in this mountain solitude."

Compared to Gilt Edge, they were leading a busy life in Lewistown. The Hazens were a popular couple and were soon caught up in the whirl of small-town society—most of which took place in homes. With little outside entertainment, people had to make their own. Many, like Lillian,

Lillian, 1910, was active in community affairs. She joined the Lewistown Women's Club and the Eastern Star.

missed the big-city concerts and gallery openings and added what they could to their small-town existence by forming music groups and "great books" study groups.

Couples also took turns entertaining each other. They played whist, a form of bridge, and had taffy pulls. The newspaper editor described these festivities down to the last napkin as hosts and hostesses tried to outdo each other with unique games and clever table decorations.

As Lillian proceeded to go through all the proper motions of an early-twentieth-century matron, she joined the Lewistown Women's Club, which was part of the giant Federation of Women's Clubs across the United States with its 1,200 separate affiliates and 150,000 members. She also belonged to the Eastern Star, the wives' companion to the Masons, because Frank was a Mason.

These clubs were part of the social feminism true feminists rejected, because they weren't working for women's rights. They were women working together to develop common interests and to improve their communities. Lillian enjoyed this and felt useful. Andrew Carnegie, industrialist and philanthropist, offered Lewistown, as he did many communities across the country, $10,000 to build a library if the city would pledge to raise $1,000 for maintenance each year. The Women's Club helped fulfill the pledge, and the library building was completed in July 1906.

Lillian was also a faithful churchgoer, alternating between the Episcopal and Presbyterian churches. The Episcopalian minister became a frequent visitor in their home. She liked him, found him well educated, and liked his thoughtful sermons. He enjoyed their discussions, as did Lillian, who craved intellectual conversation and the respect she once had as a syndicated columnist.

His church was her favorite, although it was tiny—barely accommodating a hundred people. It had been inexpensive to build with its simple construction. The walls were stone set with small stained glass windows, tasteful, with the only design a small amethyst-colored cross in the center of each. The pews, chancel rail, and pulpit were all the same dark-colored wood. The font was plain stone, and a hand-pumped organ supplied the music.

Lillian and the minister had an ongoing friendly argument for years, because she refused to take communion from the single communal cup offered in his little church. She always went down the street to the Presbyterian church for communion, where each participant had an individual cup.

The minister chided her, saying, "If you are a true believer you won't catch a disease."

Lillian always answered, "God helps those who help themselves."

— TWENTY —

No Ordinary Sight

Our mothers sung in their lonely bowers,
And struggled their narrow sphere to keep.
But, now, I'm glad in this world of ours
We, girls, don't follow the ancient ways,
Our tastes have changed in these modern days.

Lillian's journal. 1910

Nowhere in her writings did Lillian ever voice regrets at leaving New York City. The western woman's life suited her and other eastern women who headed west at the turn of the century. As early as 1889, editor Henry B. Blackwell of the *Woman's Journal* promised the Montana constitutional convention that giving women the right to vote would bring "immigration of a large number of good women to the territory."

The right to vote, however, was not the main reason women were moving west in record numbers. They came seeking their fortunes, like Lillian and Frank, and a better life, either with or without a mate. Some wanted to do things women couldn't do in the East—take up homesteads and run their own ranches.

The right to vote was not on Lillian's mind either. In fact, some of her early "Lillian's Letters" indicate she was a bit mixed up about women's rights. As early as 1888, she wrote: "Belva Lockwood intends making herself conspicuous again this year. I believe in women's rights but not in women who try to obtain men's rights."

Belva Lockwood became the first woman lawyer to argue before the Supreme Court in 1879. When in 1884 the National Equal Rights Party, formed by a group of women in California, nominated her for president, she received 4,149 votes in six states. After running for president again in 1888, she resumed practicing law.

In December of 1894, Lillian was still mulling over whether women should have the right to vote: "With regard to woman's suffrage, I have never yet been able to make up my mind which side of the question to take. Although if taxation without representation is tyranny, why should women be taxed and have no vote?"

It was a diverse group of women Lillian got to know and admire in the early days of the twentieth century in Montana—strong, independent women fending for themselves. One was Nellie Belland Fraser, who at age nineteen came to Montana in 1905 from the Red River Valley in Minnesota. Her father was a Norwegian sea captain. Nellie later told her story in *The Heritage Book of the Fergus County Area:*

> I inherited my spirit of adventure and determination from my father. My brother worked for the Northern Pacific Railroad and sent me pictures of Montana's mountainous scenery when I was a little girl and I fell in love with it. I vowed I'd live there some day.

In 1910, she actually took up a homestead claim near Kendall, Montana, where she and her sister, Mamie, built a cabin. They would get up early in the morning and walk the six miles from town to the homestead site to work all day. After a real struggle, they finally erected the two-by-four frame for their twelve-by-eighteen-foot cabin and walked back to town.

The next morning they again walked the six "weary" miles back to their land only to find that during the night, the cattle had knocked down the frame by scratching their backs on it. Old-fashioned stubbornness and hard work helped these ambitious young women finish the cabin so they could live in it and not have to walk six miles every day. Mamie, however, had had enough. She went home.

Nellie actually lived on her claim the required length of time, three years, and even raised a crop of flax. She didn't realize much profit but "had a beautiful blue field."

For many women, anything was better than their eastern urban lives, where many earned their livings either as factory workers, domestic servants, or boardinghouse keepers. Unfortunately, jobs were scarce for women in the early 1900s in the western states, too. Montana ranchers were not progressive enough to hire women to wrangle cattle and do hard ranch labor even if women dared apply for the jobs. Few were as brave as Nellie Fraser.

That left the working woman few ways of earning a living other than school teaching or being a waitress or cook in the few restaurants. She also could hire out as a domestic helper to a rancher's wife or, if a rancher were single, she would be the sole cook and cleaner. These were called "hired girls," who lived "in" on ranches. The 1963 movie *Hud*, which takes place in Texas, is a good example of one woman's life as a hired girl on a ranch.

Women tried any and everything to survive. An old newspaper ad tells of one Lewistown woman's search for income in 1902. She, a "widow lady," advertised, "Thanksgiving turkey dinner, price 35 cents."

Albeit there was one woman's business in the West that flourished—prostitution. "Ladies of pleasure" were some of the first white women into Judith Basin, and all Montana towns had booming "red light" districts. Lewistown was no exception. Because it was the center for the mining districts and the surrounding ranches, these women made good money.

When the cowpuncher came to town, he didn't go to church or to the library; he went to the dance hall or a house. Often, however, the hired men moved on after a night on the town, and good ranch hands were hard to find. One resourceful rancher always made arrangements with one of the madams to bring her "girls" and lots of whiskey to his ranch on payday so his men wouldn't have to go to town.

Lillian told a story of one of these madams, who sometimes wintered in the Hawaiian Islands in the early 1900s. She posed as the wife of a rich cattle baron. This charade worked until Dr. and Mrs. Long of Lewistown, who traveled extensively each year, arrived in the islands for the winter. The Hawaiian attorney general gave a big banquet and introduced the madam to Mrs. Long as the wife of a famous cattleman in the same town as the Longs came from—Lewistown, Montana.

Mrs. Long snorted, "Wife of a cattleman! She runs the most prosperous brothel in Lewistown. That's what she does."

Because Frank was cashier of the bank, the local prostitutes were often his clients. Much later, Richard said they all liked to deal with him, because he treated them like ladies. One day, one of the most beautiful, and the most businesslike, madams came to him and said her son was coming to visit her. She wanted to bring him into the bank to transact some business and asked Frank to call her by her real name. She supported her son in a private school in Seattle, and he didn't know how she earned her living.

Usually the folks in western towns were tolerant of different lifestyles and the pursuit of pleasure, but the Lewistown city council eventually passed an ordinance that said, "Any man who permits minors or lewd women to frequent his place will be liable to a revocation of his saloon license."

Thus an era had passed. When Charlie Russell, the western painter, wrote a book about some Lewistown citizens and local gossip concerning their patronage of various houses, he illustrated the story so there was no question about the identity of each character. The targeted citizens were mortified and irate, much to Lillian's delight for she herself didn't care how people dealt with their sexuality as long as they were good citizens. She looked upon such revelations as "much ado about nothing."

At the turn of the century, as many women searched for and found constructive ways to express themselves, there were some who, frustrated, released their anger in destructive ways. Small-town newspapers of the era and area, including Lewistown's, carried accounts of women picked up for acts of public violence and vandalism like smashing store windows. The sheriff usually carted the vandal off to a local hospital mental ward, if there was one, or gave her a one-way ticket on the next train out of town.

There were other women who challenged prudish Victorian rules in a more forthright way. Some incidents made hilarious reading, such as a 1905 article in the *Fergus County Democrat* called "Brutes Seduce Young Girls."

It seems an irate father called the sheriff and told him his two daughters were being held prisoner by two men in an old building. When the sheriff arrived at the scene, there was a scuffle and one of the girls was accidentally hit over the head. It seems the girls were not "reluctant captives," but were having a lovers' tryst: "Smith escaped but was compelled to leave his trousers and other essential wearing apparel in the building."

Lillian was like many American women who, as the twentieth century began, were fast shedding their Victorian plumage and attitudes. Fashions were beginning to relax. Women were coming out from under all those layers of clothes. Dresses were getting shorter, to the midcalf length. Styles were changing to accommodate women leading busy lives who couldn't cope with long skirts and heavy hairdos.

But American women were still spending $14 million a year on corsets. In fact, at age eighty, Lillian did not consider herself dressed without a corset. By that time, she needed one to hold her muscles in place. In the early 1900s, a Dr. Phillippe Marechale of Paris made American headlines when he tried to introduce a bill into the French parliament placing corset manufacturers under state control.

Before a crowded auditorium filled with physiologists and women's clubs, Marechale declared that many young women who wore corsets died of pulmonary diseases or suffered from organic derangement through their entire life:

> The first article of the proposed measure forbids women below 30 years of age to wear any kind of corset under penalty of three months in prison and a fine of not more than 1000 francs ($193). The second article permits women older than 30 to wear corsets.

Europeans were trying to prevent women binding their bodies at the same time as the Chinese government was trying to stop women binding their feet. In both cases, the issue was what men considered erotic and beautiful. American men liked the hourglass figure, and Chinese men considered the "lotus," the broken bound foot, most sensuous.

In the early 1900s, other female issues were being analyzed and regulated. Although many of the early-twentieth-century women's magazines urged women to get out, exercise, eat healthy foods, and quit pleading ill health, these same magazines were filled with the patent medicine ads. The *Ladies' Home Journal* stopped carrying these ads and a reporter, Mark Sullivan, wrote a series for the magazine condemning patent drugs. Then Sullivan, the magazine, and President Theodore Roosevelt helped the passage of a 1906 regulation prohibiting patent medicine advertising in magazines. This meant they couldn't be sold by mail. Although this helped curb their sale, it didn't eliminate their over-the-counter sales.

Women were banned from clubs, saloons, and tobacco shops. In some states, an unescorted female might, by law, be refused a meal at a restaurant or a room in a hotel. In 1904, women were arrested in New York City for smoking in public, another vice Lillian indulged in occasionally.

In 1900, half of the states still denied women the right to own property. One-third of the states allowed her no claim on her own earnings. Four-fifths of the states denied her equal share of guardianship, and, of course, she couldn't vote. It was not against the law, however, for either a man or woman to advertise for a mate. In Lewistown, every issue of the *Fergus County Democrat* carried lonely singles' personal ads like the following one:

> Ladies, Take Notice! A gentleman of good character and habits desires to form the acquaintance of a lady of suitable age, with a view to early marriage. Will exchange photos and full particulars in the first letter. Address: Box 145, Lewistown, Montana.

In those first years of the twentieth century, Fergus County residents were marrying in record numbers, usually in the spring before crops were planted or in the fall after crops were harvested. Couples didn't hold fancy weddings. They wandered casually into the courthouse, got their licenses, and then went around the corner to a justice of the peace and were married. Obviously, men thought women added quite a bit to the quality of western life. Detailed birth announcements filled a good part of each edition of the paper, too. Women were having large babies, some weighing over ten pounds.

Many of these marriages ended in divorce, which could be had for the asking. Desertion was the leading cause, as both wives and husbands found it easy to drop from sight in that day and age of unsophisticated record keeping, communications, and travel. Wives, however, often found themselves impoverished when their husbands divorced them. If they were prominent members of the community, newspapers like the *Fergus County Democrat* covered the divorce actions, both the legal aspects and the gossip, as did most newspapers in the early 1900s.

Margaret Fleming of Moore, Montana, filed for a divorce from Albert Fleming, saying he was a cruel husband. Again, the *Democrat News* published the details in "The Trials of Married Life," saying the Flemings were married in Great Falls on July 11, 1896.

The paper reported Mrs. Fleming said, "He has $600 a year income from the ranch. He has 40 head of cattle and ten head of horses and makes $100 a month from the Moore saloon."

Mrs. Fleming said she had earned her share of it—no details on whether she ever got it.

Although Lillian still followed women's issues and chafed at their lack of progress, she was more concerned with her life at this point.

— TWENTY-ONE —

Through a Glass Darkly

*All children yearn for the little extras—tassels on her
boots, a fancy sewing basket—all costing a little more.
Fripperies have their place in the great scheme of creation. If
anyone doubts it, let him note how the bare, hard rocks are
usually softened by vines and mosses, how exquisitely
tinted weeds and wild flowers with their luminous green
leaves and tendrils, brighten, yet harmonize with, the ugly
rust of old tin cans in a garbage heap on a vacant lot.*

"Sympathetic Understanding." 1904

Lillian was a serious parent. The one thing she treasured, in spite of her
disappointing marriage, was her children, and not only did she take good
physical care of them but she did her best to socialize them. She took a
real interest in every aspect of their lives.

A part of this attitude was her kindness to and interest in their teachers. One might wonder if Lillian saw herself, if she hadn't married, in
these single women, who more often than not led lonely lives in boardinghouse rooms. The Hazens often entertained them, and the *Democrat*
duly reported these events: "Little Miss Barbara Hazen and Master
Richard Hazen entertained their teachers, Miss Newell and Miss Hughey,
at dinner on Saturday."

Lillian complained few mothers took any interest in their children's teachers. Sometimes they didn't even take the trouble to get acquainted with them. There was a downside to this, however, because Richard, years later, said she spent a great deal of time monitoring his classes, which embarrassed him. This didn't make her popular with the school administration either. She thought more women should be on the school boards, because then they would have some say in selecting teachers. Of course, she admitted, not many women had any interest in being on a school board.

Even then, in the early twentieth century, Lillian complained about domestic science and manual training added to the high school curriculum.

She said, "Educators should concentrate their energies on teaching young people mathematics, science, history, languages, and the much abused classics, which, as Thoreau says, are 'usually decried by people unfamiliar with them.'"

She felt that even if students went on to vocational school or learned a craft, they would have a good foundation after being taught the three Rs. This last statement is interesting because Richard, as an adult, read the newspaper and comic books. I never saw him read a novel or book of any kind.

Lillian was also against sex education in the schools.

"Some of the lectures delivered in schools, 'For Boys Only,' or 'For Girls Only,' are fairly steeped in the putrid atmosphere of moral rottenness. In the name of common decency, why don't parents protest against having their children's minds contaminated in such a way?"

She said, "A child should have its natural curiosity on the mysteries of birth and life gratified. The information, however, should be given individually, not collectively. What may be one child's meat, may be poison for another. People in the nineteenth century may have kept silent on certain subjects to the point of prudishness, but they are certainly swinging to the other extreme in the twentieth."

She went on to say that one novelist defended his "obscene stories" by saying, "I made vice so revolting so people would shun it in horror."

Lillian answered thus, "It is not necessary for people to wallow in mud and filth to learn the advisability of keeping their bodies clean; and sullying a child's mind with thoughts of vice and impurity is not calculated to improve his morality no matter how vividly the results of immorality are depicted."

Everything in the Hazen household was geared to the children's welfare. Lillian's emotional state might have been more balanced if her marriage had been a happy one. As it was, she appeared convinced that being a mother was her most important mission in life, and she was a kind mother.

Lillian also thought love, more than food or shelter, made a child thrive. She agreed with the experts who said the first seven years laid the foundation of a child's life, that a firm foundation would withstand any adversity. Years later, she wrote about a child-care pamphlet that state health departments sent to every family registering a birth. She said it was supposed to be science's last word on bringing up a child properly: how much sleep is needed, how the child should be dressed, and what food should be fed.

She concluded those under age two need nurturing more than food and rest. She quoted a famous doctor, head of an orphanage, who said that although the children in his institution lived in the best of conditions with scientific feeding and trained nurses, "the infant mortality was so high we were appalled." One of the nurses suggested finding foster homes for these babies "in the tenement district where poor, but clean and respectable, women would 'mother' them." The children thrived. The doctors and nurses then realized the babies had died because they needed "mothering."

It's certain both Hazens loved their children. Although Frank was quiet and undemonstrative, it didn't mean he cared any less. Sometimes he brought balance to Lillian's unbalanced mothering by sticking up for one or the other. Although both Barbara and Richard were beautiful, intelligent children with sensitive faces, Barbara was the light of Lillian's life. She identified with her daughter even as she tried not to play favorites, tried to show equal love and affection to both her children.

The little she wrote about Richard described him as "stubborn and naughty." She didn't see a normal, smart little boy being obstinate. She saw her husband in miniature. At some level, she was aware of this and consciously tried to control her biased feelings, but Richard had to have felt ignored, shut out, more often than he would admit when he was old. The bond between Barbara and her mother was so strong.

Through a Glass Darkly

And I hear the fond assurance
That you gave me months ago
With your little arms around me
Then you whispered, "Don't you know
There is nothing, nothing, Mamma,
Nothing that could ever be
Could keep me from loving Mamma
Who I always know loves me."

When eight-year-old Barbara died on January 10, 1905, Lillian wanted to die, too. Capillary bronchitis was the immediate cause of death. Their daughter had fallen ill about three weeks earlier with pneumonia and whooping cough. She was improving when a relapse occurred, and she developed bronchitis. As they hovered over her, she assured them she felt much better, and so Frank and Lillian returned to their bedroom to catch some much needed sleep.

Within a few minutes, they heard Barbara choking. When they got to her bedside, she was dead.

It was the greatest tragedy of Lillian's life, one that was to mark her for the rest of her days. On November 24, 1905, the *Great Falls Tribune* published Lillian's poem "Through a Glass Darkly." The following is the first stanza:

She is safer in His keeping than she ever
was in mine;
Yet I cannot help the longing for a visible sure
sign.
Was it given me, I wonder, when I first
Knew she was gone.
As I followed through the shadows that
For me would meet no dawn?

Again she used the byline M. D. Gaines and listed Gilt Edge as her home address. Because Lillian took the best physical care of Richard and Barbara, they were rarely sick, but even she was powerless in the face of some illnesses in the days before antibiotics.

Lillian later wrote, "I could not bear to see her lying there, so cold and still."

Some way, somehow, she thought she might have saved Barbara, but in the early 1900s, people had little control over whether a sick person lived or died. Usually it was just a "wait and hope" situation. People relied on the local doctor, "folk" cures, and patent medicines. But in this instance, even homeopathy failed her.

Lillian's belief in another life after death and the promise of Barbara and her being reunited in the hereafter helped her deal with her grief. From a poem, "To One Beyond," written on June 24, 1906, Lillian describes her positive attitude toward death:

And is Death but one more name, dear, for the new mystic birth? Then again I dream that heaven is not far away at all . . . That you have not really left me, and do I feel your presence near,

And I know you do not wish me to despair and grieve, and cry, for though very weak and little, you were not afraid to die.

It's obvious Lillian's faith and belief in God helped her find her way back to a degree of normalcy. Although she had been extremely religious all her life, she did not belong to any one denomination but always observed the Sabbath by either reading the Bible or going to church or both. Later, she wouldn't even go to movies on Sunday and that was a real sacrifice. She believed the seventh day was a day of complete rest, "a time for marshalling one's defenses against life's adversities."

After Barbara's funeral, Lillian appeared to go on with life and its many projects and acquaintances, but her daughter's death probably was yet another blow to her and Frank's shaky relationship. Each withdrew into a private world. Lillian's grief lay in wait, ever ready to surface, while Frank, as usual, was silent. Lillian mentions him only by using the word "we" when writing of their pain. He appeared to come and go, doing his thing as he had always done.

When he was home, he sat quietly in his oak-and-leather rocker in the sunny bay window, reading his newspaper or a book, the same one over and over—a tattered but elegant copy of Charles Dickens's *Tale of Two Cities*.

Lillian's most serious reaction to Barbara's death was her overprotection of Richard. Soon after the tragedy, anytime he was out of her sight, anxiety overwhelmed her. She tried to protect him from all small boy traumas and, at first, didn't allow him to do the things normal western boys did like sledding, horseback riding, and hiking. She watched over him with fierce zeal.

She always came to his rescue and thus turned him into a "child" man. Insight into her overprotection of Richard in all areas is illustrated by her story of the "missed" spelling word.

"A little boy studied and struggled for a 100% in his spelling examination and was marked 98%."

Almost in tears, Richard brought his exam paper home to Lillian to prove all the words were spelled right. She saw, at once, that one of them was written so poorly that, with a hasty glance, it would appear incorrect. Right away, "the loving mother's heart" understood that the words had been dictated so fast the little inexperienced fingers had no time to write plainly and that in his eagerness to get all the words, Richard's hand had slipped and misformed a letter.

Lillian went to the teacher, who didn't deny the word was spelled correctly but said the writing was not plain.

"I understand you told the children the writing was not to be considered in the test," protested Lillian.

The teacher said, "I shall not change the mark."

Lillian said she was indignant and went to the principal—"a timid man who did not like any altercation with his teachers."

"It is such a little thing," he said. "Let the lower mark stand."

"It is not a little thing," Lillian told him sharply, "to cheat a child out of his mark when he has worked hard to earn it."

"Teachers sometimes make mistakes," murmured the flabby principal.

"Of course, they do, but, when possible, they ought to rectify them."

If this were an isolated incident, not much damage would have been done, but it wasn't an isolated incident. Lillian always came out of her corner fighting for Richard when she thought he had been slighted, and unfortunately, Richard grew up with little respect for his mother.

In 1906, Frank left the clerk and recorder job to become assistant to a bank president. Then in 1908, he took over management of the bank as vice president and head cashier. Bank patrons liked him, and he made a good salary. While Frank was managing the bank, he caught an employee, in charge of savings accounts, stealing $100,000. From the moment an auditor detected irregularities, Lillian said she knew he was the culprit, because he was living so far above his means, buying horses and a movie theater.

For the first time in their married life, the Hazens had enough money to live in comfort with a few luxuries. Lillian also was active in community affairs, with a degree of success of her own. There's no record of when she became a member of the school board, but she held the post until Richard was out of high school. In June 1909, she also was elected vice president of the state's eastern division of the Federation of Women.

At about the same time, her father made headlines all over the country. On March 15, 1909, Edward Payson Weston, at age seventy, began a walk from New York City to San Francisco, 3,895 miles over rough country roads and mountains, fighting tornadoes and blizzards. He covered the distance in 104 days and seven hours.

The next year, on February 1, 1910, he began the return trip from Santa Monica to New York City. This time he followed the Atchison, Topeka and Santa Fe Railroad tracks for 2,500 miles, covering the distance in seventy-six days and twenty-three hours, and celebrated his seventy-first birthday by walking seventy-one miles in one day.

He was a picturesque figure with his white hair, white mustache, velvet black tunic, and high gaiters. Everyone in the country, even in Lewistown, followed his feats, but no one knew Weston was Lillian's father. Although she hadn't seen him since he left her mother in 1893, she was proud of being his daughter. Her feelings were hurt when she wasn't listed as one of his children in the many newspaper articles. She continued to follow his career in the newspapers, a career that lasted almost until the day he died in 1929. *Strength Magazine* published her personal story about Weston in 1924.

Although Lillian appeared to return to a normal existence years after Barbara's death, her grief always engulfed her when she visited the little

Weston, a seventy-one-year-old pedestrian, appeared as dapper as ever when he finished his cross-country walk, 3,500 miles, in 1910.

cemetery to place fresh flowers before the Washington Monument—style headstone carved with the dates of Barbara's short life.

Once again, however, a new adventure rescued her and Frank's relationship from disintegration just as it had when they first headed west.

TWENTY-TWO

New Beginnings

> *The freshness of the early morning; the acres of emerald*
> *green alfalfa, the fields of golden stubble studded thick with*
> *shocks of wheat, contrasted with the deep rich brown of the*
> *summer fallowed ground were beautiful beyond description*
> *tinged as they were by the fair, faint colors that precede the*
> *rising sun.*
>
> "Ranch Notes." 1912

Lillian, ever the gambler, saw land sales booming and urged Frank to buy a ranch as early as 1909. Programmed as an inquiring reporter, she realized wheat and cattle were Montana's future as it moved into the twentieth century. From his vantage seat at the bank, Frank saw Judith Basin land double and triple in value. He saw ranchers making big money and thought about trying it, but he took forever to make up his mind. Lillian nagged and he pondered.

There had been a steady influx of cattle herds into Montana from before the time the Hazens first moved west. In the mid-1800s, early cattlemen Richard Grant and his partners gathered herds at Fort Hall in southern Idaho. Each fall, they paid a small price per head for underfed trail-weary cattle settlers were driving through on the Oregon Trail to the

West Coast. Grant then drove these skinny animals north into grassy valleys for the winter, fed them up, and sold them to other settlers for a good profit. He also drove some six hundred head of these cattle into Montana in the 1850s.

At the same time, Texas ranchers, who had been driving their herds to Dodge City and Abilene, Kansas, to railheads, began herding their rangy, wild longhorns north to Montana's Judith Basin, where lush grasslands maintained the cattle's weight until they were shipped east by railroad.

People were also streaming into the state to collect free land. In 1909, the new Homestead Act became law and allowed the head of a family to claim 320 acres free, a fourth of which had to be cultivated. Inexperienced easterners were dazzled by the promise of large crops on free land.

Between 1910 and 1918 were the big homestead years in the Judith Basin. James J. Hill, the promoter who built the Great Northern Railroad across Montana, developed the immigrant car system. For $50, a settler could rent a boxcar to transport his family, furniture, household goods, farm implements, fence posts, horses, mules, cows, and even a few chickens—all things needed to start a ranch in Montana. Gone were the covered wagons and the hard trek west, but these latter-day pioneers still ended up in a rough country living in shacks, dugouts, sod huts, or lean-tos.

The Hazens never considered homesteading, because they knew they couldn't make a living on 320 acres of Montana land where there was no irrigation and little rainfall each season.

By 1911, Frank and Lillian had lived in Lewistown for ten years, something of a record stay for Lillian. She'd be the first to admit she needed change and variety from time to time, and so they decided to join Frank's brother, John, on a trip to Glacier Park, but she didn't sell her story of the trip until 1919.

"It was the most interesting vacation I ever had, a 10-day camping trip through Glacier Park, and the day we crossed Gunsight Pass (10,000 feet above sea level) will never fade from my memory."

There is a photo of a jaunty Lillian in some kind of knickers, wearing a man's cap, riding a horse up a trail. A woman could never have survived on such a trip, much of it on horseback, in the usual skirt. She described leaving their camp on Gunsight Lake—how they went along a level path for two or three hundred yards, then scrambled across a river,

The guide and Lillian on horses and Frank walking on vacation in Glacier Park, 1912.

filled beyond its banks with melting snow, and began ascending the mountain. The guide rode one horse and drove the three packhorses in front of him, but the rest of the vacationers felt safer walking and leading their horses, especially in the steepest places, where Lillian said she crawled on all fours.

The footpath zigzagged up the mountain with the guide above them. Once in a while they had to stop so as not to be right under him in case one of his horses slipped. Every season some horses died going over Gunsight Pass. Finally it became too steep for even the guide to ride. He dismounted and helped the horses over steep, slippery rocks, where a tumble meant death. Up and up they climbed—Lillian lost her breath. She wrote it was a terrible feeling, like being suffocated by smoke or having one's head underwater. By this time, they were swathed in a dense fog.

"I groaned and stopped—they waited for me. I tried again, and stopped again. At last I got what my guide called my 'second wind' and went on."

Lillian wrote, "Suddenly, I found the path going across a kind of glacier—a great wall of snow, so high we could not see the top, and so deep we could not see the bottom. We were supposed to walk a sixteen-inch ledge of snow along the side. My head whirled. 'I cannot do it,' I said. 'I shall surely fall.'"

The guide and horses led the way and went over safely. Still, Lillian lingered and felt as though she had to walk a tightrope, suspended hundreds of feet above the earth. She couldn't make herself move until thirteen-year-old Richard stepped in front of her and told her to hang on to his coat. Then Frank walked close behind, holding her coat. Thus she crossed the most difficult place on Gunsight Pass.

Because few tourists visited Glacier Park at the time, Lillian found the quiet landscape unspoiled—beautiful foliage and wildflowers, pine and fir trees, swift rivers and streams. She mentioned that the park grew 250 varieties of plants not yet discovered.

After their return from Glacier Park, Frank finally bought 520 undeveloped acres twenty miles from Lewistown in 1912. It was also three miles from the little town of Ware, with its few weathered buildings—a log cabin post office (still standing today), a grain elevator, a railroad water tank, and two small houses squatting on the flat prairie. The town actually had two names. The government's post office name of the town was Acushnet, whereas the railroad company called it Ware.

Frank leased his land to a local rancher, who ran stock on it.

Again the Hazens were on the move in June 1914, when Frank, Lillian, and Richard took their first trip east since coming to Montana. They shipped their Cole automobile by train and picked it up in Buffalo, New York. Then they drove to New York City, Boston, and around the New England states.

Six weeks later, they drove home to Lewistown via South Dakota and the Yellowstone Trail, which must have been an adventurous trip, fraught with problems on the primitive roads of the time. In 1914, a car had to be cranked if the motor died, and it often died. Service stations were few and far between and there were no motels. They probably stopped in small-town hotels on their way. No details of their trip survive, but there must have been many stressful moments.

In 1915, Richard went off to Dartmouth College but returned after a year to take up ranching with his father, who in 1916 bought 520 acres more until they owned a total of 1,040 acres. Frank hoped to make his fortune, with World War I wheat prices at $2 a bushel.

Lillian, as usual, looked forward to the new adventure of living on a ranch. She was almost her buoyant self of yesteryear as they prepared to move. Indeed, from the moment she first saw their ranch, with its gently rolling hills and wide-open spaces, the purple mountains in the distance, she was smitten.

TWENTY-THREE

Starting a Ranch from Scratch

> *The average farmer's wife is expected to combine the avoca-*
> *tions of cook, nurse, dressmaker, poultry raiser, dairyman,*
> *and other vocations, any one of which is sufficient to*
> *occupy all the working hours of any one person.*
>
> "Slighting Work." 1917

Everything seemed to go wrong when the Hazens, at last, started working their ranch. The smallest tasks became large ones. Although Frank
was an expert horseman and grew up on a "gentleman's" farm in
Vermont, he had no idea how to plan a western ranch from scratch. He
loved working in the soil and viewed the ranch as a big garden, but he
hadn't done enough research or he would have known what a challeng-
ing profession dryland farming was, what a serious game of chance they
had wandered into.

Montana's climate is one of extremes, where temperatures range as
high as 117 degrees in the summer and as low as minus forty degrees in
the winter. Sometimes hail is big enough to kill chickens and behaves in
strange ways. It may wipe out one rancher's wheat crop and not bend a
blade of grass on a neighboring rancher's land. Crops rely on rainfall for
all their moisture, yet the area normally has little precipitation.

Montana ranchers get used to getting up each morning and peering at the brassy sun in an azure blue sky as they pray for rain, which seldom comes. But there are rare years when plenty of rain falls. The year 1916 was a vintage one when a few ranchers produced as much as eighty bushels of wheat per acre. The average in an average year was about twenty-five bushels per acre.

Aside from worrying about weather, water, stock, and crops, the Hazens also had to find time to help and encourage the carpenter, a local rancher, to finish building their small square house on a knoll overlooking the barnyard. Because the rancher-carpenter had his own crops to worry about, it was slow going.

But they had to have the house. No one could survive a Montana winter in a tent, and someone had to live on the ranch, year-round, to water and feed the cattle and horses. It was equally imperative they have a barn, but things went wrong with that project from the first. It cost more than Frank anticipated, but, of course, it had to be finished.

By the time winter "socked in," the house and barn were, more or less, completed, the house standing above the barn on a slight hill, a simple square building with a small porch on one end. At least they were habitable, and so Richard and his friend Johnny Daley settled down for a long lonely winter. In their spare time, they finished, with the help of the carpenter, the insides of the buildings and painted the inside walls of the little ranch house.

Then Lillian and Frank gradually hauled furniture from Lewistown. The main room, the kitchen, had wooden chairs and a blue-and-white-checked oilcloth-covered table, a wood- or coal-burning cookstove, a cabinet for dishes and food, and an oak stand with a basin on its top and a pail and dipper beside it for washing hands.

There were a couple of rag rugs on the wooden floors. The curtains were Montgomery Ward specials. The kitchen was the largest room and the most lived in. It was where all company and family congregated. In the winter, everyone usually huddled around the big stove in one corner. The only time people had time to visit was in the coldest weather. There was a lean-to attached to the back of the house for the cream separator. In subzero weather, one had to work fast or suffer frostbite.

They furnished each of the two bedrooms with two single beds and a basic five-drawer chest. There was, of course, the necessary chamber pot under each bed to supplement the outhouse in the side yard, one Lillian was to burn down several times deodorizing with hot ashes from the kitchen stove.

The bedrooms opened off a small living room with a stove in the center, a chesterfield (a leather-and-wood couch), and an old easy chair. Unless it was very cold, they didn't bother to light the stove. Lillian's old oak desk with her ancient typewriter sat in a corner of the room next to a small bookcase. A comfortable oak office chair was to receive much use over the next sixteen years.

After Lillian and Frank and their dogs—a Boston terrier, Mike, and a collie puppy, Buster—joined Richard on the ranch in the spring of 1917, ranch life shocked Lillian almost daily, but she didn't dare complain to Frank. After all, she had urged him to buy the ranch, and he was having his own problems with allergies like hay fever, much aggravated by the dust and pollen in his field work.

She soon realized she was not living the tranquil agrarian life she had envisioned when they moved to the ranch. Most people start to slow down in their fifties, but here Frank and Lillian were living a basic life in a simple bare-bones environment, working eighteen hours a day. Neither Lillian nor Frank had considered the amount of manual labor they would have to do, day in and day out, during the growing season. Real life on a western ranch shocked them all.

Her first harvesttime in 1917 turned Lillian's days into one long nightmare. All the available "girls" had been hired by the time she went looking for one, and so, for over a month that season, she fed from three to eight hired men every meal in addition to her husband, her son, and one hired man. Soon after she moved to the ranch she learned how important good food was to help the men do the heavy ranch work. They were always hungry and wanted three square meals a day.

She observed most ranchers ate too much pork, because it was easily cured to keep it from spoiling, whereas a butchered steer would spoil if it weren't eaten soon. In fact, she said most consumed great quantities of greasy fried foods.

She often said, "Country people are not healthier than their city cousins."

King, Lillian's favorite horse, shares shade with Buster and Mike on the ranch.

She criticized the ranch wives' canning all their fresh fruits and vegetables in summer—eating little of the fresh produce—so they could have more for winter use. They ignored the fact that oranges, apples, lemons, and root vegetables were healthier than the canned food in the winter, and they could eat summer fruits and leafy vegetables as they ripened in the summer.

Many ranchers were too busy raising wheat to deal with the health-giving, unprofitable task of tending a garden. They expected their wives and children to do it; thus, sometimes there were no gardens and most ranchers' wives served only potatoes as a vegetable.

After Lillian's first harvest ordeal was over she, of course, wrote about it. She sold "Hints for Harvest Time" to a farm paper.

"At first, my task appalled me. . . . Then out of necessity I began to think and plan how to work."

Although she usually made her bread, she bought it that month. She also bought larger pots and pans so she would have no more to wash for nine men than for three. After that, she carefully planned her menus, "healthy and tasty but not much trouble to cook." She was a good cook, a skill learned so late in life after her marriage, and probably many a hired hand stuck around to eat from her table.

> For breakfast, I had a cooked and uncooked cereal, fried or creamed potatoes, cold meat, eggs, and biscuits or Johnny Cake [cornmeal bread] and coffee. I always took care to have enough meat and potatoes left over from supper the night before so I could serve hash browns for breakfast.

Before washing the breakfast dishes, and while the oven, in the woodstove, was still hot, she made a pound cake and a pudding that would be cooked by the time she finished tidying the kitchen. It's hard to imagine she would have all the ingredients needed to bake a rich pound cake, which calls for almost a dozen eggs and a pound of butter. If the men didn't work as hard as they did, this diet would have killed them.

Early in her ranch life, Lillian found most working men liked two desserts a day, and so she devised a system for making several cakes at once. She used what she called the old "1-2-3-4 rule of one cup of butter, two cups of sugar, three cups of flour, four eggs, three teaspoons of baking powder, a teaspoon of vanilla, an additional cup of flour, and about two cups of liquid, milk or water." Then she had enough dough to make four layers and one loaf. Frequently she put two layers together with chocolate filling and two with lemon. Usually there was a little lemon mixture left over, which she stirred into the remains of the dough to flavor the loaf cake. She added a bit more flour if the dough wasn't stiff enough.

In the saucepan that held the chocolate filling, she added a quart of milk, some sugar, and breadcrumbs with a beaten egg, poured the mixture into a baking pan, and so produced a tasty chocolate pudding with little extra labor.

She served the loaf cake with lemon or chocolate sauce, berries, cut-up bananas, or stewed fruit and gingerbread with whipped cream. For supper she served various dried fruit puddings made like apple dumplings and served with egg and sugar whipped together with a little lemon rind. Bread puddings, which took five minutes to prepare, flavored with chocolate, coconut, or spice with raisins, were also tasty desserts.

Watermelon and cantaloupe were also easy desserts and "a treat for hot, tired men."

Instead of onions, carrots, turnips, greens, and other vegetables that took so long to prepare and cook and used precious water, she served corn on the cob, baked beans and potatoes, macaroni and cheese, sliced cucumbers and tomatoes, and coleslaw. She boiled a whole ham and then baked it and served it hot one day and cold the next. If she served chicken, she didn't use fryers. She turned a fat, old hen into a hearty potpie and served it with dumplings and plenty of rich gravy.

Lillian made it through their first harvest cycle but told Frank, "I don't know how."

After this first season, Lillian thought she needed help, and so they decided the most practical solution to their labor problems was to hire a couple and let them live in the bunkhouse. The man would help Frank and Richard, and the woman would help Lillian. It sounded good in theory but didn't work out. They found a couple and happily hired them. A few days after the man and woman moved into the bunkhouse and started work, Frank confided to Lillian he didn't dare drive a team the man hitched up without carefully examining the harness. He always found "a buckle too tight or too loose, or unfastened, which was likely to mean disaster with our spirited young horses."

Frank, however, said he would keep the man if the woman was so good Lillian couldn't do without her.

Lillian told Frank, "The woman isn't worth her salt either. She loves cleaning, even down to scrubbing the coal bucket, but her cooking is atrocious. She has a positive genius for spoiling good food."

She went on to say that if she had to do the cooking, she would rather cook for four than five, so he could hire a bachelor, with her blessing, and let the married couple go. She then cooked for a succession of hired men before they found one that suited them. These people who wandered through their isolated section of the country fascinated her. Any ranch wife, for that matter, needed to be an astute judge of character, because usually no one knew where the hired men came from or what their backgrounds were. Often a ranch woman was left alone while her husband was several miles away either tending fields or livestock or mending fences. If there were a rapist among their hired men, he would know exactly when the woman was alone.

Because she wrote about them, Lillian, of course, looked at these men with a more inquiring eye than other ranch wives. She was also lonely and starved for good conversation. Some had manners and education and wouldn't give their real names. Some had drinking problems. Some told strange tales of other lands. Few seemed accustomed to being around women. Lillian remembered an Irish boy with great affection. He could ride anything on four legs and didn't eat with his knife. He liked animals and was a smooth talker.

She wrote in one *Scribners* article: "We had real heart to heart talks around our little kitchen table, though, which gave me new insight into human nature."

They hired one man, who rarely spoke for the first few meals, but when Lillian mentioned the Bolsheviks, his tongue was untied and he turned on a torrent of words. She found him quite eloquent on the subject of Russia's liberation from the tyranny of capitalistic czars. It was during the era when Lenin and Trotsky were riding the crest of popularity.

Later, Lillian wrote:

> I listened attentively to this laboring man's ideas. I found that like most of us he resented being looked down upon by people of wealth and education. He did not object to working for a living if other people were also working on the lines for which they were best fitted. He did not object to going without luxuries and comforts if other people only took what they earned honestly, but he did object to being looked down upon and exploited by parasites.

The man didn't stay long, because he had his own homestead to work. Lillian regretted not being able to ask him what he thought about the disastrous results of the Lenin-Trotsky regime.

In his search for a good hired hand, Frank found all kinds called themselves cowpunchers. Some were lazy, some knew nothing about ranch work, and some were mean to the horses. One of these last made quite an impression on the Hazens.

Twenty-Three

His ideas were peculiar from a religious standpoint. He was firmly convinced he resembled the pictures he had seen of Jesus and so wore his hair and beard in accordance with this belief. He thought it was wicked to go to the theater or play cards, so his sole recreation was playing a harmonica.

Lillian said, "He drew forth sounds calculated to make one long to be afflicted with deafness."

One morning, Frank and he were plowing in the same field when the words, "Mad dog, you, mad dog, you," broke the spring quiet.

Frank left his plow to investigate the racket when the man burst forth with another tirade about the stupidity of that "mad dog" horse. He finished by hitting the animal over the head with a board, saying he would "learn" him "by dog." Frank gave him his time right then and there, as he didn't approve of hitting horses over the head. Before the man left, however, they learned he thought it was wicked to swear, so he reversed curse words and spelling to quiet his conscience.

In the end, they found there was no way to hire a permanent worker. If one was good, they figured they were lucky to have him a couple of years, and they had to have help.

Life Is as Water

Would be ranchers should have practical advice from farm papers,
or someone, about the elusive water supply in the north west.

"Counting the Drops." 1916

The Hazens, unfortunately, discovered a serious, and irreversible, situation after buying the ranch. Their land did not have a developed source of water for their household and stock needs. Access to water should have determined their purchase, but it appears they didn't even think about it. Frank was sure they could sink a well anywhere on their property and hit water. It's not like their ranch was some kind of waterless rarity in the middle of an oasis. Researching after the fact, Lillian found water was scarce on all Montana ranches.

She learned one rancher might find good water at twenty or thirty feet—although this was rare—while his neighbor in the next quarter section had gone down ten times as far and found nothing but a dry hole or perhaps water so full of alkali it was undrinkable.

Lillian discovered one small town in the vicinity hauled its entire supply in railroad tank cars. In the Hazens' district, a rancher was considered fortunate if he had a good drinking water well near his house. Unfortunately, his neighbors expected to share it with him and came for water any hour of the day or night, and as Lillian said, "There were times when the happy owner saw his well as something of a mixed blessing."

Water, or the lack of it, determined success or failure in almost every ranch endeavor. When the Hazens first moved to the country, there was still some "open range," defined as "grazing lands" owned either by the federal government or state or county governments. These were combined into large pastures or grazing tracts and leased to the local ranchers. The Hazens leased two state sections for $30 per year, per section. Lillian wrote:

> Although it was a cheap way to feed cattle in the summer, we found by experience that most of the cheap grazing land had little water and that the only way we could be sure of good summer pasture was to control water adjacent to the grazing land we used.

It was a rugged landscape with many steep coulees. Lillian wrote that an ideal solution to the problem would be to throw up a small dirt dam at the mouth of a stream flowing down a coulee and form a small pond. But that was expensive. They didn't see how they could afford to put in a dam when they didn't know how long they could hold the lease.

One of the first things Frank did was hire a well driller who was sure he would have no problem finding water, but things went wrong from the start. At first, the driller announced he was sure he had struck the vein of sand rock, so the Hazens returned to Lewistown that night sure they would have plenty of water in the morning.

But the driller went down 670 feet, right through the sand rock, and struck shale. He stopped drilling, stepped into his car, and started for town. On the way, he met Frank and Lillian returning to the ranch.

Later, Lillian wrote, "He broke the news delicately by stopping his car and hollering, 'I 'spose you want to know about that well of yours—there ain't a drop of water in it.'"

The Hazens were shocked—and dismayed. It had already cost them a thousand dollars and still no water. Frank suggested drilling in another place.

Lillian wrote, "The well-driller was an honest man, who keenly felt our disappointment, and when he appeared at the ranch a couple of days later, he brought the area's expert well-driller, who approved the job. The expert said the sand rock had undoubtedly been struck but there must be a fault in the formation, because we didn't have water."

Lillian agreed with him, "I didn't know a much worse fault in a well than having no water in it."

In the end, the Hazens spent about $2,000 on drilling wells, an almost useless exercise. They didn't find any water fit for human consumption, only "brackish stuff fit for the livestock." They finally resigned themselves to using a spring a half mile from the ranch in the nearby hills on government pastureland. For the next sixteen years, they hauled all their household water.

Although their well drilling produced water for their stock, this didn't solve all their problems. They ordered a windmill to pump the livestock's water to the surface. Each day, until the windmill arrived, they had to bring up as much water as they could with a hand pump, and they could never get enough to quench their animals' thirst throughout the long hot nights.

The frantic animals ran around the pasture, making the night hideous with their cries as they pawed the earth madly in their efforts to find a little moisture. Finally Richard couldn't stand the cattle's suffering, so he tied up the valuable bull next to a tub of water and opened the gates so the other animals could go to the spring. He thought it better to lose them than have them suffer.

When the windmill finally came, it was a difficult job assembling and erecting it "plumb" with the well. The thought, however, of how they could sit by idly and watch the wind pump the water once they had it up spurred them on. But when it finally stood, tall on a usually windy hill, there wasn't enough breeze to stir the grasses. Up to that point, the wind had blown so hard it almost flattened their tents. Then they had to disconnect the windmill and hook up the hand pump again.

For three weeks of the hottest weather, the wind went on strike and everyone, including Lillian and Frank when they were at the ranch on weekends, took turns pumping water for the thirsty cattle and horses. It was also the busiest season. The work was never ending as Richard and Johnny, with some help from Frank, harvested grain, cut hay, punched cattle, wrangled horses, and built fences from 4:30 A.M. to 10:30 P.M.

Twenty-Four

After Lillian and Frank moved to the ranch, she soon found housework, which was not her favorite sport anyway, different, difficult, and plentiful.

She wrote, "Dryland housekeeping is nearly as hard to learn as dryland farming."

As she learned to "count the drops," she was proud of each success in coping with her adverse conditions. She said that any woman transported from the city, where water is obtained by turning a faucet, to a homesteader's shack in the semiarid lands of the northwest region, would find the situation almost unbearable. A big challenge was cleaning house without water, and her supply depended entirely on whether the men had the time or inclination to haul it. When they weren't busy, they delivered a full barrel and two five-gallon cream cans of water every day, but more often Lillian had to get along for twenty-four hours with only ten gallons.

This meant she had to adjust to a new standard of cleanliness. Luckily, she hated routine, had never followed a tradition of "wash on Monday," "iron on Tuesday," and "bake on Wednesday." This gave her a good excuse to avoid it. She thought it beneath herself to be obsessed with "cleanliness and order."

She wrote, "The cleanliness complex makes children leave home early. A woman could wear herself out cleaning."

But even though Lillian refused to waste time on housekeeping, she did have certain standards. Dryland housekeeping, however, threatened even those. She soon saw she would have to forgo spotless floors and crisp curtains, but she liked a shining clean cooking area, utensils, and dishes.

Although washing the dishes was a major project, Lillian rose to the challenge and began devising unique solutions. When she fried ham or bacon, she didn't wash the frying pan until after the next meal. She then used it for cooking potatoes or an omelet, thereby saving money, usually spent on lard or butter, and time and water in washing the frying pan.

Lillian saved the rinse water from one meal to use as the wash water for the next meal's dishes by heating it on the coal cookstove. She substituted kerosene-soaked rags for water and mopped out the washbasin and cut the grease in the bottom of pans. Then she burned the rags.

Lillian said, "I used up a lot of rags that way and so wasn't expected to make rag rugs."

Life Is as Water

She also liked fresh, crisp bed linens, but it looked like these were a thing of the past until she thought of yet another water-saving device— the Lewistown laundry. The ranch's water shortage gave her an excuse to skip a chore she detested. She got all their clothes washed as well as their sheets, tablecloths, towels, handkerchiefs, pillowcases, and napkins ironed for a dollar a week. On dollar bundles, the laundry paid return postage, so, for a few cents more than a dollar a week, she had her hardest work done for her. She eliminated backbreaking, nerve-racking Monday wash-days. Thus she didn't have to maintain a kitchen fire in hot weather nor hang laundry out to freeze in the winter.

Because someone in the family usually went to town once a week, they dropped the laundry off and it was returned on the train.

"Personal cleanliness," she wrote, "however, sometimes got to be a problem."

A daily bath was out. Everyone was lucky to have a weekly bath with sponge baths in between. Lillian wrote she was ashamed to admit that sometimes, after feeding a hungry crew, calves taken from their mothers, and the chickens, she even passed up the sponge bath.

Winter—with snow and temperatures of twenty or thirty degrees below zero—was the only time Lillian ever had enough water. Everyone would pitch in to dig the bright, clean snow and melt it. Although it was flat and tasteless to drink, it did make good coffee, tea, soup, and cooked vegetables.

Melting snow made the kitchen a mess, but Lillian happily mopped daily: "It was wonderful for my skin, hands and complexion, and my hair."

The only trouble was—work slowed to a standstill in the winter. Lillian didn't have to feed harvest hands or extra men, and Richard and Frank had plenty of time to haul water.

Sometimes Lillian tried going for water by herself during the busy season, but it was hardly worth the trip, because all she could manage to load were two half-full five-gallon cream cans. When she could find another person to help her, they could load full ones.

When someone like her sister, Maude, visited, they would go to the spring by themselves. In the first years, they drove a horse and wagon. Later, they used a small truck made from an old jitney. The trip scared Maude, but Lillian was to drive over that ridge so often it soon held no terrors for her. At first, the drive was one of "hair raising" thrills—up a nearly perpendicular hill, then along a rough road through a wheat field into a pasture and up a steep ridge at a forty-five-degree angle.

A three-inch pipe shoved into the hillside spouted a steady stream of water into a natural basin to form a large pond full of cattails and frogs, prime hunting for the Hazen dogs. They looked forward to the water runs and would hop in and out of the vehicle as it made its slow way to the spring. Then they would romp through the cattails catching frogs just as they romped over the nearby hills catching gophers.

The spring's overflow formed a tiny sparkling stream that joined a good-sized creek rushing along the bottom of the coulee. Although it was less than a half-mile from their barn and house, the spring pond and coulee were so hemmed in by steep ridges that "everything pertaining to civilization seemed miles away." Lillian found it the most beautiful, restful spot on the ranch.

The Hazens were lucky. They were closer to the spring than any of the other ranchers. One of their neighbors, with a large family, didn't have a car and had to drive horses and a wagon two miles to pick up water. They usually sent two of their teenage daughters, who filled a collection of barrels, kegs, and cans. Because it took a long time to drive a team two miles, the girls had to haul a lot of water to quench the thirst of milk cows, workhorses, and chickens. They also hauled water to do the large family laundry.

Lillian told her sister, Maude, that those neighbors were poor homesteaders with no money and lots of children. They were ignorant of birth control and other modern improvements, "flat failures, in fact, from a worldly point of view, but notwithstanding, seem to extract a lot of joy out of life."

Maude told them all she didn't understand how anyone could enjoy living on a ranch. She thought it was about as bad as life could get. Lillian took her sister's complaints with good humor and told her, "If you stayed here long enough, you might learn to understand the lure of the land of the Shining Mountains."

TWENTY-FIVE

Riding the Range

Old timers told us, "You should've gone at sunup or
sunset—cattle always stay in the shrubs in the heat of the
day to get away from the flies." They always gave such
valuable information after the tenderfoot has learned by
experience.

"Hearts and Herds." 1919

Punching cattle was one of the Hazens' more difficult chores. When Richard was eighty years old, he remembered it sure wasn't all "poetry and roses," and being novices made every day more difficult. Because the Hazens were a bit different from the usual Montana rancher, the old hands living on the surrounding ranches enjoyed their problems.

In their first year on the ranch, almost daily, Richard and Frank chased their cattle for eight hours up benches and down coulees until the sweat poured off them and their horses looked like they had waded ten rivers. They never saw such "artful dodgers" as those ornery heifers. The local cowpunchers watched and chuckled until they got to know the Hazens. Then they told Frank they should have rounded up the cattle early in the morning before they settled into the heavy brush for the heat of the day.

Nevertheless, all their neighbors pitched in to help the Hazens with roundup chores. This meant Frank and Richard, out of necessity, had to learn cowboy skills so they could take their turn in the various neighbors' roundups. Even as technology and mechanization took over some routine chores, in the early 1900s the cattle business remained a hands-on business of rounding up the animals, branding them, dehorning them, and driving them to a railhead for marketing.

At first, Frank and Richard followed the local practice of roping and throwing the animals, but after one season, Frank devised a series of corrals and a branding chute that made the work easier on both the men and the cattle. They also ran the calves into a chute where they were castrated, branded, vaccinated for "black leg," and dehorned and had their ears split, all in one operation. It was not pleasant for them, especially the bull calves, but the little fellows recuperated from most of these necessary operations except, sometimes, dehorning. If the horn was cut too close to a calf's head, it would affect his brain.

After castrating the calves, the cowboys would save the testicles in their bags and drop them into the fire, where the bag was seared and popped open and the testicles browned like so many chestnuts. These are still called "Rocky Mountain oysters" in butcher shops.

Years later, Richard said, "I had to be a good sport and eat my share, but I needed a lot of bourbon or beer to wash them down."

Because the local ranchers pitched in and helped the Hazens, they also expected either Richard or Frank to return the favor by riding for them. Because Richard was young, it made sense that he join the roundup chores on other ranches. At first, he dreaded fulfilling this obligation because, being a rank tenderfoot, he was the butt of many a practical joke, and cowboys loved practical jokes. His first time out on a roundup, each person riding in the camp had four or five horses assigned him. Because Richard was inexperienced, the older riders arranged for him to draw the worst horse in the "string."

Then, in the morning when it was chilly, these same old-timers would see that it was the first horse he rode that day. The horse would buck until it finally threw Richard, but that was not the end. The other cowhands would catch the wayward horse, and he would have to get back on and ride again.

After a couple of years, however, Richard became a seasoned hand and came to look forward to joining in a roundup. He enjoyed the camaraderie, the joking around and the change from living quietly with his parents. He never found the cowboys boring.

In fact, Richard said he knew one guy who could tell dirty stories all day and never repeat one. "I counted 264 different stories. . . . Cowboys also played endless games of poker and knew all the cusswords there were to know."

Richard also loved to tell cowboy tales, which he exaggerated just a bit. A favorite was "Why Cowboys Wore Guns":

A lot of cowboys carried a Colt .45 six-shooter in a holster tied down by a leather string around the thigh. But the gun wasn't for killing men. He wore it to protect himself in another way. If he was out punching cattle and running his horse as hard as he could and it stepped in a gopher hole or it stumbled and fell, it could get up and, if the cowpuncher didn't get his foot out of the stirrup, he could be dragged to death. So he always carried a revolver so he could shoot the horse if it began dragging him. He also used his gun for killing rattlesnakes.

Some historians labeled the cowpunchers "one notch above a tramp" or "saddle tramps." Charlie Russell, the western artist and writer, didn't see them this way. In his book *Paper Talk: Illustrated Letters,* he described the cowboy as a man who followed the cows, who was willing to try almost anything once:

A plain everyday, bowlegged human—carefree, courageous man. . . . The cowboy's religion is his code. It calls for courage, loyalty, cheerfulness, uncomplaining, laughter at danger and hardships, lack of curiosity about other's pasts, respect for womanhood.

Some of Montana's early cowboys, like Granville Stuart and his DHS partners, became captains of industry in the Northwest. They improved breeds, both horses and cattle, influenced state legislation, practiced diplomacy with the Indians and government officials, and opened credit channels to the financial centers in the East.

Charlie Russell, for a time, worked as a cowboy for Granville Stuart on the DHS spread. He wandered Judith Basin for many years after starting work as a sheepherder in 1880, when he was only sixteen years old. Later, he hired out as a wrangler, tending horses by night and painting by day.

Barbed wire fences, invented in the late 1800s, put many cowboys out of work by the time the Hazens moved to the ranch. At the same time, homesteaders were eliminating Montana's spacious free ranges by fencing their plots of 160 or, later, 320 acres. Most land was fenced by the time the Hazens began ranching. Although someone had "to ride fence" to see if repairs were needed, a child on a plow horse could do that.

Sometimes fences caused disputes between close neighbors. Occasionally, one neighbor took advantage of another and a rancher had to stick up for his rights. Frank soon found spring was the time when a cattleman had to check his fences most carefully, making sure they had four strong wires well stapled to posts, not over fifteen feet apart, to keep others' hungry livestock out. Even then, the wires were sometimes cut or a gate left open.

Their closest neighbor, whose land bordered their property, irritated Lillian because he never repaired his fences, for a good reason. He made no effort to keep his milk cow at home and happily let her munch the Hazens' home pasture.

Frank complained, but the neighbor told him the cow would go through a four-wire fence if she saw good feed on the other side. Frank seemed to believe him, but not Lillian. One day, when the men went to the fields, she decided to put one over on that "smart aleck." After a struggle, she managed to open the gate between the home pasture and the range, which extended, fenceless, for miles. Then she drove the trespassing cow through.

Lillian wrote, "I smiled maliciously at the thought of the long walk or ride my sponging neighbor would be obliged to take before he milked that night."

About six o'clock that evening, she heard Buster bark and a child scream. She looked out of the window and saw her neighbor's five-year-old stepdaughter running as fast as she could toward home. Lillian looked over at the range gate, and there stood the wandering milk cow. She had returned by herself to be milked at the usual time, as cows will do.

Lillian waited and, in a few minutes, heard Buster bark again. Going outdoors, she saw the little girl approaching the range gate. She was trying to soothe Buster by saying in a trembling voice, "Good doggie, good doggie," as she patted his shaggy coat. Tears streamed down her cheeks. Of course, Lillian knew Buster wouldn't hurt the little girl. He barked to let Lillian know a stranger was on their land, but she told him to be quiet and asked the child what she wanted.

"Dad sent me for the cow," she said.

"Why didn't he come himself?" Lillian asked. "You were here before, weren't you?"

"Yes, but the dog scared me so I went back home."

"What did your dad say?"

"Asked why in hell I didn't bring the cow and told me to go get it," she answered.

The curse word startled Lillian but, looking into the child's hazel eyes, she saw the little girl didn't know she had said anything wrong and was more afraid of her mother's husband than the collie. Lillian took her into the kitchen and gave her some cookies, which she shared with Buster. Lillian then went to the gate and tugged and strained to open it.

"As I watched the little girl happily following the cow home, I felt like one who 'had gone out for wool and come home shorn.' I laughed though, thinking of the easy, clever way my neighbor had out-witted me."

Another close neighbor, Buck Ruby, who was a real movie-style western bad man, used all the tricks of the beef trade at one time or another. He would turn a hundred head of cattle into a pasture that wouldn't feed twenty-five adjoining the Hazen ranch, and "those critters soon found the weak spots in our fence," wrote an exasperated Lillian.

One time Richard bought twenty calves and drove them home late in the day. He put them in a pasture next to the barn, thinking he would brand them first thing the next morning, but when he got up, they were gone. He rode around the neighborhood until he found them in Buck Ruby's pasture. By that time, Ruby had imprinted his brand on all their rumps.

If Buck was sometimes a shifty neighbor, he was interesting. He was one of a few leftovers from an earlier, less civilized era full of people who lived by their own codes, men who came in with the late-1800s cattle drives from Texas. Many tales circulated about his antics. It was rumored he came from Montana's Deer Lodge Penitentiary to homestead 160 acres, before a new homestead law allowed 320 acres, on Indian Creek. Then he hired a bunch of his cowpuncher friends to homestead additional 160-acre plots until he had quite a spread west of the Hazens. Local gossip said he never hired a man who hadn't been in the penitentiary for horse stealing or cattle rustling.

Lillian lived on the ranch for months before she even saw him. Frank and Richard assured her he looked just like an ordinary rancher, but it was obvious the neighboring ranchers—and this included Frank and Richard—didn't trust Ruby. When word went out Buck Ruby was going to round up his horses one fall, Richard and Frank quickly rounded up their own, as did all their neighbors.

Finally Lillian met the man face-to-face when he came over and said, "I've rounded up my horses, and there're a few that don't belong to me. Would you or your husband come over and see if the animals belong to you?"

In a tape he made about ranch life, Richard said, "Ruby was a good horse thief and was quite proud of this fact. He started from Wyoming one time with twenty head of horses he'd paid for. When he arrived at his ranch, he had 160 head. He kept out of serious trouble by following a few of his own rules. He would never steal a uniquely marked horse such as a pinto. He would never steal a horse with a brand he couldn't change to one of his brands."

In those days, a ranch owner paid $5 a brand and filed it with the state. One person could have as many brands as he wanted as long as somebody else didn't already use the same one.

One day, Ruby stole a saddle horse from a horse buyer in Lewistown. The dealer thought Buck was the thief, so he asked the sheriff to ride out to the Ruby ranch with him. When Buck saw them coming, he saddled up the stolen horse and rode out to meet them. The sheriff told Buck the dealer accused him of stealing a horse.

Buck said, "Okay, let's go out and look. If you find it, I'll admit it."

They inspected the herd but couldn't find the horse. Neither the sheriff nor the horse buyer noticed Buck's mount.

Riding the Range

They said, "Sorry . . . ," and returned to town.

Buck went back to his barn, unsaddled his new horse, and later sold her for a good price.

The Hazens did trade horses with Buck Ruby when they first moved to the ranch, probably before they knew too much about him. Early on, they had ended up with a dangerous horse with the benign name of Blackie, because a neighbor put one over on them. He had hitched her to a wagon with another horse and drove her around, so Frank thought she was "broke, as he affirmed," and "gentle as a kitten." But after they brought her home, she showed "a disposition that made it like handling a stick of dynamite to put a halter on her."

She kicked and bit, struck and bucked if anyone tried to persuade her to earn her living. Once Lillian tried to lead her from one pasture to another and forgot to wind the rope around the pommel of her saddle. The horse turned with the "speed of lightning" and was off, running the rope through Lillian's hand so fast it left a burn. It was good luck Lillian didn't have the rope fastened to her saddle, as the horse she was riding weighed about five hundred pounds less than the maverick. Nobody knows what would have happened if she hadn't been able to break away. The horse was as intelligent as she was mean.

One day, Buck Ruby suggested trading horses with Richard and agreed to take the outlaw, Blackie. Lillian was glad to get the horse off the ranch, because she never felt easy when one of her menfolks rode it. They had to blindfold Blackie before two men could saddle her. Then after that feat was accomplished, the height of Blackie's ambition was to throw anyone who tried to climb aboard.

Although Ruby was noted as a horse swapper and rarely got the worst of a trade, Richard said, "I don't see how we could get anything worse than Blackie," as they watched their neighbor lead a pretty white mare into their barnyard.

"But have you told him what kind of animal Blackie is," Lillian whispered anxiously, "because I'd feel guilty if the horse threw him?"

Richard laughed. "Don't you worry. The horse was never foaled that could throw Ruby. Besides, he knows Blackie as well or better than I do, knows he is perfectly sound and capable of hard work. He has some hard riding to do and wants a good strong cow pony."

The exchange was made and, for several weeks, Richard watched the new horse, expecting it to display some vicious tricks or physical defects, but she seemed all right. At the end of the month, Buck rode over on Blackie to see the Hazens. No one was home at the time, but when Lillian and Frank returned from the post office, they found Buck sitting on the corral fence, watching some newly weaned calves and chewing an enormous quid of tobacco.

"Say," he said, "ain't you folks got any moonshine? I been all over the house to find some. Saw a demi-john in the kitchen and lit on it like a bee on a rose, and there wasn't nothing but vinegar in it."

He made a wry face.

Lillian laughed and told him, "We haven't been over to Hattie's lately."

He pretended to look sad and laughed. "I really came over to ask, 'What's the matter with Blackie?' I'm always suspicious of a horse trade, but I can't find nothin' wrong with her."

Then he rode the horse around to show them what a gentle, well-mannered specimen she was. Lillian looked on in speechless amazement, but Richard whispered, "Blackie hasn't forgotten how to strike and buck and bolt—she's just found her master and knows it. Ruby is welcome to her."

Actually, the Hazens had to overlook local folklore to sell Ruby a horse, no matter how mean it was. According to old-timers, Ruby himself had a wide mean streak. One story concerned a maverick horse Buck suspended in a well for several days. When he brought it up, it never bucked again, but it was never much of a horse after that.

Neighborhood gossip had it that he didn't treat his family much better. He had a wife for a while, but she died. She left him with two boys. One story tells of his teaching his son to ride a mean horse. It bucked and the child jumped off.

Buck said, "What did you do that for?"

His son said, "I didn't want the horse to kill me."

Then Buck said, "If that's the way you feel about it, I'll show you how it feels to be killed."

He grabbed the boy by his feet and banged his head against the side of the barn until the child was unconscious.

Buck Ruby, however, met an untimely end several years after the Hazens moved to their ranch. He was running bonded whiskey in from Canada and bootlegging it in Great Falls, Montana. He got caught and just before he was to go to prison, he had one last fling.

He went to a brothel in Great Falls and chose the prettiest woman there. Then he took her to the Manhattan Café, the best restaurant in town, where they sat in a booth. He ordered the biggest steaks on the menu. When the food was on the table, Ruby pulled out his gun and shot himself.

— TWENTY-SIX —

Neighboring in Lonesome Places

*Neighbors are a considerable factor in adding to or detract-
ing from the pleasures of a rancher's life as country people
are very "interdependent" because of necessity.*

"Obliging Neighbors." 1918

None of their other neighbors were as flamboyant as Buck Ruby. Most
were regular people trying to survive a rough environment and make a
decent living. All learned they needed to depend on one another. Lillian
found few neighbors tried to take advantage of the situation. In fact, she
was eternally surprised at how much people would do for one another.
When the Hazens moved to their ranch, Montana averaged about four
people per square mile. A person's life could depend on one's neighbor.
Although the ranchers worked long hours with little time to spare, they
would always stop to help one another.

Before Lillian realized this, she was irritated by how often their
neighbors seemed to borrow tools or ask for their help. Her favorite quote
was, "Give and take, borrow and lend is the Law of the Open Spaces."
Anyone who had a surplus of some necessity expected to share it with a
less fortunate neighbor. Of course, hard feelings were sometimes the
result of this indiscriminate borrowing and lending.

Lillian, however, found that the person who was honest with himself usually remembered he had not returned borrowed articles to his neighbors in a timely manner. One time she fumed when Frank had to hitch up and go after a plow he had loaned to someone three miles away. But then her anger evaporated when she saw that other person's wagon standing in their yard and remembered that several days earlier, they promised to return it.

She also remembered the sick horse a neighbor, learned in the ways of horses, cured at a fraction of the cost of a veterinarian. This kept her from telling him "where he got off" when he borrowed a saddle and kept it for weeks. More than Lillian would like, the Hazens also had to ask for help. Because cash was scarce, they weren't any better organized than other ranchers. Two necessary supplies on any ranch were gasoline and oil. Everyone bought them in barrels but often procrastinated ordering a new supply until the old was gone. Then a neighbor with a full keg was convenient. Generally, "like the Wise Virgins," the Hazens bought in time to avoid borrowing but were sometimes careless, as Lillian discovered one cloudy night when she and Richard headed for the post office three miles away in their old jitney.

For a couple of miles, they rolled along as fast as those old cars could go. Then she heard a mechanical murmur. Was the engine hitting on two cylinders, or was it short of oil? Inwardly, Lillian groaned but said nothing. They were about halfway to their destination, and walking a mile or two along the lonely, dusty road did not appeal to her. Their speed changed from that of a "carrier pigeon to a lame duck," but finally they arrived at the post office.

There weren't any gas stations in Ware, and so Richard went to one of the houses and rousted out the bachelor owner while Lillian sat in the car. She watched the two men wander the yard in search of a container to draw oil from the barrel and pour in their troubled engine. The dilapidated lantern they were carrying went out several times, until the owner told Richard to keep his hand over the broken top to prevent the wind from extinguishing the flame. At last, they found an old coffeepot and filled it with oil.

The donor refused to take any pay, saying he was likely any day to be in the same plight and would expect the same treatment. Richard didn't insist, fearing he might hurt the man's feelings by not receiving the gift in the same spirit as it was offered. Emergency help was, indeed, passed from one to another like a chain letter—perhaps one would never have occasion to repay a direct donor but would repay, indirectly, by doing a kindness for someone else.

They thanked him and went on their way. The machine purred softly and the car resumed "its birdlike flight" as they headed homeward. But then their lights went out. Lillian grumbled while Richard tinkered under the jitney's hood but couldn't get the lights to work.

He said, "We'll have to drive home without lights."

This scared Lillian, because there wasn't even a full moon. She could scarcely believe their good fortune when, safe and sound, they arrived at their next-door neighbor's house, a half mile down the road from their house. Lillian knocked at the door and asked to borrow a lantern. The rancher was in bed, but his wife was up, washing dishes, and told her it was hanging in the barn. When Lillian got back to the car, Richard was furious. He couldn't start the car.

"You may be out of gas," Lillian suggested.

"No, I'm not," Richard said.

"You'd better take this lantern and look."

Richard followed her advice and found—an empty tank.

"We'll have to borrow some gas," Lillian said.

"I won't borrow anything more," said Richard. "I haven't the gall to ask anyone for gas at this time of night. I'd rather walk home."

"Well, I wouldn't," Lillian snapped. "I'm too tired to walk, but I'll borrow the gas."

She went back to the house and was given a bucket and told where to find the gas barrel. She filled the pail and took it back to Richard, who, "growling like an angry bear," poured the gas into the tank. Then they continued on their way.

Ranchers and their families depended on one another like members of a large family depend on one another for companionship and emotional sustenance. Although in the summer no one had time to socialize, in the winter they got together as much as possible. Boredom and monotonous days were real threats to emotional stability on these isolated ranches. When they had time, they thought nothing of driving miles in a bobsled through a blizzard to join neighbors at cards. Pinochle, poker, hearts, or whist, a form of bridge, were favorite pastimes where neighbors would get together, serve refreshments, and play the night away.

But the most popular event was the country dance, usually held in the local schoolhouse. The Hazens rarely missed one and always included the current hired man living in the bunkhouse. In good weather, they would ride to the dance on horseback or in a car. In the wintertime, they would go in a bobsled with sideboards and a tarpaulin over the top. Often it was twenty degrees below zero, and one partygoer would have to drive the team with his head out in the weather.

It was not unusual to drive twenty miles to the dance, a two-hour trip each way when it was slow going through heavy snow. The dance would last until 3 A.M. By the time the group got back to the ranch house, it would be time to milk the cows and feed the stock. They never got to bed until the next night.

All were welcome at these dances, even the children, who danced until they were tired and then were bedded down with the coats.

Often a new barn was the site of a dance—any building with a good wood floor. Richard told an amusing tale of a local man who bought the Mennonite ranch, where there was a large dining hall with nice hardwood floors. He prepared it to be the main dance hall for the region. The only problem was the sticky floor. Evidently, the Mennonites used a lot of honey in their meals and had spilled it on the floor. It took the owner a long time to clean it up, to turn the wood floor into a slick dance surface.

Music was furnished by anyone who could play an instrument. There was usually a violin, sometimes a horn, and either an organ or piano. If a man was a good fiddler, he was immediately drafted. The players banged their feet on the wooden platform in time to their own music, and the dancers rocked the whole building with such rollicking tunes as "Turkey in the Straw," "Redwing," "Buffalo Gal," "Irish Washerwoman," "Over the Waves," and "Arkansas Traveler."

Men and women, old and young, moved around the dance floor, trying to keep time to the syncopated noise, while a few wallflowers sat on wooden benches lining the walls on three sides.

Dancing, from the time of the first settlers, was a popular Montana entertainment. In fact, the state's folk music is based on the fiddle music of the earliest country dances. Because the violin was easy to carry, it was the first instrument brought into the territory. When a man would ride through a settlement with a violin tied to his saddle, the local residents would draft him for dance service and promised "the moon" or at least board and room if he would stay around for a night or two of partying. If a blizzard blew in, so much the better. The dancing would go on for days.

At first, the only women available were the Indian women, but there weren't enough of them to go around. This, however, didn't discourage the men. They would designate some men as "women" and tie kerchiefs around their upper arms. A man would dance the woman's part for a few dances, and then it would be another's turn to assume the woman's role.

The young Indian women looked forward to these festivities too and spent days beading special buckskin dresses for the occasion.

Lillian also looked forward to the dances and wrote: "Country people in the pursuit of pleasure think nothing of staying out all night, or, at least, until the wee small hours two or three times a week."

Most partygoers were friendly and wanted everyone to have a good time. One spring night, two young bachelors gave a dance at the schoolhouse in Ware. As usual, they invited everyone in the neighborhood, and one was a newcomer, a homesteader, who spoke English with a heavy Scotch brogue. He was anything but a graceful dancer and was shabbily dressed. The two hosts soon discovered he wasn't having a good time, because the women ignored him.

One of the men lured the homesteader outside on the porch while inside the other made a speech to the guests. "The woman who dances with Lawrence the most often will win a prize."

When Lawrence returned to the party, the host called, "Ladies' choice."

Lillian wrote, "The girls, catching the spirit of kindness and good will shown by their hosts, vied with each other in giving the newcomer the time of his life."

Most of the local bootleggers made much of their money at these dances, where everyone lived it up after a summer of hard work. Each person would pay one dollar for a ticket to get in and one dollar for all the beer he or she could drink, while moonshine was passed from hand to hand in the parking lot. Certain people, usually the same people each

Happy hour, cowboy style, on the ranch. Even though it was Prohibition time, everyone found a way to drink.

week, got blind drunk and ended up sleeping it off in a car or buggy out-side if it wasn't too cold. In bitter weather, they passed out in the cloak-room with the children.

It was a hard-drinking neighborhood that, in western tradition, found a way to drink, Prohibition or no Prohibition. Some liquor was imported from Canada, but most was made right in the Ware area in nearby ravines and caves, where telltale stills could be well hidden from the federal agents, "hooch hounds." A $50 outfit could make liquor sell-ing for $8 a gallon.

In later years, Richard liked to tell moonshine stories. There was Guy Johnson, who found a steam engine to run the liquor through. It was complicated but it worked, and he could make a lot of whiskey most said was pure wood alcohol. He ran it out into a ten-gallon garbage can. When a customer went down to see him, he just helped himself to a sample with a tin cup hanging on the edge of the can. It didn't taste good, but Richard said it would make a person just as drunk as any other kind of alcohol.

And then there was a man named Combs, a bachelor down on the river. Richard thought he made the best whiskey, because he put it in charred wooden ten-gallon barrels. He would fasten ten of them on a rope and put them in the Judith River so they'd rock back and forth. He claimed he could make eight-year-old whiskey in three weeks that way. Richard thought that was so, because European importers put charred kegs of whiskey on sailboats from Europe to New York and by the time the liquor arrived it would be eight-year-old whiskey.

Lillian worried, because she knew Richard and Johnny were making and selling whiskey, but when she confronted Richard, he always denied it. When he was an old man, he admitted he and Johnny had a coyote den on Indian Creek where they stashed their jugs of whiskey carried over on horseback. He said no one ever found it, although the sheriff was suspicious of him. He would send a deputy out to buy a pint of whiskey from Richard or Johnny, but they were too smart to sell to him.

Many of the men in the area were making corn whiskey, but Hattie Ryder was the only woman. She was a widow, fat and blowsy with bright red hair and a raucous laugh. Her land adjoined the Hazen property. Many years earlier, she had been a successful businesswoman, when she owned and ran the hotel at a stage stop on the prairie between Great Falls and Lewistown.

Local rumor had it she also ran the "girls" who were residents of her hotel. She eventually married, but her husband died. At that point, Hattie was getting older and was forced to change her lifestyle. When a woman found herself widowed in turn-of-the-century Montana, with no mate to help her, she had to make a living the best way she knew how.

Hattie saved her money and bought eighty acres along the Judith River. It was good land except for the field on the edge of the river, which never produced a good wheat crop. Because there's so little rain in Montana, the ranchers depend on the snow melting off and staying in the soil. When the land borders a river, the moisture seeps off the crops into the water.

She built a little house at the top of a hill a hundred feet above the river and leased her land to a tenant to raise wheat. In those days, the owner got a third of the wheat crop and the renter, who furnished his own seed and labor, got two-thirds of the crop.

Money was scarce, but Hattie had an old horse, a wagon, and a buggy and did what she could to earn extra income. She raised chickens and turkeys, but this didn't earn much, and so she started making whiskey. Because it was good whiskey, it was much in demand. Unfortunately, one night her still blew up and her house burned down. The thing that upset her the most was the loss of a ring her husband had given her. She and her neighbors, including Richard, helped her sift through the ashes for two days, trying to find the diamond. She never found it.

Hattie then moved into her chicken coup and continued to "run mash." It was just a one-room shack, and, according to Richard's story, she had to keep the chickens in there too because it was the only place they had to stay. Local folklore tells of chickens perched everywhere—on the edge of the mash barrel, even on the brass headboard of her old bedstead.

Frank didn't buy from her, because he wasn't much of a drinker. Lillian drank but didn't like homemade whiskey. She preferred the commercial kind, but it was too expensive during Prohibition, so she bought moonshine from Hattie. She also liked to visit with the bootlegger and saw nothing wrong with her profession.

As early as November 22, 1894, Lillian had written her opinion of Prohibition. "Temperance means moderation and Prohibitionists are not moderate; they are tyrannical, and tyranny in anything is an abomination. . . . I knew one lady who regretted she gave her dying husband a few drops of brandy at the doctor's instigation. . . . All good carried too far may become an evil. Let us have temperance in all things."

More Than Pets

*My neighbors are respected and liked by me according to the
way they treat their stock, and I don't make any secret of
that fact. . . . I was glad when tractors came into general
use because it had made my heart ache to see horses overworked and mistreated.*

"Our Obligations to Animals." 1920

Many Montana ranchers seemed to have developed a tolerance for cruelty to both men and beasts. After all, it had only been thirty years or
less since Stuart's Stranglers, a group of vigilantes formed by rancher
Granville Stuart to bring law and order to Fergus County, took justice
into their own hands by hanging cattle rustlers from the nearest tree.

Although Frank would occasionally sell a horse, as he did to Buck
Ruby, he would not lend the family horses. In fact, they were the only
possessions the Hazens refused their neighbors. Lillian said a creature
could not tell how he was treated, could not be repaired like a piece of
machinery, and, above all, had feelings and faith in its owner.

"Our four-footed servants are our friends."

Lillian watched some ranchers work their teams long hours without
rest or food. They would come in at noon after eight hours of work and

leave workhorses standing, still in harness, with no food. Lillian figured their animal helpers needed a rest the same as their human supervisors. Animals caused a lot of Lillian's extra work, but she didn't care. She found her animal relationships the biggest compensation for living the difficult ranch life. Lillian had few pets when she was growing up, and so, for the first time in her life, she could surround herself with animals.

As did most ranchers, the Hazens early acquired a full crew necessary for efficient ranch operation—two dogs, many barn cats, several horses, and the usual assortment of pigs and cows.

In 1918, she wrote: "Companionship and keen, if unspoken, sympathy of four-footed folks can brighten weary hours and sweeten bitter trials."

Lillian loved them all. She poured her mothering instincts into their care, and the animals, in turn, responded to her kindness. She rolled up her sleeves and pitched in to feed motherless baby animals or nurse ailing creatures back to health.

"A fellow wants four legs to get any attention around here," Frank's brother, John, grumbled.

"This observation," Lillian said, "was provoked by being obliged to wait for his dinner while I doctored a sick cow."

It also appeared to be Lillian's job to tend to the daily wants of the horses. According to her diary, she fed them, let them in and out of the barn, and chased them around the pasture to catch them for work purposes. She also rode them when weather permitted.

"A ride on King was a joy."

She fed them grain and sometimes forked hay to them. She doctored them when they needed it and fed them salt. She watched over them—Peanuts, Pinkie, Mary Ann, King. In most cases, one has to read between the lines of her diary to realize what is really happening with her. On March 9, 1925, there was a blizzard. An anxiety-charged March 19 entry read: "Mary Ann sick. Took her into barn and fed her."

After that, each entry for over a week read, "Mary Ann still sick."

Lillian helped Frank give Mary Ann daily doses of medicine. She also mentioned Frank found another cow almost dead on the range.

Two weeks later, she wrote, "Mary Ann seems better. Fed her."

People have always had and always will have their own personal biases when it comes to cruelty or kindness to animals. For instance, Lillian didn't agree with John that branding cattle was cruel. He was still visiting the Hazens every two years and often participated in ranch chores.

Lillian wrote:

> This same man called it "sport" to chase and kill a deer. He stalked one mountain sheep for hours and was so proud of killing the brave old patriarch. He had the head mounted and sent to the museum in Bronx Park with his name prominently displayed as the victor in his most unfair battle with this unoffending, aged creature of the wilderness.

Who is cruel, he or the western cattlemen? Stock has to be branded in order to distinguish them from their neighbors' cows when mixed on the open range.

Montana, however, was a harsh environment for all animals. Every winter, Lillian worried about the animals left on the range to starve in severe weather. Some ranch neighbors pooh-poohed her fears, but Lillian knew this happened more than they would like to admit—and usually at regular intervals over a decade. She had read the accounts of Montana range disasters, like the one that began in 1885, when a dry winter to the south had forced some two hundred thousand head north and the Montana ranges were crammed with cattle.

Then in the summer of 1886, hot winds baked the overcrowded meadows, and there was no grass. By fall, there was still no rain, and in November, winter settled in and stayed. In late January 1887, temperatures averaged twenty degrees below zero, sometimes plunging to forty degrees below zero, and remained there for a month. This was when Charlie Russell painted his now famous *Waiting for the Chinook* while working in the Judith Basin for Helena cattlemen Kaufman and Stadler.

That year, it was March before the chinook, warm winds, finally came and, as always, melted the snow and ice almost overnight. During a chinook wind, the thermometer can shoot up thirty or forty degrees in an hour. The word *chinook* is defined in the dictionary as a moist southwest wind blowing from the sea onto the Oregon and Washington coasts in winter and spring or a dry wind blowing down the eastern slope of the Rocky Mountains at recurring intervals.

After the snow melted, the cowmen rode out over the ranges to find their cattle. In every gully, along the streambeds, in the fence corners, and on the level plains, they found thousands of rotting carcasses. Granville Stuart lost 65 percent of his herd and was so sickened he vowed never to ranch again.

A severe storm always took its toll. A sensitive Lillian never got used to watching her beloved animals suffer:

> Wide expanse of frozen snow,
> The icy blasts of winter blow
> The cattle stand and starve and wait
> For the Chinook that comes too late.
> So they must perish—slowly die,
> New stock costs less than hay to buy.

To Lillian, the coming of spring meant new, abundant pasture food for the winter-starved stock. She knew tree branches seldom showed green before May, but every year she began looking for the welcome color in March and was often gratified by glimpses of green grass in the coulees long before anyone else expected spring. She hailed every green spear she found with "unfeigned delight."

Springtime also brought new animals. Lillian loved birthing time on the ranch and found most animal mothers devoted to their offspring: "One time when a cow rushed up to the barn bellowing, it took us some time to learn just what she wanted."

Her calf had been with her not half an hour before and so could not be far away. Still, she acted as though she had lost it. Lillian and the hired man looked everywhere but could not find the calf. The distracted mother kept on bellowing and came up to the house after they left the barn. Finally Lillian noticed she always returned to the straw stack. It was about three hundred yards from the barn and so, at last, Lillian understood.

There had been a slide at the stack, and the cow's calf was buried under straw. The hired man laughed when Lillian insisted he take a pitchfork and go investigate. The cow followed. As Glenn neared the stack, he heard the calf mooing faintly in answer to the cow's bellowing. Sure enough, the little fellow was buried in the stack, and Glenn pitched off a wagonload of straw to rescue him.

The Hazen farm animals trusted their human owners to solve their problems, and Lillian formed a special bond with most of them. In a story for *Scribners,* she described how an old mare gave birth to her colt in a coulee near the house. Because no one had seen the horse for a couple of days, Lillian started to worry and went for a long walk to search for her. She found the mare standing with her head down over the body of her dead baby. After putting her arms around the animal's neck and giving her a hug, she wrapped her apron around the old mare's neck and led her away, with some gentle tugging, from the colt's body.

As the weather improved and the ranch work expanded to fill every waking hour, Lillian, on horseback, also helped keep track of the newborn calves out on the range. Sometimes one was born in subzero weather, before spring arrived. Stubbs was one of these who entered life on a bitter cold, winter morning just outside the barn. The thermometer was thirty below zero and, undoubtedly, the old cow had hoped to find the barn doors open, but they were closed.

She had to wait for shelter until the men came down to milk and, by that time, her poor little calf had nearly frozen to death. Its tail, ear tips, and feet were frostbitten. The men carried it into the barn because it was too numb with cold to walk. A few days later, the calf's feet, tail, and ears were in bad shape. Frank decided to put it to sleep, but it was such a lovable little animal he kept delaying "the evil day."

All their neighbors gave advice. Some said she was a strong, healthy calf, her frostbites would all heal in time, and she would be none the worse for them. The Hazens named her Stubbs, because of her abbreviated tail, and let her live. But long before the prairies were green with grass, they knew Stubbs would never recover. Her tail was only about a third as long as it should be, so she couldn't even swish away flies. Severe frostbite had crippled one foot, so that it was nearly useless. She could never forage around the pasture, like other cattle, and so would have to be cared for all her life.

The Hazens thought of "beefing" her for meat, but they couldn't bring themselves to do it. She was their pet. They all waited on her after she was weaned; gave her the nicest hay and the freshest water and generous feeds of grain. In the season when flies tormented the cattle the worst, they put her in the cool, dark box stall during the heat of the day. At other times, she had the free run of the barn and yard and would hobble around to where the grass was the best, then lie down and contentedly chew her cud. But Stubbs was not a total loss as a beef animal. She earned her keep by giving birth to a superior calf each spring.

In the early 1900s, a rancher didn't have a veterinarian's services handy. They had to do what they could for a sick and ailing animal. Lillian had more patience and took more time than the men to coax an animal to health. One of these was a motherless colt, called Billy, who had "joint disease." He was a walking skeleton covered with open sores. Lillian doctored him and fed him a bottle. He thrived and grew into a huge draft horse, behaving like a giant dog, who followed her everywhere when she did outside chores. Richard and Frank had to hang the full milk pails on a high hook, because Billy drank the milk as fast as they produced it. On the ranch, Billy slept under Lillian's bedroom window every night.

Frank also cherished their animals and was very fond of his herd of Jersey cows. He used to sit on the fence and watch them graze. But he wasn't in the milk business, so he sold them to a neighbor. To his sorrow, more than half the herd had to be destroyed because they developed tuberculosis through sloppy care.

Lillian saw her animal world as a microcosm of the real world as humanlike scenarios were acted out on the ranch each day. "Animals, in many ways, behave just as people do."

Many a time she saw fifteen or twenty yearlings (young cows) rush over the bench toward the sound of clashing horns and scuffling feet to see two steers fighting in a coulee.

"For all the world, they were like small boys running to see a fight."

Lillian never ceased to be amazed at animals' intelligence. She described how one horse learned to open the granary door and let a half dozen horse friends in to feast on the grain.

She was convinced animals responded to kind treatment and the more one loved them, the easier it was to understand their wants. She wrote, "Our stock seemed to have such absolute faith in our willingness and ability to help them when they get into trouble. . . . They always come home if anything is the matter with them."

Twenty-Seven

Lillian and Chapp, her Airedale, begin a water run to the spring, 1920s.

One night when a horse limped into the corral from the pasture just as Frank and Richard were going to bed, they investigated and found she had stepped on a board with a nail in it. The nail was so deeply imbedded in her hoof it was all a strong man could do to pull it out. They doctored her, fed her, and kept her in the barn for a day or two so she would not be obliged to step on her sore foot to graze.

Although Lillian pampered all the livestock, their dogs were her favorites. By 1925, both Mike and Buster had died and were replaced by one dog, Chapp. He figures prominently in Lillian's diary and stories, as the family auto rarely left the ranch without him.

He was a feisty, intelligent Airedale and Lillian loved him. She often mentions driving to the post office with Frank and Chapp in the bobsled in bad weather and in the old Studebaker in fair weather. She also complained because Chapp constantly got into trouble because of a serious obedience flaw. He would not come when called unless he happened to feel like it. Dog trainers of the era suggested they whip him if he did not mind them, but if he saw someone coming with a stick or strap, he would run away and stay away.

Because of his disobedience, he almost met an untimely end. One day, Frank and Lillian rode out on the range to round up the workhorses. They found them a mile away and turned them toward home. Suddenly the animals scattered in all directions, running blindly. Lillian's horse also ran, jumped, and reared until she thought he would throw her.

Finally, when the horses calmed down, Lillian and Frank could see the cause of the commotion. Chapp had discovered a horse's carcass, dead a year or more. He was digging around it and shaking the bones until the skeleton seemed to rise up off the ground. No wonder the horses ran; the bones seemed to have a life of their own. When Frank and Lillian finally started home again, Lillian thought it strange Chapp didn't follow them. She called and Frank whistled, but the dog wouldn't come. He kept worrying the pile of bones.

"Come on," Frank called to Lillian. "We've got to hurry and get the horses ready for the field if I'm to do any plowing this morning. Chapp will follow us when he gets good and ready, which may not be soon. The skeleton is a new plaything."

Reluctantly, Lillian followed Frank. Several hours passed, and the dog didn't come home. She thought of searching for him but was afraid to ride alone so far away from the house. When Frank came in for his noon meal, she met him before he could get the horses fed and told him Chapp was still missing.

"Maybe a coyote has got him," Lillian said.

Frank looked worried too and said, "I'll just eat a bite, and then we'll look for him."

Lillian couldn't eat, she was so worried. After dinner, they saddled their horses and began backtracking to where they had left the dog. As they neared the skeleton, they could hear him barking.

"Great guns!" yelled Frank, suddenly spurring his horse to a gallop. "I'll bet that in spite of all my threats and the signs I've posted, somebody set a trap by that carcass, and the pup's caught in it."

Sure enough, poor Chapp was held fast in a coyote trap that had been wired to the neck and tail of the skeleton. His attempts to pull free had caused the lifelike motions of the skeleton.

"Lucky he only got one toe in," Frank said as he struggled to release the dog. "Otherwise it would have meant a broken leg for him."

"Poor, dear Chapp," said Lillian as she stroked the dog while he

Twenty-Seven

licked his hurt paw, "I'm so sorry—I never dreamed you didn't come because you couldn't come."

"Serves him right," snapped Frank. "If he always came when he was called, we wouldn't have left him. We would have known something was wrong and checked to see what it was."

Although he was angry and his words were harsh, Lillian noticed he lifted Chapp carefully to his saddle, trying to make him comfortable while the three of them rode home.

Over the years, Chapp constantly found trouble. He was a most curious dog, always investigating things. One day, he saw a strange animal moving near the chicken house. It had queer-looking hair that seemed to bob up and down as it walked. It was springtime and the little chicks were running around the coops. As Chapp watched the creature, he barked furiously, but no one came. The animal paid no attention to Chapp, so the dog grabbed for him and never knew what happened. Suddenly his muzzle was filled with sharp spinelike things he couldn't rub off.

The encyclopedia describes the porcupine as an animal about two feet long to the tail, which is seven inches long, covered with a mass of white spines. It says nothing, however, about the misery the creature inflicts on western ranchers' dogs and stock.

Horses and cattle who get those bearded-tipped spines in their soft, tender noses are liable to die of starvation in good pastures unless their owner finds and extracts the porcupine quills, because their mouths and noses get too sore for them to crop the grass.

It usually takes two men to pull the quills out: one holds the animal while the other removes the fishhooklike spines with a pair of pliers. It's so difficult, it can be compared with a dentist pulling teeth. One of the Hazen neighbors shot his dog. He said he didn't have the heart to torture his friend by pulling out so many quills. Some ranchers in areas infested with porcupines would not keep a dog. When Frank saw Chapp, he reached into a drawer for a pair of pliers. Chapp saw what he had in his hand and tried to get out of the kitchen, but they held him down for two hours while Frank pulled the quills out of his nose, mouth, throat, head, and shoulders.

After it was all over and Frank was consoling the dog, he said, "That'll teach you to mix with a porcupine."

A Day in the Life of an Idle Ranch Woman

As time went on, I was informed on different occasions by my husband and my son, how the wife of one neighbor plowed, another ran a binder, another shocked grain . . . all could milk and make butter, not to mention pitch hay for the stock and harness horses.

"A Day with an Idle(?) Ranch Woman"
Scribners. September 13, 1922

Frank and Richard nagged Lillian daily to spend more time on routine chores. The last straw was when Richard told her their hired man said she did the least of any rancher's wife he ever saw. Nobody likes to be considered lazy, and this remark made Lillian angry. She found ranch chores never ending, and although her husband and son wanted her to spend even more time helping them, she soon realized she had to escape from the real world for an hour or two each day to retain her sanity. She was determined to continue writing. In fact, it assumed an addictive quality. The more she wrote, the more she wanted to write, but she was frustrated.

While still living in Lewistown, before they moved to the ranch, she tried her hand at fiction and continued her efforts on the ranch. She produced page after page of soppy love stories and trite confessions, the kind she thought she saw published in the "pulps." Her contrived short-story plots seem to be her fantasies. Here again the "Bewitching Mrs. Gay," a rich, sophisticated older woman from the East, comes west for romance and adventure, appearing under various names and in different situations. Lillian's heroes were all good and her villains were all bad. Although later she said she knew people were a complicated mixture of good and evil intentions, she couldn't seem to put the subtle nuances of character into words.

In a story published in *Scribners,* "Aspirations and Inspirations of a Ranch Woman," she talked about how hard it was to find time to write. The first day she sat down at the typewriter, the two dogs, Mike and Buster, got into a dogfight. She put ammonia on a cloth and waved it under the dogs' noses. That stopped the dogfight.

As she was going back to her typewriter, she heard a commotion in the henhouse. A calf had wandered in and lain down in the fresh straw, and she drove him out. Then she noticed a tiny chick had fallen into the water bowl. She rescued it, wrapped it in cotton batting, and put it in a Nabisco Shredded Wheat box behind the stove to dry out.

She wrote, "I don't know what I should do without shredded wheat boxes when my hens are hatching. They are just about the right size to serve as chicken hospitals, carriers, and nurseries. They cost nothing, so can be thrown away the minute they get dirty. I recommend empty shredded wheat boxes to anyone raising poultry."

Finally, one morning a few days later, she got under way again and had written several pages when she looked out and, to her horror, saw Richard and Frank headed for the house. She looked at the clock. It was noon. She hustled into the kitchen and threw together a lunch of boiled eggs and potatoes left over from the night before, some canned peaches, and "store bought" gingersnaps and tea.

"They were not enthusiastic over the repast, and asked me what was the matter. I confessed I had been writing a story."

They laughed at her and she vowed not to tell them anymore, especially when she started getting checks. However, as quickly as she mailed a short story, it came back like a boomerang.

She wrote, "I never realized how efficient the postal service is."

For a year she wrote without any success except with her poetry, written for the sheer joy of it, which sold for pennies per line. She had to produce something for a real paying market.

She, of course, cut a few corners in order to find time to write, usually at night after all her chores were done. Then Richard and Frank complained about the old typewriter's noise. In fact, they made it just as difficult as they could for her to continue writing. They thought her literary efforts an entire waste of time and would roll their eyes when they heard her clacking away in the corner of the living room. When they picked up her rejected manuscripts instead of slim envelopes containing checks at the little Ware post office, they were embarrassed. They knew the postmaster was the center of the neighborhood gossip network and were ashamed of her failures. They both told her she could put her time to better use, like doing more ranch work.

One day, when a neighbor came by to ask her advice about successful chicken care, Lillian gave her some pointers. After the friend left, she sat down at the typewriter and wrote up the advice, counted the words on a line, number of lines on a page, and the number of pages and figured she had a five-hundred-word manuscript. She sent it to a farm paper paying one-half a cent per word. By return mail, she received a check for $2.49, her first ranch story sale.

Frank kidded her about her small earning capacity, but she felt good. For once, she had stepped out of the "interminable circle of rejection." She had written something an editor wanted to buy. In her struggle to produce a salable story, she said she forgot a cardinal rule of writing. "You have to write what you know."

Because she had been a successful writer earlier in her life, she was sure she could be one again. Every day, she observed great story ideas; tragedy and comedy were the stuff of ranch life, but she couldn't seem to capture them on paper. It's little wonder, considering she had to fit it in where she could around her work schedule, which began at 4:30 A.M. and ended at 10 P.M.

"Gradually, as the idea dawned upon me my family and neighbors thought I was leading a very idle life . . . I determined to keep an exact account of how I spent my hours and minutes for one day, at least, for purposes of self-defense."

She started a journal. One day, while reviewing it, she realized it might make a good story. In the end, she wrote several articles based on it and *Scribners* published them, earning her a much-needed $150 per story. When the *Lewistown Democrat News* also published them, she became something of a local celebrity.

Her first story, "A Day with an Idle(?) Ranch Woman," began on a typical summer day when the Big Ben alarm clock went off at 4:30 A.M. on August 24. She got up, dressed, and went to the kitchen to begin breakfast. As she made coffee, toast, cereal, and fried potatoes and eggs, she also set bread to rise and put up two lunches, one for her son, who was going to work on a distant part of the ranch and couldn't come home for his midday meal. The other was for his shocker, a worker who cut and bound the grain so it could dry upright in the field. "His appetite made one wonder if he had three stomachs like a cow," Lillian commented.

She wrote that she wanted to stop her work long enough to watch the sunrise, "the faint colors of the dawn always give me keen delight," but there was no time. She didn't even take a few minutes to step outside and feel the light, fresh, early morning breeze. She had six motherless little chicks she kept boxed up in the kitchen at night. They had to be fed, watered, and put outside. Mike, their Boston terrier, was barking loudly for admission at the living room door. He always went there when she was in the kitchen and vice versa. The table had to be set and the kitchen swept and tidied, not to mention feeding the chickens and letting them out of the henhouse.

Six o'clock, breakfast time, came all too soon, but when the four men sat down at the table, the meal was ready. She served them, and, when they finished eating and lighted their cigarettes, she went down to the barn, about a hundred yards from the house. By that time, her saddle horse, King, used to catch the workhorses, had finished his oats, and Lillian felt, after being shut up in the barn all the long hot night, the animal should have a chance to run and roll about the pasture. She put the horse out, checked the water tanks, and turned the water on in one that was almost empty.

She returned to the house and cleared the table of breakfast dishes. She had started to wash them when Richard called her. Lillian went to the door and saw him between the house and barn, hitching four horses to a binder. He wanted her to hand him his gloves as he passed the house. He didn't dare leave his team standing alone, because, although they were gentle, they were easily spooked.

It was 7:30 A.M. when she returned to the dishpan. Then she plucked and prepared a chicken for frying and had barely finished this job when Frank called and asked her to help him catch a horse that needed doctoring. They finally managed to get a halter on the animal, and Lillian held the rope while Frank treated him. She was about to return to the kitchen when Frank said he had to sack a lot of oats and could get through much quicker if she would help him, so she stayed. After they finished, Lillian remembered her bread and again started for the kitchen.

Then Frank asked her to come back in a half hour to open and shut the corral gate so none of the animals got out as he drove through with a load of seed wheat for the hired man, who had commenced to drill (plant) wheat. Lillian returned to the kitchen, kneaded her bread, put it in pans, made cinnamon rolls, and returned to the corral in time to "render the needed assistance."

Frank gave her further orders: "I think the windmill ought to be turned on, and I'm afraid the reservoir is nearly empty. Oh! And would you mind feeding Lord Brae and Stubbs some grain."

Lillian immediately climbed the steep hill to the windmill opposite the house, a difficult quarter-of-a-mile walk. By then, it was 10 A.M. As she was returning to the house and her indoor duties, she saw King looking toward her from the other side of the pasture fence. She often took him into the barn and fed him oats, so could not resist his longing expression and spent twenty minutes with him.

At last, returning to the kitchen, Lillian found her bread was ready for the oven. She brought in wood, rebuilt the fire, and then began making pies. On hot days she tried to bake everything at one time so she could let the fire go out. She was glad to sit down to peel the apples, as she was tired, and Frank and the hired man would be in at twelve-thirty, expecting a hearty dinner.

August in Montana is hot, sometimes a hundred degrees in the shade. Heat waves shimmered off the wheat fields as Lillian set the table behind the house in its cool shade. Dinner was ready on time, but she shuddered at the pile of cooking dishes to be washed after the meal. She started the

home, watered and fed him, it was nearly six o'clock. Frank would have watered and fed him, but Lillian liked to attend to his "creature comforts" when she brought him from the pasture so he would continue to come to her.

She finally left him, carried wood into the kitchen, and started her fire. The meal was ready at seven. Frank, the hired man, and the shocker sat down at the table, but Richard sent word he should work late, having lost so much time chasing the cattle out of the oats. Lillian was disappointed because he particularly liked her menu for that night—fried chicken, creamed potatoes, stewed corn, fresh bread, cinnamon rolls, green apple pie, cheese, and coffee.

She had to make more trips to the woodpile to keep his dinner warm. She had paused in picking up the sticks to watch the fading sunset when she realized both dogs were waiting for supper. The terrier expressed his impatience with short angry barks. The collie was silent but turned expectant, amber-colored eyes in her direction, more compelling than the little dog's fretful yaps.

It was dark when Richard came in for supper. "He was too tired to know whether he was eating fried chicken or boiled horse meat."

About the same time, Frank brought in the milk. Lillian strained it, then washed the dishes. It was after 9 P.M. when she laid her weary body on the bed. Thinking how short the time before Big Ben would again ring out 4:30 A.M., she had a fellow feeling with the man who said he got up so early he met himself going to bed.

She was just drowsing off when she remembered she had forgotten to fill the collie's water dish, and on such a hot night, he would need plenty to drink. She got out of bed, slipped into a robe and slippers, hurried into the kitchen to the water pail, then outdoors with a dipper full. Just then, she heard the wavering call of a coyote and remembered she had not shut the door of the chicken house. Groping her way twenty or thirty yards in the darkness, she closed it and returned to the house.

"As I lay down again, one of Irving Berlin's popular songs rang in my inner ear, and I felt a strong desire to ask him if he had ever really lived on 'that farm in Michigan.'"

— TWENTY-NINE —

And the Earth . . . Shall Be Iron

> *There had been little snow the past winter and so there wasn't*
> *enough moisture to make good pasture. . . . The soil resembles*
> *powdered ashes and rises in a great cloud of dust as the stock*
> *wander from range to range in the hope of finding sustenance.*
> *The poor creatures look like animated bags of bones as they*
> *seek the coulees they remember as rank with life-giving pasture*
> *after the benches are denuded of grass and weeds.*
>
> "Hearts and Herds." 1919

Lillian also wrote, "It seemed like we were just getting the hang of the ranching business when bad times set in."

All that May, every morning the sun climbed over the mountains, "robed in its cloth of gold," while the blue of the sky was usually unclouded, and the heat was oppressive for that time of year. The grass was still green, but dust followed the steps of men and animals even in the pasture, while dust hung like a curtain over the plowed fields if there was much wind. Even the wildflowers were veiled in dust, and Lillian had to shake or blow it off the blossoms before entering her house with them.

Night after night, she lay awake, longing to hear the patter of raindrops on the roof or the drip, drip of water from the eaves, but no such welcome sound broke the stillness of the lonely hours of darkness, intensified by the light of the moon and stars.

Everyone gave up all hopes of a crop by the middle of July 1919 as a drought rolled over their land. Lillian never forgot watching the unbelievable suffering of ranch animals when their owners ran out of food and money. The weather was blazing hot, night and day. It reminded Lillian of the ancient curse: "Thy heaven that is over thy head shall be brass, and the earth that is under thee shall be iron."

She watched in horror as the drought took over.

When the Hazens bought their first 520 acres in 1912, Montana's Judith Basin was in one of its periodic wet periods. Good, high-protein wheat and abundant pastures flourished. A great many people, including the agricultural experts, forgot this was most unusual weather for that part of the Great Plains. Normal conditions were semiarid. They didn't understand the long rhythm of the Great Plains, that drought is part of its ancient cycle.

A few experts issued dire warnings about the feasibility of dry farming in Montana. R. N. Sutherlin, editor of the *Rocky Mountain Husbandman*, wrote, "There is no district in Montana of any considerable size where crops can be grown safely and successfully one year after the other without artificial watering."

To begin with, the dry-farming system depends on at least fifteen inches of annual rainfall. If the rains come as needed, crops are green, lush, and four feet tall. But if it is dry, the wheat only grows a few inches, turns a pale yellow, and dies. It was precisely these "ifs" that were ignored. Promoters, and the Hazens, sincerely believed an agricultural, technical breakthrough had occurred. Scientists, speculators, railroad officials, western chambers of commerce, and locators went to work to spread the word.

Congress passed the Enlarged Homestead Act of 1909, which should have struck the average plainsman as a laughable piece of legislation. All it did, in essence, was increase the acreage obtainable under the old Homestead Act of 1862 from 160 to 320 acres, still far too few to support a rancher on semiarid land. To make a living on 320 acres, a farmer would need an unlimited supply of water to nourish every inch of the land filled with cash crops. As it was, every plant depended on enough rainfall. Although the Hazens chose not to take up claims on government land as homesteaders but purchased 1,040 acres from private sources, they faced the same circumstances as the hapless homesteader: too little acreage to earn a living.

Many of their homesteader neighbors were the sad victims of the massive propaganda effort to populate the region. James J. Hill began the program as early as 1890, when he built the Great Northern Railway into Montana's Milk River region. Both the railroad and the local press began advertising the great opportunity to acquire a free farm just by filing a claim and living on the land for five years. Later, the time to prove up one's claim varied from three to five years.

People flooded into western North and South Dakota and Montana. To the average easterner, scrabbling a bare living on ten or twenty acres, 320 acres just for the taking sounded like utopia to him or, in some cases, her. To inexperienced city dwellers, it sounded like the only chance they would have to acquire property.

No one knows how many people came, because the census of 1910 was taken before the influx was well under way and the census of 1920 occurred when the out-migration had already become a flood. But by sampling county records and land office filings in key areas, it's a conservative estimate to say that between 1909 and 1917, eighty thousand homesteaders inundated Montana.

Just as these hopeful farmers were settling on their tiny plots of land with barely enough to eat, living in primitive homesteader shacks or sod huts, the drought began in the far north in 1917. It started small and inched southward, destroying all in its path, even the insects. Sometimes it behaved in mysterious ways, leaving green, productive islands in the wasteland. In 1918, it appeared in central Montana in glowing spots. By 1919 it had spread all across the state. There were brief periods of remission in some places, but it never completely abated.

There was one thing it did not kill—the seeds of native grass. Those seeds lay dormant, hard as tiny pebbles, just beneath the surface of the cracked earth. They would not sprout until the rains came again, and they did not sprout for a long time. But domestic seeds like wheat can be coaxed to sprout by the hint of moisture. They emerge to be seared, never to sprout again.

Twenty-Nine

Eleven thousand Montana farms blew away eastward on the edge of the blast furnace winds of 1919. In some places the humidity hovered at 4 percent. Skin cracked, boards warped, and sand blasted buildings in the new towns, making them look a century old in a year's time.

Lillian wrote, "It is impossible to picture the helpless, hopeless misery of a drought-stricken community. Men stand around and talk and smile and laugh, but no one is deceived by the ghastly merriment with which they try to while away the weary hours of enforced idleness. A grim, awful dread overshadows everything and everybody."

The clouds gathered frequently, sometimes tempering the heat of the sun for an hour or two, then passed away without giving a drop of water to the parched ground, where the vegetation was dying. Day after day, the people waited, disappointed.

At the time, Frank and Richard were only tilling six hundred acres of their land. Frank believed in letting half of the land remain fallow (unplanted) for a year. The next year they would plow and plant that half of the ranch. After a summer of no rain in 1919, they took only 160 bushels of wheat off six hundred acres, enough to feed their chickens for the year. There was no feed for the cattle.

Richard said, "We should have harvested 15,000 bushels."

Many ranchers decided to sell their cattle, but there was a delay in getting railroad cars to ship their livestock, and the starving animals quickly decreased in value and their owners lost a lot of money. Some cattlemen tried to rent pasture in other states, but they were unable to get transportation for their animals.

In late summer, Lillian and Richard urged Frank to sell their two hundred head of cattle rather than borrow money to buy expensive feed all winter. He chose to listen to the bank officials, who urged him to borrow the money for hay and grain. They, and Frank, thought the price of beef would go up in the spring.

Unfortunately, the winter of 1919–20 started early in October and was severe. Lillian described the grim scene. "The price of hay began to soar, and the feed men, in town, bought new automobiles that year. Forty dollars a ton for hay as coarse as rushes, and filled with all kinds of weeds, thistles, cattails, and brambles. Occasionally, one even found pressed snakes and frogs in the bales."

The starving cattle would eat the miserable fodder but could not live on it so owners, including the Hazens, who could borrow enough money gave each animal a measure of grain every day to keep life in their bodies through the terrible winter. The poorer ranchers who lacked cash and credit had simply to watch their horses and cattle starve to death if they chose to keep their animals. Lillian would never forget the agony of watching animals die on the prairie. The cattle would just fall from weakness and die quietly, usually on the range out of sight and sound, but the horses hung around near home, having faith their owners would feed them.

She wrote:

> A horse stands up until he is a living skeleton, one can almost see through him. Then, when his weak legs will uphold him no longer, he sinks to the earth but keeps his head up, still watching, waiting, hoping for help that doesn't come. At last, the head sinks down on the ground, the legs stretch out, the large patient eyes close, a shudder, and the poor brute has ceased to suffer.
>
> Sometimes, a horse with uncommon vitality, even after he is down, will make such a heroic effort to stand up that he thrashes his eyes out of his head before the end comes. Many of the ranchers shot their horses rather than have their feelings harrowed by the sight of their dumb friends' sufferings.

The Hazens owed the bank $35,000 by spring. The calf crop might have saved them, but because of the poor feed, most of the calves were born dead. The price of beef plummeted, and, after borrowing money to feed the cattle all winter, Frank sold them for $70 a cow, less than what he would have gotten in the preceding fall.

Opportunists waited on the sidelines to take advantage of the ranchers' problems. A representative of one of the smaller packinghouses went to many of the homesteaders and poorer ranchers, offering to buy their cattle, ship them, and pay the market price the day the animals arrived at his stockyards.

Lillian wrote that farmers were usually simple, honest men; consequently, they were easy marks for the packinghouse representatives. They thought the offer to buy their cattle was an opportunity they couldn't pass up. Few of them had even one carload of cattle, which meant several of them would have to join together to ship, but there were no available cars most of the time. So they let the supposedly benevolent agents drive off their stock. The day the cattle reached the stockyards, the market ranged from three to seven cents a pound and these ranchers, regardless of the condition of their animals, received three cents a pound.

Lillian wrote, "They would not have made any profit, this year, at seven cents a pound, but three cents was a regular holdup for anything like a good steer."

Many homesteaders gave up. They gathered together what little they had left in the way of belongings—no one had any money—and escaped before they and their families starved to death like their animals. North, south, east, west, some sixty thousand Montana homesteaders began to flee. They left in tilting Model T Fords, their household goods tied and piled on handmade roof racks. They left in buggies and wagons. They left behind them dead and dying towns and the range dotted with abandoned homestead shacks.

The winter of 1919–20, though long and cold, produced enough snow to momentarily end the drought. Then began the remaining ranchers', including the Hazens', struggle to plant crops. Because the snow had been a foot deep on the level for five months, there was plenty of moisture in the ground, but few had the cash to even buy seed. Most had so little cash they couldn't even afford life's necessities.

Everyone was so poor, many found themselves doing things they wouldn't ordinarily do. Fifty years later, Richard admitted he and the hired man butchered other ranchers' cows if they found them on their land. They would cut them up in a coulee and then bury the evidence. A new meat market opened in Lewistown, selling what must have been stolen meat, because the butcher was selling it so cheap. Rumor had it that the brother of the new butcher had been arrested for cattle rustling before he came to Lewistown.

Established ranchers like the Hazens did manage to get their seed in the ground and to produce a good crop, thirty bushels of grain to an acre, in 1920. About this time, however, something else happened in Fergus County that made it even more difficult for the struggling ranchers. Oil was discovered. Overnight, the area boomed.

Every week the *Fergus County Argus* published a column, "Week's Review of the Oil Situation." "The farmers were struggling with a drought, but the oil men were so 'flush' they were practically lighting their cigars with $20 bills." The price of all consumer goods in town shot up.

Lillian was disgusted with the oilmen's flamboyant acts. In fact, she wrote an article for the *Oil and Gas Journal* in 1920: "Lewistown is crowded with oil men from all over the country. . . . The whole population is oil mad."

Although most ranchers had steady help, they still needed to hire extra hands for harvesttime, as did all the surrounding ranches. Even in a depressed economy, good temporary workers were scarce, but now the ranchers had to compete with the oil companies. It was just one more problem added to the impossible burdens of the last year.

Everyone vied to hire any available transient shockers who wandered through. Of all years, 1920 was a crucial one for harvesting the crops after the bad year that had just passed. Most shockers would work two or three days, draw their pay, and loaf around Lewistown until their money was gone, and then they would "ride the rods," ride railway freight cars, as far as they could and shock a couple of days more at another ranch.

Sometimes if a storm came up, making shocking impossible until the grain dried, the men would take their pay and go to town to spend it. Ranchers tried to make them promise to return when the weather improved, but although they always promised, most never came back. Sometimes the rancher would drive to town and try to collar the former employees and drag them all back to the ranch to help with threshing the grain.

If the weather cooperated, shocking would usually last for several weeks. After that, the rancher would ask the men to join the threshing crew. Then the Hazens, along with their neighbors, hired rigs with twenty-man crews that threshed everyone's fields out. A contractor would bring in a steam-engine-powered threshing machine and ten or twelve bundle wagons to haul the wheat to the grain elevator in Ware.

Lillian often mentioned what a relief it was when they heard the engine whistle at 6 A.M. on a summer morning as the threshing crew appeared in the field and the machine came over the hill. When it stopped, there was another whistle to warn the grain haulers to be ready with their wagons because threshing was about to begin. Everything was "hurry and scurry" because, even though the whole state had just passed through a devastating drought, rainy weather often appeared when least convenient. At that time of year, one could expect a long storm any day, and all the ranchers waited impatiently for the threshing crew. They were anxious to get their grain under shelter as soon as possible.

The crews went from one place to another as fast as they could. Once the engine was started, it stopped for nothing except water or a breakdown. If a wagon was under the spout to catch the grain, well and good, but if it was late in getting into place, the wheat went on the ground. One bundle wagon on each side of the threshing machine caught the grain as it threshed out. If it was a big rig, producing a stream of wheat forty-two inches wide, it took twelve wagons to keep up with its output. The haul to Ware was five miles round-trip, and grain wagons loaded with 150 bushels, pulled by four horses, didn't go as fast as trucks do.

Lillian spoke of the relief when "at last, the grain was threshed, the wheat hauled to the elevator, and the oats and barley dumped in the granary."

But because ranchers thresh late in the Northwest, some of them, including the Hazens, didn't have their wheat in the elevators when the price, $1.95 per bushel, went down with a rush in 1920. Government supports, during and after World War I, kept wheat prices high, but by 1920, prices began to fall. The farmer needed larger markets abroad and help at home in marketing produce and obtaining credit.

Frank decided to keep his wheat until the next spring, thinking to make more per bushel. He paid one-half cent per bushel that winter of 1920–21 to the elevator company to store his grain. Then, in the spring of 1921, he ended up selling it for 60 cents a bushel.

Montana moved into an early depression. The tariff of 1922 made it impossible for Europeans to sell goods in the United States, thus making it impossible for them to buy American agricultural surpluses.

Lillian wrote, "The 1919 devastating drought virtually ruined many of the ranchers and cattlemen in the northwest, and yet, at the time, city people were sending thousands and thousands of dollars to help war sufferers in Europe without a thought of aiding their drought stricken neighbors at home."

It was not until the 1930s that the federal government's National Conservation Commission belatedly classified the land of the Northern Plains, fixing with certainty according to the productive value of the surface, a reasonable home-making area for each class of agricultural land. It was ascertained that in general, 320 acres of humid-area land was roughly equivalent in productivity to 5,120 acres of semiarid land like that found in Montana.

The Hazens didn't realize it, and none of their neighbors realized they were trying to make a living on too few acres. No matter how efficient they were or how hard they worked, they were doomed to failure through no fault of their own. How could Lillian and Frank hope to earn a living on 1,040 semiarid acres? And no question about it, everyone was working as hard as he or she could. They kept hoping for more good times, but an era of abundant moisture had passed. The weather and the land reverted back to its normal state: one or two wet years followed by one or two dry years.

THIRTY

No Turning Back

Two principal factors have caused what Mr. McAdoo calls "the present tragic agricultural situation"—arbitrary prices set on farm produce that bear no relation to the cost of production and the high interest rate farmers are obliged to pay on borrowed money.

"Farmer's Finance"
Dearborn Independent. 1923

All three Hazens were healthy, but they were small people. They couldn't do as much work or work as long hours a day as some of their brawnier neighbors. They worked as hard as they could, but it just wasn't good enough. By 1919, they were heartsick as they realized their desperate situation. They had sunk every penny they had into their ranch. They couldn't turn back. The land was mortgaged to the hilt, as was most of their neighbors' land. They had to try to recoup some of their losses.

Lillian realized Frank and Richard were as unhappy and scared as she was, but her life was just as difficult as theirs, and she thought she deserved more than their constant criticism. In an angry unpublished story, Lillian described Frank as a "wizened, gray-haired little man with a deep sense of his own importance."

Add this to the fact that the dynamics of ranch life gave Frank an excuse to boss Lillian around. She wrote, "He turned into a sly tyrant."

Early on, Frank set the rules of the family "game" by never backing up Lillian's discipline of their son. He, in fact, encouraged Richard to be as obnoxious as he liked to his mother. But the worst thing about Frank and Lillian's attitude toward each other was the effect it had on Richard over the years. He respected neither and was drinking more of the moonshine he made in a nearby coulee than he should be. Lillian was afraid the revenuers would find out about the still, even though she knew most of their neighbors were turning out various alcoholic beverages.

Frank's silence on the subject exasperated Lillian. When she protested his making whiskey, Richard at first denied it and then ignored her. He was hiding his whiskey in a coyote den in the hills and was sure the government investigators would never catch him, and, evidently, they never did.

The following incident illustrates Richard's attitude toward his mother.

"I thought we were having chicken today," Richard said one noon.

Lillian glared at him. "You said you didn't have time to kill one this morning."

"Well, I don't see why you can't kill the chickens you cook yourself. All the other old women around here do it."

Lillian told him, "If you wait until I kill a chicken, it will be a long time before you'll eat one."

She always appeared to forgive his mean remarks, but perhaps she felt helpless in dealing with this aspect of family dynamics. A charmer could always charm Lillian, and her son was definitely charming when he wanted to be. In her various unpublished stories, Lillian seemed to wish his bad behavior away by ignoring it. Many of her fictional at-home-on-the-ranch stories talked of an "adoring son." Richard, however, never even pretended to be that, and it's doubtful she thought he was even as she penned her wistful thoughts.

Lillian has one of the protagonists in her stories say,

Mother and wife, the closest relationships of man and woman. If a wife could bring into his life a fraction of the happiness his mother's

Thirty

companionship had given him—he recalled the pleasant surprises his mother was always planning for his benefit; their little sacrifices for each other that had seemed merely new ways for demonstrating their affection. How he wished they could sit down together and have one of their long, intimate talks. . . . She had inculcated in him a chivalric tenderness towards women.

That Lillian thought an intimate relationship with his mother would produce the ideal man is surprising for an intelligent, educated woman, although she was born before psychiatry became a recognized profession. This attitude plus Richard's remarks as an old man about conversations with her about her sex life border on incest. Lillian laid a heavy emotional burden on Richard with her "intimate" talks. If he still remembered them in detail when he was eighty-five years old, they left an impression.

Lillian must have felt very alone as she wrestled with ranch life with no emotional support from either her husband or son. All were just existing from day to day. Each night she fell into bed, exhausted. Sometimes she yearned for a free day and night where she didn't have any demands on her time. She was as quick as she could be at age fifty-five, sometimes to the point of being sloppy. She just had too much to do. She also had arthritis, and her feet always hurt, especially as she gained weight with age. It's a real wonder she accomplished as much as she did.

Frank was well organized but methodical and slow. He had no idea what Lillian did each day and never accepted what appeared, to him, to be her haphazard approach to daily routine. As did most farm wives, Lillian did all the things to feed her family as cheaply as possible and help the men with their work during the busy growing season. She planted and maintained a large vegetable garden, not an easy job on a dryland ranch, where watering was done by hand. She canned hundreds of jars of fruits and vegetables and made jellies and jams to feed them all winter.

When the men were busy, she fed the livestock and cleaned out the barn. It was also her job to round up the milk cows at night and then drive the jitney out to pick up Frank wherever he was plowing. Neither man seemed to notice, or care, that he constantly interrupted her work with his demands. Because Lillian was never quite caught up on her chores, an unexpected time-consuming task would put her behind for days. It seemed to Lillian she ran errands for the men all day, every day and still they complained.

The tractor broke down almost daily, and Frank wasn't much of a mechanic. He would walk the miles to the house and send Lillian to town to have a part repaired or welded.

She noted in her diary, "Frank irritated because I wouldn't drop everything and drive to town."

The twenty-mile-trip to Lewistown took an hour each way. She had to carry a large can of water in the car, because the radiator leaked, and she had to stop often to fill it. When she arrived, she always found a couple of her neighbors waiting to have a piece welded, too. Everyone was trying to make do with the least amount of expense, and, of course, this caused constant breakdowns as equipment wore out.

By the time they had lived on the ranch for five years, Lillian knew as much about farming as the men, but this only made her life more difficult. If she saw them making a mistake, she didn't dare say anything about it, or, if she did, they ignored her. And so she learned to suffer in silence. By that time, Richard also knew as much about ranching as Frank, but Frank would never listen to him either.

After Lillian's first *Scribners* sale, Frank and Richard were quick to admit, in those tight money days with the slump in the wheat and cattle markets, an inspiration worth $150 was not to be despised. They assured her any time she felt a high-priced idea coming on they would gladly fix their own dinners and clean the chicken coop. Nothing, however, changed. She continued to clean the chicken coop and Frank and Richard continued to expect three square meals on the table at the usual times.

Her *Scribners* articles were the beginning of many sales as she also analyzed ranch economics for such magazines as *The Deerborne Gazette* and *The Dearborn Independent,* a Ford magazine.

She asked the question, "Why was a successful rancher successful?"

She wrote that one farmer, in a bad year, might harvest twenty-five to thirty bushels an acre while his neighbor just across the road, on the same kind of land, harvested only eight to twelve in the same season. Although his neighbors said it was luck, Lillian saw it as anything but mere luck when both had the same soil and climactic conditions.

Haying time on the ranch was a busy, labor-intensive chore.

In "Diversified Farming," she wrote some ranchers tried to farm more land than they had labor, equipment, or management ability to cultivate. She saw these same farmers wasting their off-season rather than doing necessary chores like repairing buildings and fences and renovating machines, harnesses, and implements. They wasted income buying new things to replace those ruined for lack of timely care. She wrote that efficient farmers performed routine maintenance work when the weather made field work impossible. Often the inefficient rancher was forced to do maintenance at the peak of the harvest season, causing delay to crucial projects:

> His grain may be cut too late so much of it is wasted by scattering. His hay may be spoiled because it isn't stacked soon enough, and increased stock inventory is likely to die for lack of proper shelter.

Lillian continued to write fiction but sold few pieces. When she stuck to nonfiction, she earned at least a hundred dollars per story. Although these dollars helped the Hazens survive, the money instantly disappeared into the "black hole" of their ranch finances. It's a sure bet Lillian was working through some frustration as she watched Frank and Richard's farming methods. In some fiction, she writes of constant breakdowns of machinery and vehicles—of flat tires and empty gas tanks. Their equipment was patched together, literally, with "spit and baling wire." Every season had its special problems, and the rancher had to be alert to every possibility. At least in the summer, the roads were dry and hard, whereas springtime was a nightmare of racing to transport all goods between the last snow and the spring thaw, before the weather warmed up and the roads turned to mud.

Lillian wrote about hauling barley in the early spring when the temperature was about thirty degrees above zero. They would start getting the truck ready before sunrise so as to be on the road while the ground was still frozen hard. Often, they woke up to a flat tire on the old truck.

One small mistake, one inefficient project and a farmer could lose all, because he operated on such limited capital. Lillian didn't think one man in a hundred could be "master of his fate" to this extent and succeed: "Most can't act wisely on their own initiative nor can they overcome indolence, extravagance, and other vices common to mankind."

The drought of 1919 was so serious many merchants and banks in Lewistown started faltering. Then the townspeople began to realize the dire poverty of their rancher customers might affect them.

"Up until this point," Lillian observed, "townspeople not only showed little sympathy with their country cousins but used this opportunity to plunder them."

She gives the example of a young woman from town who stopped by the ranch and wanted to buy a chicken to take back to town. She evidently didn't like Lillian's price and said, "Why do you ask so much, when it costs you nothing to raise it?"

Lillian made no comment on this ignorant statement, but she thought of the hours of backbreaking work necessary for raising chickens, not to mention the actual cash expenses for well-bred cocks to improve the breed, incubators for the chicks, and feed.

The town fathers knew they had to do something to help the ranchers survive. They encouraged them to diversify and suggested various moneymaking projects. The Hazens were way ahead of them. When bad times started, they actively looked around for another crop, another source of income.

Thirty

"Say it with cows" was one Lewistown chamber of commerce slogan as it urged Fergus County ranchers to invest in dairy cattle as a hedge against a failed wheat crop. The Hazens never had more than a couple of milk cows for their family table needs. When they decided to take the chamber's suggestions seriously and diversify still further, they borrowed money to buy three more milch cows and then found out how much care and trouble their dairy herd would be.

Lillian concluded city dwellers didn't understand that, with the possible exception of a racehorse, nothing requires so much intelligent care as a milch cow. She wrote:

> Many townspeople think all a farmer has to do to get milk is to milk the cow who, presumably, eats grass and rustles its own living. The members of the Chamber of Commerce, in a certain Montana town, shipped in a number of bovines to sell to their country cousins at cost, ignoring the fact that the ranchers in that vicinity did not grow, and could not afford to buy, the proper food to feed milch cows in the winter.

Not only do they need lots of expensive fodder, they have to be well protected in bad weather. Stuffy lean-tos or makeshift sheds won't do. Cows fed for large milk production can contract tuberculosis unless they live in clean, well-ventilated barns. They have to be milked twice a day, every day, and milked dry, or the milk supply will decrease rapidly.

She heard a young rancher neighbor say, "Milking is simply a matter of conscience," and later, when he found his cows drying up, he concluded his hired man had no conscience.

Lillian wrote, "One had to overcome the temptation to stay in bed late Sunday mornings, if one desired a profit from milk, because cows are as temperamental as prima donnas, and any divergence from the accustomed routine affects their milk supply."

Their five animals produced nine gallons of milk every twenty-four hours. The Hazens got out their old separator and found they produced enough cream to make twenty pounds of butter a week to sell in addition to what they used on their own table. Butter brought 45 cents a pound in the winter. A farmer had to figure his profits in relation to the cost of food production. Cream, like wine or tea, is graded by the taste, but in 1920 the cause of its variations in flavor couldn't be determined.

A few ranchers were a bit shifty when dealing with Lewistown's grocery store managers. One, where Lillian sold her dairy produce, told a story of a ranch woman who sent her little girl in with butter to sell, and, before they had concluded the bargain, the child tried to buy back a couple of pounds from the store.

"Why didn't your mother keep some of this?" the storeowner asked.

The little girl told him, "Ma found a dead mouse in the cream so she didn't want to eat the butter made from it."

He told her, "And I don't want to sell it for other people to eat."

So he wrapped it up and handed it back to her.

Once Lillian became a country person, she was irked to find that few city people realized the time, labor, and hard cash the farmer used to raise his produce.

"Well, how are things on the ranch?" asked one of Lillian's Lewistown acquaintances.

"About as well as can be expected as long as we have to feed you city people for nothing."

Lillian had just left ten pounds of butter at the store and received credit for nine. She later discovered a defect in her mold that accounted for the shortage. The storekeeper, however, charged his customers the full pound price and, therefore, made a pound clear gain on Lillian. He didn't give her cash for her products, either. She was paid in credit from his store.

For eggs, he gave her credit at market price, minus five cents a dozen. She couldn't get cash for them unless she shipped by the case. Few small farmers had enough hens to ship thirty dozen at a time, so she had to "trade out" her butter and eggs, and the storekeeper made a profit both ways.

If the town butcher bought a steer from a rancher, he expected to buy it at the market price. For instance, he paid 7 cents "on the hoof" and sold the cheapest cuts for 14 cents, but he sold the choice cuts for 35 cents a pound. He also made money on the hide and by-products. Although a steer dressed down 40 percent of its weight, he still made a good profit, but all the cattleman made by selling at the home market was the amount of the freight to Chicago or Omaha.

Thirty

After a few months of producing dairy products, Lillian, who had been keeping meticulous records on their profits, found they were making only 26 cents per day per cow, even when butter fat brought the highest prices.

At the same time that the Lewistown chamber of commerce suggested milking cows as a way to diversify, they also suggested another "money making scheme." After selling his cream, the rancher could feed the skim milk to his hogs, but Lillian and Frank, faithfully trying to diversify, found this didn't always produce a profit. Pigs couldn't live on skim milk alone and required a measure of grain to fatten them. Wheat, when the price was high, couldn't be fed at a profit, and unless a farmer lived where he could raise corn easily and cheaply, he lost money raising pork.

The Hazens learned all these lessons the hard way. They saved the "butter" money for three weeks and bought eight little pigs, Durocs, from a neighbor for $3 each. Right away, one smothered on the way home. They put the little pigs in a box stall, because they didn't have the pigpen ready yet. Then, when they let them out in the corral for exercise, one ran away.

After numerous misadventures with the original eight animals, Frank decided the only way to make a profit raising hogs was to buy a sow, breed her, and raise little pigs "from scratch." A year went by, and they discovered they weren't making any money from them either. At first, they thought they were making a profit when they received an $800 check twice a year for the animals sold, but this didn't really meet the expense of acquiring the pigs and feeding them.

Lillian also tried to diversify her poultry business—again as suggested by the Lewistown chamber of commerce. Raising turkeys was profitable if a man understood the business. For instance, in grasshopper season, the turkeys not only fed themselves but rid the wheat of a destructive pest. Young turkeys, however, are delicate and dumb.

Lillian wrote, "You have to keep on the job all the time for until the red begins to show in their throats, they're awfully easy to kill. Lots of mine got sick."

One sudden hailstorm or thunderstorm might kill large numbers of them unless they were protected. And Lillian had to be ever vigilant to thwart coyotes and other wild things that shared man's love for turkey meat. She found turkeys were "an everlasting nuisance." She thought she'd have two hundred to sell one year, and they petered down to twenty before it was time to market them.

She lost sixteen at one whack, drowned in the watering tank. She usually kept a board in the water, but someone took it out. She didn't notice it was gone when she went to town early in the morning and came back late at night. Frank found the birds floating around in the water—"between 50 and 60 dollars worth."

Another time a "cold snap" came just after eight hatched out. Lillian got up early and went out the next morning, but they were all dead, frozen to death. The coyotes got some, and the gobbler killed several.

Lillian realized there were lots of products the dryland farmer could produce that would bring in an income and never could understand why the so-called experts encouraged the rancher to milk cows or raise pigs and turkeys. She saw many a farmer saved from disaster by a good potato crop and saw others supplement their incomes by raising strawberries and honey, but one needed water to raise this kind of produce.

She wasn't on the ranch long before she realized the only way a rancher had any hope of succeeding was to use all scientific methods available at the time, summon up and use all the common sense he had, and work harder than he thought possible. Her life was taxing every ounce of strength she could muster, but she realized it was even worse for Frank. Compare the pictures of a debonair, well-dressed new Dartmouth graduate with the ranch photos of a seedy-looking little man in need of a haircut and hair comb, wearing bib overalls, the barren prairie a backdrop to the dreary picture.

— THIRTY-ONE —

A Bit of Sustenance

Fed hens, got twenty-one eggs; let Jane out, fed King and Jane and took them in. Fed Peanuts and took him in . . . wrote.

Lillian's diary. March 13, 1925

Lillian kept track of her whole life in her small, gold-embossed red diaries with her strong, angular but intellectual, sometimes illegible handwriting scratched out with black ink dipped from an inkwell. Her entries, however, were factual accounts of ranch life. It's as if she were ever aware someone might read her diaries. She never wrote any personal revelations or description of her feelings—just matter-of-fact recordings of events and weather.

By this time, Richard had married nineteen-year-old Vallie Duvall, daughter of a nearby ranch family, and anyone who knew the Hazen family dynamics could guess this new daughter-in-law would not have an easy life. Earlier, Lillian had written in a piece of unpublished fiction with thinly disguised characters, "My husband was not congenial, but I idolized my son. He was my world—my all—and I had lost him. Perhaps I had sinned in lavishing so much affection on him, and this was my punishment."

227

Add that to the fact that from the time Richard was sixteen and beginning to develop as a man, there was almost constant friction between Frank and Richard. Then, when he married Vallie, Lillian, of course, was not happy with his choice. The Duvall girls and their mother had dubious reputations, determined by local gossips and the era's strict standards. They were pretty and sensual, with dark hair, dark eyes, and seductive moves. Lillian had hoped Richard would marry one of the so-called good girls in the neighborhood.

The little ranch house turned into a tension-filled environment after the newlyweds moved into Richard's room. There appeared to be some kind of a working arrangement between Frank and Richard, and although they weren't getting rich, they seemed to be making a shabby living.

It must have been hard for Vallie to face Lillian's constant disapproval. She was young and up-to-date, a flapper with bobbed hair, short skirts, and a yen for fun. Lillian, who had always depicted herself as totally liberal and liberated, looked down her nose at Vallie, who was very aware of this. Her family was too, and they resented Lillian thinking she was better than they were.

After Richard married, they didn't include Lillian in their recreation any more than they had to. Even in old age, Lillian was up for new experiences. Anytime Richard and Vallie left the ranch to play cards or go dancing, Lillian wanted to go, too. Sadie, Vallie's sister, complained about this when she herself was eighty-five years old.

The couple ran with a hard-drinking, wild crowd and spent a lot of time partying, which, of course, didn't help Richard do his share of work. Vallie did as little as she could get away with, which infuriated Lillian. She described trying to tell Vallie she and Richard had to get serious about earning a living on the ranch.

Later, Lillian wrote, "I can see her now as she sat before me in a dress barely reaching her knees; her bold gray eyes looking defiantly into mine, as she lounged in a rocking chair and crossed her long, silk clad legs. Her strong point was sex appeal, and she knew it. She simply laughed."

Duvall family stories tell of Frank often taking Vallie's side if she and Lillian disagreed. Obviously, Frank could be manipulated by a pretty face, too, and those Duvall girls were knockouts. At about the same time,

Thirty-One

Johnnie Daly married Sadie, and his mother was not thrilled with his choice either when she said to Lillian, "I judge you are trying to make the best of Vallie as I am of Sadie."

In the early fall, Lillian wrote, tersely, about going out each day to watch the harvest—300 bushels of wheat in a day, 300 bushels of oats. So much depended on the harvest at this point. They literally had nothing. In the end, she recorded that they harvested 4,700 bushels of wheat but crossed that out and inserted 3,000. That meant they harvested only two-thirds of what they expected. But even if the amount had been 4,700 bushels, that was a third of what they usually harvested in a good year.

It appeared to be one of the worst financial years for the Hazens. In 1925, Lillian submitted many manuscripts but sold few for small sums. She kept track of money spent on postage. Times were tough, but postage was cheap: 2 cents per ounce with postcards costing 1 cent.

On Sundays she didn't write. She listened to the radio broadcast by the Metropolitan Opera House from New York City. She also allowed herself the luxury of reading the Bible and her subscription magazines—*Cosmopolitan, Good Housekeeping, Liberty, Literary Digest, Colliers, Saturday Evening Post, Red Book, Physical Culture, Country Gentleman*—and a Minneapolis newspaper. Frank read the farm journals and the newspaper. Lillian must have read the farm journals too because she sold articles to them.

In her diaries, she always listed the temperature and described the day: "fair, hot, drizzle, rain, or snow."

All through the summer of 1925 the thermometer hovered between eighty and one hundred degrees. She and Vallie canned peaches and serviceberries, sometimes on the hottest of days.

According to her ranch diaries, one day ran into another in sameness, especially in the winter, with weather the main topic of her entries. Lillian came to the ranch with adventure in her soul and the hope for a new beginning for her and Frank's relationship, which, of course, it wasn't. Their struggle to survive superseded every other consideration. Money was short. Everything was going wrong; each worked against the other.

Frank, however, begrudged Lillian any respite from her hard work and daily grind if he couldn't share it. Sometimes Richard and Vallie or a neighbor invited Lillian to town for the day to shop, to eat in a restaurant, and to see a movie, her particular passion. She would see one movie, sometimes two, like *Born Rich,* with Bert Lytel, at Lewistown's Judith Theater or *Little Miss Blue Beard,* with Bebe Daniels.

She enjoyed eating at the Tea Room or the Fergus Hotel dining room. In the summer, she would always have a Coke, or two, and an ice cream cone, or two, at Seiden's Drugstore, on the corner of Main Street. Life on the ranch conditioned her to enjoy the simple things. A trip to Lewistown was not complete without a trip to the library to replenish her supply of borrowed books and visit with the librarian, her good friend Miss Main.

If she hadn't been to town in a long time, she might go by train and stay at the Calvert Hotel. Sometimes Frank even forgot to pick her up when she returned to the little train station in Ware. He made it just as tough on her as he could when she made one of her infrequent "escapes." Lillian satirized his attitude in an unpublished article, "Reuben's Ranch Notes":

> Well, I declare, this new freedom for women is the bunk. How can a wife expect to keep the love of her husband when he gets home between half-past two and three in the afternoon to find a note saying she had a chance to go to town with a neighbor? It does beat all how women waste money. She was in town and saw a show not much over a month ago and she's left me with only cold victuals to eat, cold roast chicken with currant jelly, potato salad, and chocolate cake. She must know when a man is working in the field he ought to have a good warm meal. I'll even have to boil water to make tea.

Her protagonist gets grumpier as he reads he is supposed to look after the brooder fire and the incubator as his wife and her friend, Millie, are going to the talkies and so won't be home until after ten. He doesn't get the egg and chicken money, so the brooder and incubator can go haywire for all he cares. Then he wonders where she got so much money for shows and things.

"Let me see—eggs are only $5.50 a case now, but she did get a check for some a week ago. Suppose she's blowing that."

Lillian usually didn't ask for help with her feathered charges. She didn't mind being the keeper of the henhouse, because she liked chickens. She was the one who started raising them a couple of years after they

Thirty-One

moved to the ranch. She saw them as a way to earn a bit of cash of her own. Frank hadn't wanted to go into the chicken business, but Lillian promised she would never ask him for his help.

In the beginning, she didn't know a thing about chickens. She wrote, "I foolishly looked upon the poultry business as one in which no skill or knowledge is required, and so I ventured in without any preparation," when she found "to my sorrow that things are not what they seem."

Her chicken business had a rocky start and many minor problems until Lillian realized she needed help and read everything she could get her hands on. She also had long discussions with her more skilled neighbors until she finally established her thriving flock and became good at rescuing the maximum number of little chicks from each batch.

How she treasured her feathered charges! She fussed over them, making sure they led the good life—for a chicken, that is. They in turn produced for her, thus giving her some money of her own each month, but not without a battle with Frank.

"I pay for the feed. I should have any profit you make."

Lillian then asked him: "Do you like eggs for breakfast? Or fried chicken for dinner? I think I earn my share of cash on the chickens."

It was not easy raising a flock of chickens, because so many creatures loved chicken meat. She said coyotes, weasels, hawks, porcupines, cats, and snakes were all anxious to eat her charges. Lillian worked hard to protect her flock, and although Frank jealously watched each check she received for her poultry business, she stood her ground. In the end, the chickens were considered Lillian's sole responsibility in the summer, but both Frank and the hired man took turns cleaning the chicken house in the winter.

According to Lillian's articles on raising chickens successfully, a clean chicken house was a must. In fact, in January 1925 diary entries, two days in a row, she cleaned the inside of the chicken house thoroughly with kerosene. Two weeks later, Frank and Glenn were cleaning the chickens' abode again. Lice must have invaded the henhouse.

She noted how many eggs she collected each day. This had a practical purpose. It was a way to track her meager profits. In 1925, Lillian's hens laid 5,820 eggs. She sold $37.90 worth and $51.81 worth of chickens. She also wrote many amusing stories about her "feathered friends." At first, she started out with little chicks, which she bought from a neighbor who let her pick out the ones she wanted. Lillian picked the largest and ended up with half roosters. She traded them with a neighbor for hens.

The next year she had two cocks with twenty hens. One was much more aggressive than the other and the hens loved him. If his competitor tried to get near the hens, he would fight him. Every morning Lillian found the vanquished one hiding in a corner of the henhouse. When she opened the door, he would make a dash for the outside with the ornery rooster right behind him.

Then the victor would strut around the yard, surrounded by admiring hens. He would preen himself in the sunshine. Meanwhile, his rival wandered around alone most of the time unless a hen out of favor with the Great One would condescend to share some delicious tidbit with the vanquished fowl.

Lillian talked about the joy of rescuing a chick she thought was dead. When it emerged from its shell, it was slimy and scrawny looking, but it cheeped, so she put it on a piece of soft flannel in a Nabisco Shredded Wheat box in the oven. The next morning she found "instead of the skinny, horrid looking object of the night before was a beautiful, plump little chick, its yellow down shining like gold, and its bright eyes blinking up at me, gleaming and sparkling as though they were jewels."

Her joy at rescuing a baby chick symbolized Lillian's attitude toward ranch life, where she found beauty and gratification at every turn. Usually, she didn't dwell on what might have been. It was her natural inclination to take each day as it came and make the best of it, and so it's little wonder that in spite of isolation and hardships, she found much to enjoy.

In a "Ranch Woman's Guests," published in 1922 by *Scribners* magazine, she told of the camaraderie found over a burdened table surrounded by people enjoying good food. She wrote that in town, when she had dinner guests, she usually invited them several days ahead, cleaned house, polished up her silverware, took the opportunity to display her finest linen and best china, and lay awake nights trying to think of rare delicacies likely to temp their appetites.

On the ranch, if anyone happened to be there at mealtime—neighbor, stranger, hobo, or college professor—he was invited to sit down at the oilcloth-covered table in the kitchen. In town, her guests appeared in

Thirty-One

their company clothes and manners. On the ranch, hired help and guests all sat down at the festive board together in their working garb—whole, holey, or embroidered with patches, clean or dirty.

A guest was invited to eat what was set before him, fried chicken and ice cream or fried eggs and gingerbread. Lillian made a fine art of and was proud of her culinary skills learned so late in life, because she had never cooked before she married. When the men rose from her table after a meal, she bragged, "They felt satisfied—light bread rolls, and biscuits, flaky pie crusts, and delicious, not to mention, well-cooked vegetables and juicy meats."

In fact, Lillian was a very good ranch wife. After all, what could be more important than serving delicious, nourishing food, a skill many ranch wives never mastered? And she liked to share, especially if it brought interesting people to her table. Frank did, too. Any diversion was a welcome change from the monotony of their hard work.

Even though her diary doesn't describe much other than the weather and her numerous ranch chores, it says enough to indicate 1925 appeared to be one of the worst years of Lillian's life. On May 10, Lillian wrote one line: "John Hazen died of Brights Disease in Sioux Falls, South Dakota."

At about the same time, she wrote a poem called "Lost," never published but preserved among her other manuscripts:

Beloved, when they told me you were dead,
The world was empty—And I walked alone,
Bereft of all desire—for youth then fled,
My heart seemed flesh no longer, but a stone.
Yet, when I too am free from time and space,
I know that I shall find your resting place.

For months after that, her dairy entries expressed distress. On May 16, she wrote, "Felt sick but went to town to meet Frank with Richard and Vallie" when he returned from John's funeral in Sioux Falls. That's the first time Lillian ever wrote she felt sick. She appeared at this point to be suffering for a lot of reasons.

In May she wrote in her diary, "Mother ill. Sent her my diamond solitaire."

She spent a lot of time climbing the hill to the windmill. It seems to be the place where she could go to be alone and gain some peace of mind, with its serene view of the surrounding country. It must have made her angry that Maude was asking for money all the time to help her mother. Years later, Lillian angrily refused to allow Richard to bring Maude to visit her in Logan, Utah. She didn't explain her anger, but it was probably because her sister used their mother for a housekeeper and babysitter for years, but when her mother needed financial help, Lillian was expected to ante up. And she did try to help, but she didn't have any money either.

On May 29 Lillian tried to borrow $1,300 to send to her mother, but, of course, the bank wouldn't lend it to her. Their ranch was mortgaged for much more than it was worth. She scrounged money wherever she could. She sent all of her jewelry to be pawned. She paid the interest on it monthly, so she did retrieve most of it later. The only thing not retrieved was the diamond engagement ring Frank had given her so many years before. It was sold, not merely pawned. Finally, on June 3, she went to Lewistown and borrowed $300 on her life insurance policy and sent Maude a $100 draft for her mother.

Although Lillian had an upbeat approach to life and its troubles, "meet them, greet them, beat them," life seemed bleak to her at this low point in her life. She never quite succumbed to self-pity, but she did have her regrets, often voiced in poetry like "I Want":

A little love, the few years I am here;
And flowers now, not placed upon my bier.
A sympathetic knowledge of my ways—
Forgiveness too, when honest censure flays.
A little help, when everything goes wrong,
A cheering word, a jest, or some sweet song.
A little pleasure, and a little trust
Before my mortal body turns to dust.
And last, but not the least, one faithful friend
To stay beside me 'til the journey's end.

Never a Winning Hand

The farmer has to take what is given him, and give what is asked. Could any business succeed under such conditions?

"Farmer's Finance"
Dearborn Independent. 1923

Lillian knew the numbers were out of whack. She knew they and their neighbors were doing the best they could yet not making it. All went to bed each night, bone weary and worried, and rose at dawn to begin the futile routine all over again.

By October 28, 1925, the temperature was down to zero degrees with snow on the ground. On Thanksgiving Day that year, seven extra people from Vallie's family arrived unexpectedly for dinner, and Lillian fixed a second table to feed them all. That was the neighborly thing to do—especially when so many had so little. Then they all played 500, a card game, until 1 A.M.

On December 4, Lillian went to Lewistown in preparation for her trip to New York City to see her mother, who was still sick. It was her first trip back since their 1914 vacation trip. One can feel a "lift" in her diary entries as she prepares. She's looking forward to it. The night before she left, she went to see the movie *Rin Tin Tin* and wrote, "Wonderful dog!!!!" A most unusual, demonstrative entry.

On December 5, she left Lewistown on the 11:25 A.M. train for Harlowton, where she caught the 4:40 P.M. Olympian for New York City. She ate oranges and dates for lunch. She had dinner on the train: fish, bread, and tea cost a dollar, and one gets the feeling of great anxiety about each penny spent. Is she going to make it on the little money she has with her?

A man she knew casually from Lewistown asked her to dinner the next night, but she had already eaten. She arrived in New York City at 3:35 P.M. on December 8 and went right to her mother's house, where she met with the doctor. The next day, she retrieved her mother's watch from the pawnshop but pawned some of her own silver instead.

She wrote, "Mother still sick."

The next day, she pawned some gold jewelry with a brief entry the day after that, "Went to sell my bridgework."

Her diary entry lists cherished possessions pawned or sold and little else. It would be the last time she saw her mother. Abruptly, she returned to Lewistown on December 22 and wrote, "So glad to be home."

Most of all, she had worried about the men caring for her animals' special wants. Lillian never went east again although in later years, Frank made several trips. When they finally left the ranch and had more money, they often went to California.

After her return from New York, things were even worse between Vallie and Lillian, who expected more help out of her daughter-in-law than she was getting. She noted in her diary that she was furious when Vallie went off to town without helping with supper, and part of that feeling was Lillian wanted to go, too.

In 1926, the Hazens harvested 8,000 bushels of oats and 7,000 bushels of wheat. That's almost twice the yield in 1925. After the crops were in and expenses paid, Lillian went to Lewistown on a shopping spree, the only one ever mentioned in her diary. On December 6, 1926, she hitched a ride to the Ware station with Vallie's sister, Sadie, on her way to Lewistown to buy new clothes from the inside out—corset, underwear, dress, hat, and coat.

When she returned to the Ware station a day later, she had to beg a ride with a neighbor to the bottom of their road and walk the rest of the way to their house carrying a bag. One would have thought Frank could have made more of an effort to take her to town and bring her home.

Thirty-Two

Two days later, she and Frank took their first vacation from the ranch since 1917. They went to Great Falls to visit Frank's old Dartmouth roommate, O. S. Warden, who was now a prominent Montana citizen and owner of the *Great Falls Tribune*. It's easy to see why Lillian went to so much trouble to make a good appearance. It was a matter of pride. Over the years, Warden had printed many of Lillian's poems and articles. He was successful; Frank wasn't.

When they got to Great Falls, Lillian went directly to the beauty parlor for a marcel, a finger wave. Then they had dinner and spent the night with the Wardens, and O. S. took them on a tour of his printing plant the next day. Late that same day, they returned to the ranch.

Although ranchers like the Hazens managed to hang on until the 1930s, it was a constant struggle. They could never quite catch up. One good year after a couple of bad years couldn't sustain them. They, like all their neighbors, had mortgaged their land to the limit. Cash for any extras or even necessities didn't exist.

Richard, however, analyzed their problems fifty years later. First of all, the land Frank bought didn't have a good water supply. At the time, he could have bought good acreage along Spring Creek. They also didn't grow enough hay for their stock and were running about four hundred head of cattle. As long as they threshed their wheat, they had enough straw left over to keep the cattle going through the winter. But they switched to having it combined. That meant they lost the straw by-product, and so they started selling off their cattle.

Later, Lillian and Richard tried to get Frank to trade for some river bottomland, but Frank said it was too hilly for cattle and wouldn't talk about it.

Richard said, "That is how Dad handled conflict. He would just quit talking. He insisted on raising wheat. He thought he would make his fortune with wheat, but wheat is what broke us."

It was a time of great change for western ranchers because most were switching from horses to tractors. Although a tractor could do four times the work, this meant they had to run up huge debt to buy one. A rancher would make a down payment of several hundred dollars and then sign a note for the rest of the $3,000 or $4,000. Then they would try to pay it off in two or three years. In addition to the cost of oil and gas, there was the maintenance expense as the machinery aged. Sometimes an unskilled rancher didn't take care of it and would have to replace it. Again, he would sign a note for a new, improved model.

Then they found the old plows, discs, and other accessories wouldn't work with the new tractor, so they had to buy new ones. Lillian analyzed the situation for various farm business magazines, thus earning much-needed cash.

She wrote, "Montana ranchers, in the early 1920s, were beginning to think a wise man would not sit long in a game when the deck is marked and the dice loaded. They advised their sons to engage in some business where there is less risk and labor and more profit."

She thought this sad, for she saw the farmer's work as so vital to mankind's survival. The longer Lillian lived on the ranch, the more she respected the rancher.

She wrote, "The miracles of life and death are every day occurrences with him, yet he never ceases to marvel at them."

She thought American farmers were the "pluckiest men on earth," the backbone of the nation. Often in her writings, she wrote that the most courageous, hardworking rancher could not make a living under the circumstances. The more honest were, usually, the worst beaten in what Lillian saw as a crooked game. She warned that everyone would suffer if the farmers didn't get a square deal.

The federal government agencies in charge of agriculture didn't seem to have the foggiest notion what they were doing. First they passed the 1909 Homestead Law, designating too little acreage, 320 acres, for a farmer's survival on semiarid land. Then the so-called government experts, thinking they had found a new formula for farming semiarid land when in reality they had found an unusually long wet spell, urged all Montana ranchers to plow up the grasslands and plant wheat.

Sixty years later, Richard said, "Acre upon acre of that land never grew anything again, not even grass."

When the Hazens decided to take up ranching, wheat prices were skyrocketing because of World War I shortages. They and other ranchers did as the federal government suggested although they did it more for profit than for patriotic reasons. They put all available land in wheat. And did the crops grow when it rained!

Thirty-Two

In 1909, the 250,000 acres in eastern Montana planted in wheat produced only 3,560,000 bushels, but by 1924, 35,000,000 acres, all mortgaged to the hilt, produced 40,852,000 bushels. Twenty-three new Montana counties formed and, in every new town, a new bank. In all the old towns, more new banks appeared, all eager to loan the would-be ranchers money. In 1900 there were 7,000 farms in eastern Montana. By 1920 there were 46,000.

In 1922, the Hazens sold thousands of bushels of wheat at anywhere from 10 cents to 40 cents less than the cost of raising it, and they sold well-bred Hereford steers at $70 each after the animals consumed $80 worth of food. The farmer borrowed money in the spring to plant his crops, and so the money he earned in the fall for the sale of these crops and cattle was already spent.

Lillian wrote, "Even a farmer needs a little ready cash."

She also complained that when a rancher put in his crop, he had to pay the retail price for implements and machinery and the going wages for labor and everything else he needed, irrespective of his income or the price that was set on his own produce. She found the experts liked to say farmers lacked business ability and admitted perhaps most did. She suggested, however, most of them were too busy watching the weather and fighting bugs and stock diseases to learn high finance.

"The Captain of Industry," she wrote, "has not yet been born who could make money selling wheat at 80 cents a bushel if the cost of raising it came to a dollar a bushel or selling cattle at $75 a head when they cost $85 to raise.

"Senator La Follette, in one of his campaign speeches, said he was sorry for the people in a certain western state as he understood 49 percent of the ranches were mortgaged."

Lillian thought that was a conservative estimate, that most states in the Northwest had more than half the ranches mortgaged. In addition to the recorded mortgages, banks frequently held ranchers' notes to the full value of all their possessions. These were drawn for sixty or ninety days or six months at the longest and drew 10 percent interest. This was added to the principal when they were renewed, as they invariably were, because farmers had little or no money to pay debts except in the fall, when they sold their crops and cattle.

Never a Winning Hand

"Now, there may be men who can borrow money at 10 percent interest, compounded semi-annually," Lillian wrote, "and make a howling success of their business, but they are scarce as hens' teeth. The uninitiated will say, Why borrow, then? The man who lives within his means is never hurt by high interest rates."

She explained the system. If a rancher borrowed $10,000 on two thousand acres of land, he had to agree to pay $425 semiannually for twenty years, which together with $500 or $600 for taxes made about $1,500 a year, $15,000 in ten years. If the borrower, because of drought and thus crop failure, couldn't make his payment on the eleventh year, he could lose the $15,000 he had paid unless he could borrow $1,500 elsewhere to cover the payment.

One well-known Montana lawyer said he examined forty foreclosures and thought many, if not all of them, could have been avoided by a little help from the banks. How true still was the old Populist song written in 1896:

Oh, the farmer is the man, the farmer is the man
Lives on credit till the Fall.
With the interest rate so high
It's a wonder he don't die
For the mortgage man's the one
That gets it all.

It was as difficult for Frank, as it was for all ranchers, to regulate his expenditures according to his income when he didn't know what it would be. Even when his seeding in the fall or spring resulted in a good crop, prices were sometimes so low at harvesttime he virtually made nothing.

The Hazens also had to meet vital expenses. They still used some horses, which had to be fed through the winter so they would be in condition for work in the spring. Tractors were expensive. Machinery wore out and had to be replaced. Fences had to be built and maintained, stock losses replaced.

Lillian thought a man should be forgiven almost any crime when he works hard, sixteen hours a day, to pay his debts. Then, owing to crop failure and high interest rates, he fails to meet his obligations and sees his last cow led away while his hungry children are left crying for milk. She said few people realized that ruining the farmer meant ruining the country, because farming is not an industry, but "the industry of the human race." People eat to live, but where will they get food if there are no farmers?

In 1924, Lillian wrote that the American farmer objected to being reduced to a state of peonage. Even when drought stricken, hailed out, and crop prices were reduced below the cost of raising them, he did not want charity or special privileges—merely an extension of credit to tide him over hard times.

The three-year drought between 1918 and 1922 threw Montana ranchers into an early depression. On January 5, 1924, Lillian wrote, "Last month, the first National Bank of Fergus County closed its doors, and the officers and examiners thought it exceedingly doubtful if they could realize 50 percent on $1,000,000 worth of paper—that tells the story of the country people's financial condition."

A total of 214 banks failed. The average value of all farmland in Montana was cut in half by 1925. Farm mortgage indebtedness reached $175,000,000, and taxes per farm acre rose 140 percent.

Frank was not an experienced farmer, and many inexperienced farmers like him left their ranches. The survival rate of the experienced farmers was much higher. They were the ones who knew the value of water from the beginning and had purchased land accordingly so they could raise gardens, alfalfa, beans, potatoes, and truck farm products. But even they had to struggle with the same weather-based cycle—the drought years and the wet years, decade after decade.

Finally, nothing worked for the Hazens, just as nothing worked for the U.S. economy. Across the country, 100,000 businesses went under in the period 1929–32. The Hazens milked cows and sold 40-percent butterfat at three cents a pound, which, on a ten-gallon can of cream, would net about $3. They sold eggs for a nickel a dozen. Then they couldn't keep their cattle anymore and, in 1932, sold their full-blooded Hereford cows, although they weren't registered, for $5 a head.

Frank resisted giving up as long as they had any money. They both enjoyed the stay on the ranch, as difficult as it was. It was a good life in

*Lillian's daughter-in-law, Vallie, and granddaughter, Joyce,
1928.*

so many ways, an adventure close to nature. How they enjoyed the crisp
mornings of an early dawn, the night's starry radiance, the link with
their animals!

Then they lost all but a few hundred acres to the bank, and it was
all over. Frank and Lillian moved back to Lewistown in 1930, leaving
Richard with Vallie and me—I was born in 1928—to run what was left

Richard was left alone to raise a son and daughter after Vallie's death in November 1930.

of the ranch. They were flat broke but still had their house in Lewistown. It had been rented while they were on the ranch. At first, they rented an apartment until their renters moved out, and then they took up residence again at 314 Seventh Avenue South, within walking distance of the courthouse. Frank again joined Fergus County politics as a county commissioner.

*At age sixty-seven, Lillian becomes a mother again to her
grandchildren, who moved into their house in Lewistown in 1932.*

In November 1930, Vallie died when my brother, Dick, was born.
This left my father with two tiny children to raise by himself. He tried
to cope with the help of Vallie's parents, but when Lillian offered to take
us to Lewistown, he was relieved. Thus at age sixty-seven, Lillian was a
mother again, but, as with everything else, she took it in stride.

Darkness Lowers

Lillian's one attempt to turn back to her former life was her trip to New York City in 1925. Later, she wrote she "was amazed and saddened" to find she didn't belong in the city anymore when she had been such a part of it at one time. Montana really was her home. She knew she could never leave:

> At sunset, the mountains in the east are outlined by the silver light of the rising moon, the western horizon aglow with color and the stars are coming out one by one in the deep blue of the sky directly above. . . . It reminds me of "God's in His Heaven, all is right with the world."

Frank's life story might have been much the same no matter whom he married, but their marriage, undoubtedly, determined the story of Lillian's life. When she wed Frank, she thought she was marrying a handsome, attractive man with money who could give her the good upper-middle-class Victorian life. She chose with her head and then her heart and was stunned when she discovered the real Frank was not the man of her dreams after all. But it's doubtful there was ever a man like the "man of her dreams." She had to have realized how silent Frank was before she married him. His personality certainly didn't undergo a drastic change after the ceremony. She saw the personality she wanted to see.

If Frank had revealed his innermost thoughts on their marriage, he was probably just as stunned with the real Lillian. Because she appeared to be a pliant woman—soft spoken and well mannered—she attracted a man who wanted the traditional Victorian wife, a role Frank tried to force her to play, in one way or another, all her life.

For most of her marriage, she yearned for peace in her relationship with Frank but instead found herself frustrated and angry, caught in a chain of events she felt powerless to change. She was more or less at Frank's mercy when it came to the economics and physical location of their life, but she didn't relinquish any of "herself." Lillian's face never lost its youthful, sweet cast, for even with all her physical toil in a harsh climate and her long-standing disappointment in her marriage, she was still a handsome woman.

Unfortunately, she and Frank never managed to meld to make "the perfect whole," but they did manage to develop a "live and let live" attitude in their old age. Both appeared to be able to live for the moment and not dwell on the past. They were not bitter old people. How sad that she and Frank, during their fifty-four years of marriage, rarely pulled together as a team. The drastic end to their ranch venture was a good example of a resulting disaster. As early as 1909, Lillian wanted Frank to buy a ranch when prices were low, but Frank waited too long. She watched the economy and knew he was buying in at the peak of produce and land prices.

Although she wrote articles for farm papers discussing the dangerous situation the Montana ranchers faced in the 1920s, Frank never asked her opinion. He was always in charge of their finances. If Lillian voiced disapproval, that was enough to spur him on. If she urged him to cut his losses and "run," that was enough to make him stand his ground.

After leaving the ranch and returning to live in Lewistown, Lillian thought the leisure for writing would be wonderful. She said she felt like she had been "released from prison bondage" and found it utopia to have "an abundance of hot water, day and night, by simply turning a faucet." She also wrote she enjoyed picking her vegetables off a store counter instead of under a blistering sun. Best of all, she had the time and solitude to write.

But she never produced anything interesting after leaving the ranch. The small-town existence didn't seem to stimulate her creative energies,

Weston, center with white mustache, age eighty-four, walking down Fifth Avenue in New York City after finishing a five-hundred-mile walk in 1923.

or perhaps she was just tired. One wonders if she had married a compatible soul and settled down in the East to raise a family, would she have written the great American novel as she so wanted to do?

At about the same time Lillian and Frank were struggling to hold on to the ranch, her father was having his problems as an old, ailing pedestrian, a fact she read in the newspaper like everyone else and clipped the stories. When he was interviewed by a reporter, he talked of a walking comeback even though he was eighty-three years old. He said he wasn't meant to settle down after averaging nearly 1,500 miles per year for seventy years.

The reporter described Weston's collection of letters and newspaper clippings, which rivaled that of any theatrical, screen, or other athletic celebrity. Ed said he was writing his autobiography, had been writing it for fifteen years. Among prized possessions were a worn-out pair of walking boots he once used in England, a pair of shoes he used in his

1910 jaunt across the U.S. continent, and his two heavy gold watches, both gifts from admirers. He also owned several cars.

When he was eighty-eight years old and living in Philadelphia, he turned up missing for several days, and the police found him wandering dazedly around New York City. A doctor who examined him said he was in fine physical shape even though he had slept on doorsteps for four nights and had been drenched with rain several times. He didn't have any money and was destitute.

Ann Nichols, the author of the Broadway hit play *Abie's Irish Rose*, had never met Weston, but when she heard that he was old and poverty stricken, she set up a $30,000 trust fund, which produced $150 a month income for Weston. Such a sad end when one realizes he made a fortune in his lifetime, but it was all gone.

He moved to Brooklyn, and Annie O'Hagan took care of him in his last years. Unfortunately, in November 1928, he was hit by a taxicab and confined to his bed. He died in 1929 at age ninety. At that point, Lillian felt sad at his passing, but she didn't travel east for his funeral.

Often, on summer Sundays in the early 1930s, she and my grandfather loaded us into their old Dodge and headed for a picnic in the Montana mountains—sometimes Gilt Edge. We would spend the day rambling the slopes to find wildflowers for Lillian's pressed collection and then would watch as she sketched each flower, usually a buttercup or a shooting star, quite skillfully, in detail before we picked it.

Her love of books and literature was passed to us as she read such favorite children's stories as *Robinson Crusoe, The Roosevelt Bears, Alice in Wonderland*, or Sherlock Holmes tales. She loved movies, too, and we spent many a happy winter Saturday afternoon at Lewistown's Judith Theater, viewing her favorite actors and actresses—Gary Cooper, Greta Garbo, or Hopalong Cassidy. She even liked Frank Sinatra when she was in her eighties. She never missed a chance to see a movie, and one realizes why when reading about her difficult ranch life. A movie was a welcome escape into a fantasy world in the cool, dark theater from overwhelming worries and ranch drudgery.

After they lost most of the ranch acreage, Richard moved out of state, taking us with him. In 1940, Frank and Lillian began making an annual winter trek to California. They spent one winter in Pasadena, but

Frank, in his seventies, still grew his large garden, winning prizes at the county fair.

Lillian hated it and called it the "City of the Living Dead," because it was a city filled with other elderly people.

She much preferred the bustling, energetic city of Long Beach, with its free band concerts playing her favorite Sousa marches. It was also close enough to Los Angeles for her to hear such favorite performers as Jascha Heifetz. Or she could sit on the beach and relax as she watched the waves and listened to the seagulls.

Lillian, in her seventies, enjoyed life, spending her winters in California with Frank.

Each spring found them back in Lewistown in time for Frank to plant his large garden. When in 1948 he and Lillian, both in their eighties, began to lose momentum and admitted they were too tired to manage their big house and yard, my father and I went to Lewistown to help them move. We found them down to the final stages of sorting and discarding. There they sat—Frank in his rocking chair and Lillian in the blue velvet easy chair—dazed and undecided, amidst a fifty-year collection of personal treasures. We tried to help them decide what they wanted to take, to sell, or discard. It was a sad trip to wind down two eighty-three-year-old lives.

Lillian Marie Weston Hazen negotiated many a twist and turn along life's path from the teenage Lillian, who peered into her mirror and asked her mother, "Will my face ever be famous?" to the eighty-year-old woman who wrote of "blighted youthful dreams."

An important aspect of Lillian's life was her attitude toward death. To her, "physical death is merely an incident in the life of the soul. . . . The soul or spirit sheds its earthly body as a tree sheds its leaves, and creates for itself another covering, in another sphere, as the tree grows new leaves. I cannot look upon death as the end of existence, but merely as the cessation of the earthly phase of life."

She did not fear it and believed it was a corner one turned into a perfect existence, a peaceful spiritual life where she would join her long-mourned daughter.

By 1949, she and Frank were living in an apartment in Richard's house in Logan, Utah. Lillian and his second wife, who always called her "Mrs. Hazen," did not have a close, friendly relationship. If she had a problem, she probably didn't want to ask her daughter-in-law for any kind of help.

Lillian always had foot trouble, which worsened with age. Although she had tiny feet, she was proud of them and probably jammed them into too-small shoes. Corns plagued her all her life, and she trimmed them with a sharp knife. Because her eyesight was failing and it must have been an effort to even reach her feet, her knife slipped and cut her toe. By the time Richard discovered she had a bad infection, it was too late. Even then, she resisted going to the hospital, although systemic infection had set in and was shutting her whole system down. To the very end, she tried to be independent and uncomplaining even though she must have been in terrible pain. In November 1949, at age eighty-four, Lillian died.

Right after her funeral, Frank told Richard, "We lived together for fifty-five years and never said a cross word to each other."

Later, he refused to accept her death and, until his own of a heart attack in March 1952, pretended she was away for a short visit.